Managing Men Who Sexually Abuse

Managing Men Who Sexually Abuse

David Briggs and Roger Kennington

Jessica Kingsley Publishers
London and Philadelphia

First published in 2006
by Jessica Kingsley Publishers
116 Pentonville Road
London N1 9JB, UK
and
400 Market Street, Suite 400
Philadelphia, PA 19106, USA

www.jkp.com

Copyright © David Briggs and Roger Kennington 2006

The right of David Briggs and Roger Kennington to be identified as author of this
work has been asserted by them in accordance with the Copyright, Designs and
Patents Act 1988.

Library of Congress Cataloging in Publication Data
A CIP catalog record for this book is available from the Library of Congress

British Library Cataloguing in Publication Data
A CIP catalogue record for this book is available from the British Library

ISBN-13: 978 1 85302 807 6
ISBN-10: 1 85302 807 X

Printed and bound in Great Britain by
Athenaeum Press, Gateshead, Tyne and Wear

Contents

List of Figures

List of Tables

Acknowledgements

Thanks to those clients colleagues we have learnt from.

Thanks to Sharon Keeble for her skill, patience and mindreading abilities in producing the manuscript for this text.

Thanks to those whose materials we have imported or developed, to those named in the text and to those whose names were lost in the infancy of this work.

And with particular thanks to esteemed friends and fellow travellers, especially Carol Morton, Caroline Lovelock and Elizabeth Hayes.

Paddy Doyle and Tess Gooch, friends and co-authors of *Assessing Men Who Sexually Abuse*. Both have now moved to pastures new.

Managers and the committee of the National Probation Service, Northumbria for their initial vision in developing sex offender work and their continued support.

NOTA's 'Dealing with Diversity Working Party' – Alix Brown, Kevin Gibbs, Sheila Rose – for permission to reproduce their paper, and particularly Simon Hackett for material contributed to Chapter 4.

Chapter 11 of this text draws upon material developed by the Northumbria Probation Service Accredited Sex Offender GroupWork Programme with editing by Professor Don Grubin.

PART I
THE WORK IN CONTEXT

CHAPTER 1

Introductory Comments

Our first text, *Assessing Men Who Sexually Abuse* (Briggs, Doyle, Gooch and Kennington 1998), set out to address issues in the evaluation of male sexual abusers. This companion text aims to introduce the reader to issues of relevance to the management of sexual abusers following initial assessment. It is aimed at a professional though not necessarily specialist readership. Our starting point for this text is as follows.

First, we do not profess particular expertise in the management of women who sexually abuse. This text does not attempt to cover that client group. We refer readers to the work of our colleagues elsewhere (e.g. Eldridge and Saradjian 2000; Elliott 1993; Matthews 1998; Saradjian 1996). Similarly, we do not address the management of abusers with learning difficulties, and readers are referred to the work of Coleman and Haaven (1998) in this regard. Neither do we address issues relating to adolescents who sexually abuse. Texts by Erooga and Masson (1999) and Ryan and Lane (1987) form excellent starting points for those seeking information about that client group.

Second, we make deliberate choice here to refer generally to the subjects of this text as 'men who sexually abuse' rather than sexual offenders. Whilst many treatment programmes are offered to convicted sexual offenders throughout the UK (Beckett 1998), the term 'offender' tends to refer to those who have a criminal conviction and who are but a minority of abusers. Clearly other men sexually abuse; some of those are processed independently of the Criminal Justice System, many are not detected or visible at all. This text will report on what we have learnt from working with identified abusers. We acknowledge the very serious challenges facing staff in working with alleged or suspected abusers, but acknowledge that assessment and management strategies for this group are still in the early stages of development.

As noted above this text is aimed at a professional though not necessarily specialist readership. We do not intend the text to be used as a treatment

11

manual, however. Such manuals are available (e.g. National Probation Service 2001). We stress that those using this text should do so within the context of supervision and clear professional support.

In adopting the word 'managing' in the title of this text we wish to signal that whilst there is a population of abusers who wish to change their behaviour and who may respond to therapeutic interventions, there are those who are not so minded. Further, even for those who wish to change, the therapeutic interventions we have developed to date may be insufficient to bring about change. Such clients may remain risky. The 'management' of sexual abusers requires therapeutic intervention where appropriate, but may also require surveillance, supervision and monitoring. Particularly in Part II the text will focus on selected therapeutic interventions, though again it should be stressed that this is not intended to be a comprehensive treatment manual. Treatment alone, if not embedded within a proper risk management plan involving the elements of surveillance, supervision and monitoring, is unlikely to be 'safe' practice.

OUR VALUE BASE

Two white men have written this book. Inevitably our values and biases will be apparent to those who read the text. The following, however, reflects some of what we believe:

- The challenge to effective case management with sexual abusers is to identify and respect the uniqueness of the client, his context and his potential.

- Ours is a developing field, one very much in its 'adolescence' rather than maturity. Belief in an orthodoxy that we 'know' how best to manage and treat our clients is premature and potentially stifling of much needed innovation. All we can do in this text is present our observations of 'work in progress' rather than the 'truth'.

- Those who sexually abuse may contain a potential for a healthy, abuse-free lifestyle. For the sake of those who are the potential victims of such men it is important to make the effort to change and control the abuser's behaviour and to commit proper resources to such.

- No one profession can deliver all that is needed to manage an identified sexual abuser successfully. There are professions which in our view are under-represented in therapeutic endeavours with abusers (e.g. teachers and health visitors). Further, in the UK, we have made little systematic effort to evaluate the contribution of community chaperones and non-abusing partners/care givers to wider abuser management.

- It is the responsibility of those who work in this field not to abuse the abusers by way of their action or inaction. It is easy for workers to abuse the inherent power differential between themselves and their clients.

- It is the responsibility of those who manage those who work with abusers to promote the well-being, personal safety and integrity of their staff. Self care is the responsibility of all involved with sexual abusers.

- Sexual abuse is not the preserve of one social, racial or ethnic group. However, much of our practice has developed with white, convicted abusers. Texts influencing the work can often appear 'white' and 'anglophone' in character.

- Whilst we talk of 'sexual abuse' and 'sexual abusers' here, in some ways these are clumsy references. Sexual abuse, as with physical abuse and neglect, involves inevitable psychological and emotional maltreatment. Whilst we make strides forward by refining the focus of our activity within the field of sexual abuse, we must be careful not to ignore the learning to be gained from studying the allied fields of non-sexual violence, and the broader fields of child maltreatment. For example, much has been written about primary prevention (e.g. Bloom 1996) which could be extrapolated to our work with abusers.

STYLES OF INTERVENTION

Many of the men we work with have themselves been the subject of emotionally neglectful or psychologically abusive upbringings. Some (not the majority) will have been the victims of sexual and physical abuse (Murphy and Smith 1996). These men are likely to bring into the work with them little or no genuine understanding or experience of concepts such as free choice, informed consent, equality within relationships, unconditional intimacy or experience of being respected. Whilst not necessarily suffering low self-esteem they may display fragile or labile esteem. Commonly they show poor sense of self efficacy and may rate their social and interpersonal skills as poorer than is actually the case. Further, they may show poorer problem solving skills in interpersonal situations (Murphy and Smith 1996).

As our work with sexual abusers develops and we enlarge our portfolio of interventions for men who sexually abuse, we must be careful not to neglect the essential relationship between client and worker. Whilst it is crucial that we should be clear at the outset of the goals and objectives of our work with sexual abusers, and whilst we should be clear that what is offered within treatment is what is required, we should not ignore the fact that the essential substrate for change is the relationship between the client and the worker. We have an emerging literature of 'what works' with general offending behaviour and some promising suggestions as to what might work with sexual abusers. We now face the challenge of examining those interpersonal and relationship factors which might promote or retard growth and development in our clients: a 'who works' agenda.

In our consultancy work we see a range of styles adopted by workers in their approach to clients. There are indeed perhaps fashions which have been followed. Not that long ago it was quite common to see heavily confrontational approaches in this work. These approaches were characterised by workers who adopted an explicitly controlling and dominant stance in their work with clients, telling them what was expected of them and encouraging their verbal compliance. Through determined challenges clients were coerced to say that they were responsible for their offences, that they no longer denied the subtlety of their actions, that they no longer held 'rationalising cognitions', and that they were aware of victim effects. Indeed whilst these objectives were laudable, the style of intervention sadly often appeared to produce a generation of clients who had learned 'what' to say within sessions but did not perhaps experience proper emotional growth and maturity. It is hardly surprising that commentaries were critical of such styles of working; for example, the landmark text of Alan Jenkins (1990a) and the seminal paper on institutional 'nonce bashing' by Sheath (1990).

SUPPORT AND CHALLENGE

In our previous text on assessment (Briggs *et al.* 1998) we described the simple 'support and challenge' model, drawn from the change management literature, which underpins our approach to intervention. Within this framework, change is understood to occur as a consequence of the influence of two independent factors: the support the individual perceives within the change process and the perceived challenge as presented to him by the situation or persons influencing the change. Typically the combination of high challenge and low support produces behaviours representative of stress. For example, sexual abusers within treatment who receive high challenge and low support often can present as aggressive and hostile. At best they may be persuaded to say the right things and exhibit superficial compliance. Those who gain high support but little challenge can appear complacent and inappropriately 'comfortable'. Those who receive both low levels of support and low levels of challenge may appear apathetic and disengaged within the therapeutic process. It is our experience that those who perceive high challenge and high support are most likely to change. Once again it is important to emphasise that it is the client's perception of support and challenge which is crucial here, not those of the workers.

WORKER CHARACTERISTICS

The relationship between worker behaviour and treatment change has been the subject of research in recent time. As part of the evaluation of the English prison service's core programme for dealing with sexual offenders, researchers found that empathy and warmth displayed by the therapist and their directive and rewarding behaviours most strongly predicted therapeutic benefits. Further, confrontational approaches may be associated with negative outcomes (Fernandez, Yates and Mann 2001). This subject is discussed further in Chapter 5.

NURTURANCE

Mussack and Carick (2001) have written on the role of nurturance in sexual offender treatment. They suggest that many abusers have had little nurturance, particularly early in their lives. In turn, this leads the abuser to have a distorted sense of entitlement, that he 'deserves' something to compensate for the lack of early nurturance.

> These feelings provide a rationale for the abusers to take from others, regardless of the consequences, contributing to the development of a sense of self worth that can be reinforced and maintained only by engaging in abusive behaviours. (Mussack and Carick 2001, p.8)

Mussack and Carick promote the notion of 'constructive entitlement', advising that the abuser should be helped to believe he can contribute to the well-being of others, and that there are benefits for him in doing so, including the development of self worth. To achieve this the worker is advised to recognise consistently the abuser's positive value, to help the abuser by creating opportunities for him to make positive contributions to others, to acknowledge these contributions once made but also encourage others to recognise them too, to distinguish between the worth of the abuser and the wrongfulness of the offending behaviour, to expect the abuser to make positive contributions and to be consistent in this, and emphasising the abuser's accountability for the life choices he makes, be they destructive or constructive.

OBJECTIVE SETTING APPROACHES

A key element of the 'what works' agenda is that workers should be clear about the objectives to be progressed in intervention with clients. It is sensible before clients enter sessions for workers to be clear about what it is that clients are expected to achieve from those sessions. Ideally these expectations should be couched in terms of visible, behavioural outcomes.

In the arena of performance development and staff appraisal, objective setting has been guided by the principle that objectives should be

'SMART', i.e. *specific, measurable, achievable, realistic* and *timely*. This also seems to represent an ideal in respect of our work with clients, i.e. that each objective for intervention with clients should be couched in SMART terms.

Our colleague Carol Morton (personal communication) has signalled a set of issues to be considered in objective setting approaches with this group which we adapt below:

- Objectives should reflect a purpose and an intended outcome.
- Objectives should be owned. In working with abusers it is important that it is understood 'whose' objectives are being worked towards.
- Objectives must be consistent with higher strategic goals, for example, in this case the goals of public and child protection.
- Objectives should be congruent with 'organisational' policy, in this context not only reflecting the policies of individual organisations such as the Probation Service or Health Service, but also other bodies such as Area Safeguarding Boards.

Morton reminds us that:

- objectives reflect the values, biases and intentions of those who set them
- setting objectives may raise 'ethical' considerations.

Clearly clients can be exposed to multiple objectives. For example, an abuser may have a set of objectives formed in respect of his group work, but a further set of objectives formed in respect of individual work. Further, if that client is attending other programmes designed to address problems additional to his sexual abuse proclivities, objectives may be set within those other programmes. Objectives across such programmes need to be synchronised.

Often in group work with abusers there is a clear tension between the achievement of deadlines and the progression of the programme. It must be decided whether it is acceptable for clients to progress to other parts of a programme if past objectives have not been met or only partially achieved. Workers must consider issues such as the setting of deadlines for the achievement of objectives, how to choose when the deadline takes priority over content, and contingencies for those occasions when objectives are not met.

It is often assumed that programme objectives should apply to all clients. However, it is important to determine in advance whether abusers within a pre-set programme need to achieve all objectives within the programme or whether there are good reasons, identified either by workers or abusers, why an individual client may not need to attend particular modules.

SMART objectives should be measurable. If set in the language of 'visible outcomes' it should be clear, i.e. a 'yes' or 'no' decision, as to whether an objective has been achieved. The challenge here is for workers to avoid objectives such as 'the abuser will understand…', or 'the client will have learnt…', but to specify outcome behaviour e.g. 'the client will have described, when asked, at least three places within a mile radius of his home which he must avoid due to the likelihood of these situations presenting ready access to potential victims'.

In commenting upon visible outcomes above we acknowledge that behaviours and descriptions can be 'rote' learned and so may not actually illustrate depth of learning or consolidation of learning. The measurement of objectives therefore should be complemented by other continuous assessment strategies, including observations of behaviour and emotion, augmented by the use of psychometric or psycho-physiological testing where appropriate.

Our knowledge of how best to intervene with abusers continues to develop. Accordingly, mechanisms have to be in place to change and refine objectives. Practitioners are often excited by techniques and tools they have used in their work and that have worked well for them in the past. Working to an objective setting approach implies a discipline. Techniques serve the objective and not vice versa. Practitioners might well need training and supervision in how to use objective setting approaches.

If objectives are to be pursued, appropriate resources must be allocated to those doing the work to achieve these and to facilitate the work.

Objectives should reflect theories underpinning the work and should represent proven interventions. They should be robust and stand up to professional and informed challenge. They should have face validity and appear cohesive, comprehensive, relevant and clear.

In Part II we suggest objectives for the management of men who sexually abuse, and with a focus on possible risk factors. However we would not want these suggestions to be accepted uncritically and again stress that this remains 'work in progress'.

If agencies are to develop objectives for this work we strongly suggest that those who will run programmes and those who manage and monitor them should progress the work together and adapt objectives to reflect local need. Ownership of objectives and an understanding of the rationale for using such an objective setting approach are crucial in our experience to the likely successful implementation of an objective setting approach.

LIMITATIONS OF INTERVENTIONS

There is ongoing debate as to treatment effectiveness. Whilst we express an optimism that some interventions bring about change and influence the abuser's potential to reabuse, nevertheless research on treatment effectiveness is in its early stages. Modest rather than radical outcomes appear to be achieved by treatment programmes. We do not really know how to customise wholescale, multi-faceted, cognitive-behavioural interventions to the individual client. In the work of Perry (1998) it is suggested that good sex offender treatment should be responsive to the needs of those being treated. Some programmes, e.g. the Northumbria Sex Offender Groupwork Programme (National Probation Service 2001), have been structured to emphasise this principle. However, the authors would not claim that they have resolved the challenge of how to target individual need. Our experience is that many programmes tend to deliver the same interventions regardless of client need.

Modest treatment outcomes should not be of surprise to us. Setting aside differences in motivation and individual pathology which probably have a bearing on treatment outcome, we still tend to offer treatment to clients outwith the environment which supports and nurtures them. Typically, clients attend the offices and group rooms of professionals such as probation officers and psychologists to receive treatment and counselling. Rarely is any treatment offered or considered in the client's home. It is not often the case that those who live with the abuser are drawn into intensive therapy or counselling with the abuser, although examples of work with the 'non-abusing partner' can be found, e.g. in the Thames Valley programme (National Probation Service 2000) and the Partners for Protection Group in Newcastle (Butler and Hill 2002).

Those outwith the abuser's home or domestic situation who have an investment in the abuser abstaining from further abuse (e.g. members of the extended family, faith leaders or other community groups) similarly are rarely drawn into treatment in any systematic way. Also, other professionals who might monitor the abuser (including health professionals such as family doctors and health visitors) are often neglected. Opportunities for the consolidation of treatment gains as well as for surveillance and monitoring are missed.

TRENDS AND DEVELOPMENTS

When reflecting on what to include in this introductory chapter, inevitably our thoughts turned not only to the history of our work to date but also to the future. We offer some thoughts as to what we perceive to be pressing contemporary challenges, but in the confidence that five years from now we will face another raft of issues.

- Good risk management will have its roots in good risk assessment. Considerable intellectual energy and research time has been spent in the development and refinement of actuarial approaches to risk assessment, particularly the development of predictors of the likelihood of reconviction for sexual offending in known (convicted) sexual abusers. We need to accelerate our efforts to determine valid and reliable predictors of reabuse in alleged (rather than convicted) abusers. We need this to assist in risk management and the determination of the appropriateness of family placement/family resolution in alleged intra-familial abusers.

- We need to find ways to accelerate the dissemination of research information about risk assessment and risk management to front-line workers, alongside ensuring that professional training courses for those engaged in this work contain a core curriculum which equips workers to do the job.

- Prevention is better than cure. Professional organisations committed to child/public protection and the promotion of work with abusers need to increase efforts to drive the prevention agenda. For example, the internet has introduced new opportunities for abusers to support and refine their interests. It also has potential however to influence the sexuality of vulnerable individuals. Educational approaches with children and adolescents should counsel as to the dangers of accessing sexually explicit materials.

- Much attention has been paid in the UK to the development of group work programmes for sexual abusers. The development of individual programmes is needed, and thereafter the evaluation of such.

- In programme evaluation a second generation of psychometric tools is needed – robust materials standardised on relevant populations of a credible size are called for. The development of customised materials for use with non-abusing partners, community chaperones and the like should be advanced.

- Similarly, we need to develop other assessment methods. Psychometrics, by their very nature, can be transparent devices open to misuse by sophisticated clients.

- Qualitative research and single-subject experimental designs should extend current evaluation methodologies.

- Theorising about the aetiology and development of sexual offending should not merely be an intellectual exercise but should prompt the adoption and refinement of treatments.

- The evaluation of the impact of this work on the worker should be a continuing area of professional focus.

CHAPTER 2

A Context for Intervention

In recent years media attention relating to sexual abuse has tended to focus most heavily on the management of convicted (often high profile) sex offenders. The professional literature has also tended to emphasise issues relating to work with convicted offenders. This is to be expected given that they are likely to be the population most readily available with which to conduct research. However, as professionals in child protection systems are only too well aware, it is important to recognise that only a small minority of men who sexually abuse will ever be successfully prosecuted let alone be offered a treatment programme.

Whilst there are a small but growing number of programmes which offer treatment to abusers who may not be under supervision as a result of a criminal court sentence, our experience is that these programmes are still difficult to access.

THE SCOPE OF THE PROBLEM

It is clear that official reports of sexual offences significantly underestimate the actual incidence and prevalence of sexual abuse. Accurate estimates of these rates are very difficult to determine. Grubin (1998) gives an excellent review of the evidence available. Unsurprisingly, where abuse is reported, only a minority of cases result in a criminal conviction (Davis *et al.* 1999). Often this is because the evidence of victims is such that it is difficult to persuade a criminal court that the complaint is valid 'beyond reasonable doubt'.

Victims may have been traumatised by their experiences and so may not be able to give a coherent account. Courts have general difficulties in managing the evidence of young or vulnerable people, including the inappropriateness of cross-examining very young witnesses. This works against the conviction of the abuser in some cases. Perceived bias in rape trials towards men and the fear of cruel and humiliating experiences for female complainants may deter a victim pursuing prosecution (Lees 1989).

Professionals investigating sexual abuse allegations do however need to be aware that children in particular can be heavily influenced by the interviewer, particularly through the medium of 'leading questions', followed by the interviewer inadvertently reinforcing the 'right' answer (Lillee and Reed v Newcastle City Council 2001).

Research in Britain into sex offence convictions in the adult male population (Marshall 1997) indicated that 1 in 60 of a sample of men born in 1953 had a conviction for a sexual offence by age 40, and at least 110,000 men in the adult male population in 1993 had a conviction for a sex offence against a child. For these reasons it is important that the management of men who sexually abuse is set in a broader context. There have been two major developments recently which in our view do this well. They are the promotion of a 'public health' approach to the prevention of sexual abuse and the development by the Home Office of the Multi-Agency Public Protection Arrangements (MAPPA) which formalise the view that all 'work with sex offenders' should be viewed in the context of public protection.

The following is an outline of the models and resources available for the management of men who sexually abuse at the time this text was prepared (summer 2005). We introduce first two key pieces of legislation: the Sexual Offences Act of 2003 and the Human Rights Act of 1998. Laws change; however, research gives us new insights. We have no doubt that some of what we write will be superseded.

THE SEXUAL OFFENCES ACT 2003

The *Sexual Offences Act 2003* (Home Office 2003a) has recently been enacted, and we wait to see what the impact of that legislation will be. The intentions within the Act are to clarify issues of consent and to remove some discrimination that remained in relation to sexual activity between males. Consenting activity between adults will be subject to less regulation whilst offending behaviour to which the victim does not or can not consent will be proscribed more clearly. The Act defines consent for the first time in law: 'A person consents if s/he agrees by choice and has the freedom and capacity to make that choice.'

The Act expands the definition of rape to cover penetration of the mouth by a penis. It addresses consent issues where a complainant may be unconscious, asleep or under threat of violence and seeks to protect 'people with a mental disorder'. It addresses the issue of ostensibly consenting activity between children under 16, and is specific about proscribing sexual activity when one adult party is in a position of trust (including persons in families who are not blood relations) over someone who is under 18. The Act also addresses the use of children for pornography and prostitution.

The *Sexual Offences Act 2003* introduces some new orders which will be described later in this chapter. Readers who are interested to learn of the new offences the Act creates, the maximum penalties they attract and how they relate to old offences are referred to Stevenson *et al.* 2004.

THE HUMAN RIGHTS ACT 1998

All interventions must comply with the *Human Rights Act 1998* (Home Office 1998a). This lists a number of rights and freedoms which individuals hold and identifies exclusions from those rights.

Article Five asserts that everyone has the right to 'liberty and security' except upon conviction by a competent court, or if it is necessary for the purpose of bringing them before a court when there is a reasonable suspicion of them having committed an offence.

Article Eight asserts the right to 'respect for private life'. This is limited '...for the prevention of disorder or crime, for the protection of health or morals, or for the protection of the rights and freedoms of others'. In the European Court of Human Rights case of Johansen v Norway (European Court of Human Rights 1996) it was ruled that child abuse may be considered as an exclusion in this context. The authors have experience of the English courts where this case has been used to justify intervention in families because of concerns of sexual abuse.

It should be noted that all exclusions must be applied only in so far as they are *proportionate* to the issue being addressed, *legal* and *necessary* (i.e. it is not possible to address the problem by less intrusive means). Similarly, the authors have regularly attended meetings under Multi-Agency Public Protection Arrangements where these criteria are considered in relation to every multi-agency protection plan.

PUBLIC HEALTH APPROACHES TO SEXUAL OFFENDING

Public health approaches have been advocated by Richard Laws (1998) and Fran Henry (1999), Director of the 'Stop It Now!' campaign in the USA amongst others. To set such approaches within a context we need to consider approaches to prevention. Three levels of 'prevention' are referred to:

- primary – preventing something from ever happening
- secondary – identifying and targeting risk factors in individuals
- tertiary – preventing a recurrence of something.

Examples from the prevention of heart disease would be:

- primary prevention – public education to persuade members of the public to eat less saturated fat, reduce smoking and exercise more

- secondary prevention – the targeting of individuals with high risk factors such as a family history of heart disease or high blood pressure
- tertiary prevention – the effective treatment of people who had had heart attacks.

It is difficult to merely transfer the concepts uncritically to the field of sexual abuse and to place some interventions accurately within the three categories. However, it has been suggested (Laws 1998) that the analogous position with regard to sexual abuse would be, for example:

- *primary* – public education campaigns about the way that abusers behave; attention to the way that boys in our society are raised; reversing the trend towards the sexualisation of children through fashion advertising
- *secondary* – targeting of young people who show behaviours which may be precursors to sexual abuse; attention to people who show risk factors; (arguably) the treatment of first time and/or younger offenders
- *tertiary* – treatment, supervision, monitoring and incarceration of identified (including convicted) sexual abusers.

Laws (1998) has argued that too little emphasis is given to primary and secondary approaches. Both Laws and Henry describe examples of the public health approach in North America. The Association for the Treatment of Sexual Abusers (ATSA) has also promoted such an approach to the management of sexual abuse (ATSA 2004). To date, initiatives have centred on the provision of advertising and leaflets to educate members of the public, and the provision of telephone help-lines for people to call if they have concerns about their own behaviour or that of other people. The public need to learn about strategies that sex offenders use to target and groom children in order to prevent them doing so within vulnerable organisations, in public places where children congregate and in families. Children need to be taught the elements of healthy sexual behaviour. Advertising may be used to try and persuade abusers or potential abusers to seek treatment, e.g. via help-lines and voluntary treatment programmes.

In the UK and Ireland the Faithfull Foundation and the National Organisation for the Treatment of Abusers (NOTA) have drawn on the work of Laws and Henry and with other agencies have promoted the Stop It Now! campaign, the model and name being the same as those promoted by Fran Henry and colleagues in the USA (Findlater and Hughes 2004). The Home Office has given financial support to this initiative. A full time coordinator has been appointed. Public education leaflets are being circulated widely and a pilot help-line has been established for people who are concerned about their own behaviour or that of someone they know. The pilot (initially functional in the Surrey area) has become known nationally via word of mouth. Between its inception in June 2002 and March 2004, 871 separate callers had telephoned. Of these 37 per cent (325 individuals) were concerned about their own behaviour (Stop It Now! UK and Ireland 2005). Some abusers and potential abusers have been referred for assistance in managing that behaviour. These are excellent examples of primary and secondary prevention.

Another project which involves the prevention of sexual abuse and the involvement of the wider community is *Leisurewatch*, developed by the Derwent Initiative in conjunction with professionals from health, probation, police and social services in Northumbria (Derwent Initiative 2003). Training is given to staff of leisure centres and swimming pools and a protocol agreed for reporting to the police suspicious behaviour that would not in itself constitute a criminal offence. Centres are given a mark of approval. This project was also supported by Home Office funding and is being rolled out nationally. Demand for training is far outstripping supply. Leisurewatch is an excellent example of crime prevention which involves people who are not 'sex offender professionals' in the management of the issue. To April 2004 the project had been rolled out to eight local authority areas (Hogg 2004).

RISK MANAGEMENT

All work with men who sexually abuse should have risk management as its primary focus: to manage risk we have to assess it. Risk can be conceptualised as having three components (Hanson and Harris 2000):

- *static factors* that are historical and unchangeable
- *dynamic stable factors* that are long-term characteristics which can change, albeit slowly
- *dynamic acute factors* that are immediate behaviours that may change very quickly.

Assessment of the level of immediate risk an abuser presents is based on the interplay between the long-term probability of reoffending, what is happening in treatment and the current behaviour of the offender (see Figure 2.1).

A number of researchers (e.g. Hanson 1997; Thornton 2000) have identified static factors that correlate with risk of reconviction from samples of convicted offenders. Both identify previous sex offence convictions, victim characteristics (male and stranger victims), and the offender's age as risk factors (youthful offenders in their late teens and early twenties are seen as particularly risky). Thornton's 'Risk Matrix 2000' also identifies a history of other non sex offence convictions, non contact sex offences

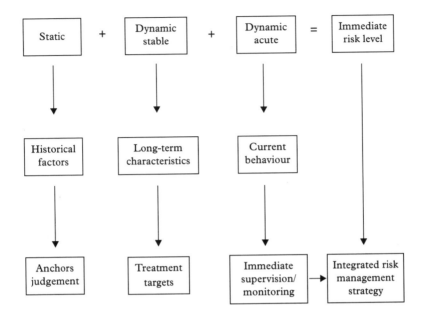

Figure 2.1: *The components of risk*

and lack of adult relationships as risk factors. Typically, the more factors found to be present the higher the risk is deemed to be. Quinsey *et al.* (1995) argued that such statistical or 'actuarial' judgements should 'anchor' judgements about risk.

High scores on measures of static risk factors tend to correlate with factors which inhibit good treatment outcomes (Beech *et al.* 1998). This means that offenders with such high scores should be regarded as being predisposed to being at high risk, however well they appear to do in treatment.

The statistical measures of risk that we have accepted to date are only applicable to adult male abusers who have been convicted. Further, they have been developed in the main with sexual offenders not convicted of internet sexual crimes. They form a baseline but do not indicate who the victim might be, what the consequences of reoffending might be, or indeed when an offence is most likely to occur. Neither do they indicate factors which might identify which statistically 'low risk' offenders may reoffend, nor do they remove professional judgement about when 'low risk' is 'low enough'. Whilst an event may be a low risk statistically, its potential consequences could be so catastrophic that no level of statistical risk will be tolerated.

'Dynamic' factors, as the name implies, are ones which may change. Dynamic stable factors are personality characteristics which may be long term. They tend to be those risk factors targeted in treatment programmes, targets which are discussed in detail in Part II of this book.

Dynamic acute factors may change quickly. Hanson and Harris (1997) studied behaviours which were apparent in the records of 200 sex offenders in the period immediately before they reoffended. They identified a number of behaviours, none of which would be regarded as 'sex offence specific'. These included manipulation of supervision arrangements, failing to be at appointed places at the correct time, drink and drug abuse, variation in some mood states and access to victims. This was a retrospective study. The exercise is being repeated prospectively in order to test whether these findings are predictive. It will be noted that these behaviours are likely to be observed by people who are not specialist sex offender workers and will be factors targeted by supervision, monitoring and, if necessary, surveillance. More detail about the practical applications of this is offered later in this chapter.

The above framework identifies different 'strands' to risk management as a function of the assessed risk that an abuser may pose. The Social Work Services Inspectorate for Scotland (1997) has described four facets of work with sex offenders which complements the above. These are:

- monitoring
- supervision
- treatment
- personal change programmes.

Monitoring is described as the 'routinised arrangements for maintaining up-to-date information about the whereabouts of convicted sex offenders'. *Supervision* is defined as the 'planned arrangements for overseeing sex offenders in the community'. *Treatment* is regarded as 'medical, psychological, or psycho-social measures following a medical diagnosis...' of illness or disability. *Personal change programmes* mean 'programmes, including residential programmes, aimed at helping offenders avoid or eradicate their criminal sexual behaviour through control or management of their drives and feelings...'. Whilst this adds clarity to thinking about various interventions, the distinction between treatment and personal change programmes has not been widely adopted (except within the Criminal Justice Act 2003 [Home Office 2003b]). Therefore we subsume the latter term, personal change programmes, under 'treatment' within this text.

HARM REDUCTION

As we discuss approaches to intervention the concept of 'harm reduction' is noteworthy. This controversial approach is based on the notion that outcomes other than absolute abstinence from reoffending may have value in tackling the problem of sexual abuse. Any reduction in degree of harm to potential victims and society is considered worthwhile, particularly as outcomes of treatment remain relatively modest (Hanson *et al.* 2002).

By extending the concept of levels of prevention (above) a fourth level can be introduced here, that referring to 'slowing the progression of the disease', or 'quaternary prevention'. With sexual abusers this level would be represented by focusing on reducing the frequency with which sexual abuse occurs (Laws 1998; Stoner and George 2000). Similarly, proponents argue that if reabuse is to occur, were treatment to be effective at this quaternary prevention level, then better the abuse be less traumatic and intensive for the victim, or that the number of victims is limited.

Harm reduction here represents 'a public health alternative to the moral and the medical or disease models of addictions, the harm reduction philosophy suggests a more pragmatic focus on the consequences or effects of the addictive behaviour rather than on the behaviour itself' (Marlatt 1996, cited by Stoner and George 2000).

INTER-AGENCY WORKING

It is apparent from the above discussion that numerous individuals and agencies should be working together in the management of a given abuser. All will have important and complementary roles. Judith Hughes, Director of the Derwent Initiative in Northumbria, has observed how the terms 'inter-agency' and 'multi-agency' are used as if they were synonymous; they are not. In her article 'Making Inter-Agency Work Work', she outlines the differences (1998). In multi-agency work, each agency takes responsibility for part of a problem, determines its own aims, assumes and maintains a lead role in its projects, and informs others of developments. In inter-agency work, all agencies take responsibility for all of the problems, subscribe to a common aim, negotiate lead roles, move in and out of lead roles as appropriate, and consult each other before developments are decided.

Inter-agency work requires that each agency puts its own house in order. Hughes cites the example where social services departments may hold information about abusers on the files of their victims, so that different staff members within the same organisation may not know that a named individual has been identified as abusing in other families. Another example was that of a police force holding information in area commands which was passed to the National Criminal Intelligence Service but was not held centrally within that force. Agencies depend on each other and must consider how their proposals fit with those of others. To this end Hughes describes how, in the Northumbria area, the Derwent Initiative has convened forums to develop inter-agency protocols, for instance, concerning the assessment of adolescent abusers, the management of information between agencies, the housing of sex offenders and the assessment and management of sex offenders with learning disabilities. The Probation Service, the Sexual Behaviour Unit in Northumbria and others have been involved in training courses involving a wide range of agencies. These initiatives have improved the likelihood that developments in the area are genuine inter-agency initiatives based on mutual trust and common understanding. This helps to address some of the tensions identified by Hughes and in the Cleveland Inquiry (Butler-Schloss 1988). These include tensions about the role of an enquiry, different value systems or theoretical perspectives, and dogmatism amongst professionals.

Within the context of the inter-agency assessment of children in need three government departments have commented on inter-agency practice:

> Inter-agency, interdisciplinary assessment practice requires an additional set of knowledge and skills to that required for working within a single agency or independently. It requires that all staff understand the roles and responsibilities of staff working in contexts different to their own. Having an understanding of the perspectives, language and culture of other professionals can inform how communication is conducted. This prevents professionals from misunderstanding one another because they use different language to describe similar concepts or because they are influenced by stereotypical perceptions of the other discipline. (DoH, DfEE, Home Office 2000)

We endorse this sentiment in consideration of inter-agency work with sexual abusers.

MANAGEMENT STRATEGIES FOR CONVICTED SEX OFFENDERS

Sentencing and registration

Since the mid 1990s, under successive governments in England and Wales, there have been legislative changes aimed at managing more successfully the risks which some sex offenders pose to the community. Many of these provisions were enacted during a period when governments were seeking to address the public reaction to sexual offending and acknowledging that, unlike other crimes where offenders tend to grow out of a pattern of behaviour, for some sexual offenders patterns of behaviours persist into old age. These legal provisions are in addition to the long-standing power of the courts to pass community orders (see later) and licences which require offenders to be under supervision after periods in custody. None of the provisions are of themselves a solution to the problem of managing convicted sexual offenders, but in total they do form a wide range of protective strategies.

COMMUNITY ORDERS

The Criminal Justice Act 2003 (Home Office 2003b) empowers courts to sentence an offender to a 'community order'. There is now only one such order which may contain a selection of requirements (guidance suggests a maximum of five) appropriate to the seriousness of the offence(s), risk posed by the offender and the offender's needs. There are 12 possible requirements:

- supervision – the offender must attend regular appointments with their probation officer
- unpaid work – for the benefit of the community
- programme attendance – e.g. an accredited group work programme
- drug rehabilitation – via the probation officer and specialist partner agencies
- alcohol treatment – with the offender required to attend for treatment
- mental health treatment – for a condition that may be susceptible to treatment
- residence – such as at approved premises, independent hostels or a private address
- specified activities – possibly relating to work or training
- exclusion – from specified areas, usually to be monitored electronically
- prohibited activity – to refrain from participating in specific activities or at specific times
- curfew – to be at an agreed place between specific hours
- attendance centre (under 25s only) – to undertake work.

PUBLIC PROTECTION SENTENCES

The Criminal Justice Act 2003 introduced two custodial sentencing provisions for dangerous violent and sexual offenders. These replace the previous powers to pass longer than commensurate sentences (Home Office 1991), extended sentences (Home Office 1998) and automatic life sentences for a second conviction for rape and some other serious sexual offences (Home Office 1997a).

The provisions are for indeterminate sentences of imprisonment for public protection (i.e. for offences other than where life is the maximum sentence), and extended sentences. These are in addition to life sentences which are available for some serious sexual offences. The following describes the provisions as they apply to sex offenders. (For more comprehensive guidance to the Act, readers are referred to Taylor *et al.* 2004.)

Indeterminate sentences of imprisonment for public protection. This section applies where:

- a person aged 18 or more is convicted of a serious offence (i.e. one where the maximum sentence is ten years or more) and

- the court is of the opinion that there is a significant risk to members of the public of serious harm occasioned by the commission by him of further specified offences.

As noted by Taylor *et al.* (2004) the definition of 'significant risk' will need to be clarified by case law. Serious harm has been previously defined (Home Office 1991) as 'death or physical injury whether physical or psychological'.

Extended sentences. This section [227] applies where:

- a person aged 18 or more is convicted of a specified offence other than a serious offence (i.e. one where the maximum sentence is between two and ten years) and

- the court is of the opinion that there is a significant risk to members of the public of serious harm occasioned by the commission by him of further specified offences.

Table 2.1: Length of registration periods under the Sex Offenders Act 1997 (Home Office 1997b)

Sentence	Length of requirement
Imprisonment 30 months or more or life	Indefinite period
Detention in hospital subject to restriction order	Indefinite period
Imprisonment More than 6 months Less than 6 months	10 years
Imprisonment 6 months and less	7 years
Detention in hospital – no restriction order	7 years
Any other sentence or order (including a caution)	5 years

Note: Terms are halved for offenders under 18 years of age.

In these circumstances the court must pass an extended sentence. This will be the appropriate custodial term (minimum 12 months) plus a period of supervision on licence of such length that the court considers necessary to protect members of the public. The maximum supervision period is eight years and the total (custodial plus supervision) must not exceed the maximum sentence for the offence(s).

Assessment of dangerousness. If the offender has not been convicted previously of a specified offence the court *must* take into account information about the offence(s), and *may* take into account information about any pattern of behaviour and about the offender, in order to decide if the above threshold has been met. If the offender has previously been convicted of a specified offence the court *must assume that* he poses a significant risk *unless* the court concludes that it would be unreasonable to conclude that there is such a risk. In reaching such a conclusion the court would take into account information about the nature of all offences, any pattern of behaviour and the offender.

Registration of sex offenders. Under the 1997 Sex Offenders Act (Home Office 1997b) amended by the Sexual Offences Act 2003 (Home Office 2003a), most people convicted of a sexual offence on or since 1 September 1997 or who were in custody, detained in hospital or under statutory supervision on that date are required to register their address with the police upon conviction or if they change address. The provisions also apply to persons who committed offences but were found not guilty by reason of insanity and those subject to guardianship orders. Failure to register is punishable by a fine or imprisonment. The length of time that the requirement remains in force relates to the type of sentence received rather than any risk which may be perceived to exist (see Table 2.1).

The guidance to the Sex Offenders Act (Home Office 1997c) and subsequent MAPPA guidelines (National Probation Directorate 2003, citing the Crime and Disorder Act 1998) allows for public disclosure as 'very much the exception to the rule'. The guidance includes criteria to be met before disclosing information. The offender must present a risk of serious harm, there must be no other practicable, less intrusive means of protecting an individual (or individuals), and failure to disclose would put them at risk. The risk to the offender must be considered (but not outweigh consideration of risk to others). The guidance also considers some of the practicalities of disclosure, such as how the information is disclosed and to whom. To date the facility of disclosure has been used only rarely.

Prior to the implementation of the 1997 Sex Offenders Act, Hebenton and Thomas (1997) undertook research into the implementation of sex offender registration in different states in the USA. They found (unsurprisingly) that where registration was merely routinised and bureaucratic it had little positive effect in managing offenders in a way which minimised the risk of reoffending. Consequently, the Home Office (1997c) resolved that all offenders should be assessed and followed up as appropriate.

Sexual offences prevention orders. The Sexual Offences Act 2003 (Home Office 2003a) combines two previous orders (sex offender orders and restraining orders) and allows for whatever prohibitions on an offender that are necessary to protect the public (e.g. a prohibition from attending certain places or undertaking certain activities). These are civil orders which nevertheless require registration. A breach of the order is punishable by imprisonment.

Prosecution for offences abroad. Part II of the Sex Offenders Act 1997 allows for the prosecution in Britain of British nationals, for sexual offences committed abroad, where the alleged acts are criminal offences in Britain and in the country concerned.

The Sexual Offences Act 2003 (Home Office 2003a) also introduced the following orders:

- *Notification Orders*, which require those convicted of sexual offences abroad to register if they come to this country

- *Foreign Travel Orders*, under which those convicted of sexual offences in this country may be banned from travelling abroad in certain circumstances

- *Risk of Sexual Harm Orders*, which may prevent sexually explicit communication by an adult towards a child.

Disqualification orders. The Criminal Justice and Court Services Act 2000 (Home Office 2000), amended by the Criminal Justice Act 2003 (Home Office 2003b), gives crown courts the power to attach an order to a sentence disqualifying an offender from working with children. The offences to which this power applies are defined in the Criminal Justice and Court Services Act as amended by the Sexual Offences Act 2003 (Home Office 2003a).

Multi-Agency Public Protection Arrangements

There has been a long history of multi-agency management of dangerous offenders (including sex offenders) involving probation services, the police and other relevant parties (e.g. Monk 1999). These have been formalised and now the management of convicted sex offenders in the community is undertaken in the context of *Multi-Agency Public Protection Arrangements* (MAPPA), which were instituted in 2001 (National Probation Directorate 2003). These arrangements require police, probation and prison services ('the responsible authority') to establish MAPPA locally. Other agencies have a 'duty to cooperate' with the responsible authority. These agencies include health authorities and trusts, housing authorities and registered social landlords, social services departments, youth offending teams, local education authorities and electronic monitoring providers. Two 'lay advisers' will be appointed to the strategic management board of each MAPPA. The MAPPA are guided by a framework which has four functions:

- the identification of MAPPA offenders
- the sharing of relevant information
- the assessment of the risk of serious harm
- the management of that risk.

MAPPA are intended for the management of registered sex offenders (see below), violent and other sex offenders and 'other offenders'. The level of risk posed is assessed by identifying static and dynamic risk factors and risk is then managed at one of three levels.

An initial actuarial (i.e. statistical) assessment of static risk factors is undertaken to screen offenders. The actuarial tool currently being used in the UK to undertake this is Risk Matrix 2000, developed by David Thornton (see above). The categories with approximate percentage reconviction rates over a 20-year follow-up are:

Low	10%
Medium	20%
High	40%
Very High	60%

Offenders screened as 'high' or 'very high' will be the subject of a meeting of a Multi-Agency Public Protection Panel (MAPPP). Those who score 'medium' or 'low' on actuarial measures may be the subject of a MAPPP meeting if dynamic risk factors indicate a heightened degree of concern.

Dynamic stable risk factors are considered, drawing from a wide variety of sources including case files, clinical interviews and observations, other observations, and psychometric tests. Mann *et al.* (2002a) (drawing on the work of Thornton) conceptualise these factors within four 'domains', which cover:

- sexual deviance and preoccupation
- attitudes that are supportive of sexual offending
- lifestyle management issues
- social and emotional regulation.

Factors within these domains accord with personality factors which are targeted in sex offender treatment and are covered at length in Part II of this text.

Notwithstanding adjustments made to the initial risk evaluation using static and dynamic stable factors, Thornton (1999) and Hanson and Harris (1997) have also identified various 'acute risk' factors (sometimes characterised as 'panic now' factors) which should urge concern to the practitioner. Amongst these are victim access behaviours such as the offender entering into hobbies that give access to victims, work that gives access to victims, domestic arrangements that give access to victims and the grooming of a specific individual or potential victim. Victim access behaviours may include the offender driving or wandering around without good purpose. It is also suggested that concern should be raised if the offender appears to reject supervision. This may be signalled by missed appointments, the offender lying to the supervising officer or alternatively being overly friendly with the supervising officer. Belligerence towards a supervising officer and the offender asking to be seen less often would also seem of concern. Finally, issues of loss are also referred to here as points of caution; for example, the offender who loses house, job or relationships, as well as the offender whose mood seems to worsen, particularly where anger increases or alcohol misuse begins.

The levels of the MAPPA referred to above into which cases are then allocated are as follows:

- *Level 1:* used where cases can be managed by one agency without actively or significantly involving other agencies

- *Level 2:* used where the active involvement of more than one agency is required. Different arrangements are likely to exist in response to each individual case

- *Level 3:* the Multi-Agency Public Protection Panel is responsible for managing the 'critical few' cases which are defined as follows:

  a) identification as being high or very high risk of serious harm *and*

  b) risks can only be managed by a plan which requires close cooperation at a senior level due to the complexity of the case and/or because of the unusual resource commitment required *or*

  c) the case may attract unusual media interest.

High or very high risk in this context means that there is a high probability of an offence occurring which will cause serious harm (i.e. which is life threatening and/or traumatic and from which recovery, whether physical or psychological, can be expected to be difficult or impossible) and that such an offence is regarded as imminent.

In 2002/3 (the second year of operation), the MAPPA managed 21,400 registered sex offenders, 29,500 'violent and other sex offenders' and 1802 'other offenders' i.e. a total of 52,702 offenders (Middleton 2003b).

Eighteen per cent of these (2843) were categorised as requiring intervention at Level 3 ('the critical few'). Of these, 468 were recalled to prison for a breach of licence, 49 were imprisoned for breach of a sex offender order (see below), and 48 (2% of the 'critical few') were charged with serious, violent or sex offences (although the figures are not clear about how many of those were convicted). In addition, it is noted from Northumbria's experience that the figures may mask the reality of what is happening on the ground (National Probation Service Northumbria 2003). One case listed as 'arson' was actually a minor fire in a 'wheelie bin' and a conviction for a sexual offence related to a historical matter predating the offence for which the offender was being supervised. It is clear that a more detailed study is required before we have a full understanding of the outcomes of interventions under the MAPPA.

As an aside at this point in the text, it is perhaps timely to indicate that whilst actuarial tools such as the Risk Matrix 2000 have currency in the risk assessment/risk management process of MAPPPs, they are not without their critics. Doren (2002) has produced an excellent overview of risk assessment evaluations, including comment on ethical issues. Other approaches to risk assessment and risk management will develop. We note, for example, at the time of the drafting of this text that training is being offered in the UK on the Risk For Sexual Violence Protocol (RSVP) (Hart *et al.* 2003), which presents a set of guidelines for practitioners in assessing risk for sexual violence. Unsurprisingly, this has met with enthusiasm by some practitioners frustrated by the bluntness of pure actuarial approaches to risk assessment. It is likely that this instrument and others like it will be developed and refined.

ACCREDITATION OF TREATMENT PROGRAMMES

In the UK during the late 1980s and early 1990s a range of facilities for dealing with convicted sex offenders was developed. The Prison Sex Offender Treatment Programme in England and Wales was launched. This is a cognitive-behavioural-based group work programme which is offered to prisoners based in specialist units within some prisons. Each establishment had to submit its programme to an international accreditation panel. Examples of accreditation criteria can be found in Beech,

Fisher and Beckett's report to the Home Office in 1998 concerning their evaluation of the prison sex offender treatment programme (Beech *et al.* 1998) and are discussed in Chapter 5.

The Correctional Services Accreditation Panel has now replaced the international accreditation panel and its successor, the Joint Prison and Probation Services Accreditation Panel. This is part of a move to promote consistency across community-based programmes and improve integration between work which is undertaken with prisoners during sentence and that conducted after release, e.g. upon licence. It had been noted, e.g. Home Office 1998b and 1999, that whilst there had been a large-scale development of sex offender programmes, particularly group work programmes within probation services in England and Wales (Flaxington and Procter 1996), there was inconsistency in the delivery of these programmes. Further, the integration of work with offenders post-custody was not always well integrated with that undertaken during sentence. It is the intention of the Home Office that eventually all treatment programmes run by the Probation Service for all offenders, not only sex offenders, will be accredited.

The National Probation Service has three accredited sex offender programmes which were designed in the Northumbria, Thames Valley and West Midlands probation areas. These are group work programmes for convicted sex offenders in the community. Typically, these are adult male offenders who are subject to supervision following release from custody or direct from court. Each probation area runs one of the three accredited programmes. Middleton (2002) has provided an overview of these programmes from the perspective of his role as Programmes Implementation Manager for sex offender programmes at the National Probation Directorate.

The roll-out of the accredited programmes has not been without concern. Whilst accredited programmes have their roots in 'evidence based practice', there are concerns that the acceptance criteria for offenders may be limiting (e.g. they have not catered for women or offenders with learning disabilities and may not be suitable for ethnic minority offenders). There are also concerns that the institutionalisation of the work into an 'accredited programme' should not stifle progress in the development of programme content (Kennington 2002). We await long-term, follow-up data on the effectiveness of these programmes as implemented away from the sites which developed them (Spencer 2000).

In Scotland, cognitive-behavioural treatment programmes have been developed in some prisons and community projects. The issue of the accreditation of programmes is currently being addressed (Spencer 2000).

Treatment of sex offenders is dealt with comprehensively in Part II of this book.

HOSTELS

There is a wide range of hostel provision which accommodates sexual abusers who are being managed by the criminal justice or mental health services. These may be provided on a statutory basis (e.g. 'approved' hostels run by or on behalf of the Probation Service), or through the voluntary sector. Hostel staff undertake an invaluable role in the monitoring and support of offenders.

Monitoring by hostel staff will involve the obvious attention to residence or curfew conditions. Hanson and Harris (1997) have noted a range of factors which are not 'sex specific' which may signal that an abuser is likely to relapse. These include increased use of substances, the development of negative attitudes to supervision or treatment, fluctuation in mood states and rule breaking (which in other contexts may appear minor). All of these may be apparent to staff in hostels and may alert supervisors to potential difficulties. The authors have observed numerous examples where trained staff have been alert to concerns about some of the 'dynamic risk factors' that have contributed to men's abusive behaviour. Examples in relation to deviant sexual interest are the reporting of a resident who had family photographs of children (including ones where his victim was prominent) in his room, and another who appeared preoccupied with children's television programmes.

In terms of support, hostel staff can clearly help with work on 'dynamic risk factors' to enhance treatment efficacy. Examples in the areas of sexual interest might include reminders to fill in homework diaries, giving advice about what to watch on television and on behaviour towards female staff. Collusive or abusive attitudes shown by clients can be checked by staff and pro-social attitudes and behaviour modelled. Support and advice may be given in terms of emotional and lifestyle management issues. Staff may be involved in supporting abusers who are attempting to become involved in new activities, either to increase general contact with adults (and thereby help to minimise preoccupation with children) or to develop social skills or self-esteem.

There are a number of other factors associated with good treatment outcome (see Chapter 5), including motivation and the ability to take responsibility for one's own actions, factors again which may be encouraged by hostel staff. It is essential that close liaison is undertaken between hostel staff, supervisors and programme providers within the context of MAPPA. We strongly recommend good training for hostel staff to maximise their ability to monitor and support abusers, but also to enhance their own safety and emotional well-being. In the experience of the authors, the provision of such training has been uneven.

CIRCLES OF SUPPORT AND ACCOUNTABILITY

An interesting development in the management of convicted sexual abusers has been that of professionally supported volunteerism in the management of high risk sexual offenders. Wilson and colleagues of the correctional services of Canada and the Mennonite Church (Wilson, Picheca and Serin 2001) have described the development of so called 'circles of support and accountability'. They have focused their attention on volunteers working with a particularly problematic group of sexual abusers, namely those who have been in prison, typically denied parole and who return to the community with few or no supports. Often they are offenders who have potential for negative media attention, given the seriousness of their offending. All have at least signalled a desire never to harm again.

The volunteers who agree to support these offenders are recruited for their stability in the community, their maturity and their availability to meet with the offender, often at unusual times of day or night in response to the offender's needs. The volunteers are deemed to have a balanced lifestyle and viewpoint towards offending, and to have sustained healthy boundaries. The volunteers are often drawn into providing support via a family member or friend who is already part of an existing order or via previous prison experience, and a significant number are drawn from the faith community.

The volunteers are trained to offer support to the offenders via an impressive raft of training. The following are cited as examples of training topics:

- overview of the criminal justice system
- restorative justice
- needs of survivors
- the circle model
- the effects of institutionalisation
- human sexuality and sexual deviance
- risk assessment
- boundaries and borders
- conflict resolution
- group dynamics
- building group cohesion
- circle functions
- client's response and preparing for critical incident stress
- working with correctional officers, police, news media and other community professionals

- needs assessment
- building a covenant
- court orders
- closing a circle.

The schedule of the volunteer's contact with the offender is driven by the offender's needs. Those volunteers forming the 'circle' offer social contact and support to the offender. In this context, the volunteers are not 'therapists'. Any counselling/advice offered is an adjunct, not primary focus of the circle meetings. The contact is community driven, not system driven.

Wilson and colleagues' research has elicited the experience of the 'core member' (the offender). Contact with the circle has been found to offer the core member a sense of support and acceptance by others. The majority of offenders report receiving practical help. At least half of those interviewed reported a sense of self worth and gaining a 'realistic perspective' on their situation. Noteworthy also, however, about two thirds of those interviewed by Wilson and colleagues reported 'increased anxiety and pressure' from contact with the circle, something which may relate to the offender experiencing a sense of accountability for their behaviour.

Wilson and colleagues are hopeful that such community 'interaction' may assist in reducing the recidivism rates of this very difficult group of offenders. Their research to date is hopeful, but is based on a small sample and recidivism rates are measured against what may have been expected using an actuarial measure. It remains to be seen whether recidivism rates will reduce long term, notably after the 'circle' has disbanded.

In the UK, the Quaker Council for Social Responsibility promoted a similar scheme which has been funded by the Home Office. The second author sat on the consultative committee representing the National Organisation for the Treatment of Abusers. Pilot schemes are being promoted in three areas with coordinators having been appointed using Home Office funding. There are differences relating to the use of the scheme and concerns that Home Office funding may engender a 'top down' approach rather than support being generated from within communities. Some volunteers have been identified and training implemented. Progress in matching of volunteers and appropriate offenders in relevant areas is proving to be slow and the number of circles established only numbered 12 as at spring 2004. It is hoped that once circles are established that developments will 'snowball'.

CHILDREN ACT PROCEEDINGS

It is noted that a wide range of measures exists to constrain the behaviour of those sexual abusers who have been convicted, particularly where current orders exist. Where abusers have old convictions or there are known abusive behaviours which have not resulted in convictions, agencies may need to resort to strategies available under civil laws, notably the Children Act 1989 (Department of Health 1989). Under this Act a local authority social services department may apply for (amongst others) a care order or supervision order. A care order may last until a child's 18th birthday and an authority may be given parental rights, e.g. to remove a child and place it in residence away from its parents, or it may leave a child with its parents but enforce rigorous supervision requirements. A supervision order may last for a year with the option of renewal for two subsequent years. As the name implies, a supervision order gives an authority power to supervise children in their home and to 'advise, assist and befriend' the parent(s).

In our earlier book, *Assessing Men Who Sexually Abuse* (Briggs *et al.* 1998, p.61) we outline the case of Re H (All England Law Reports 3.1.96) in which the House of Lords clarified that the standard of proof in care proceedings is based on the 'balance of probabilities' (i.e. lower than the criminal court standard of proof 'beyond all reasonable doubt'). It ruled that this should be based on facts not suspicion and that the burden of proof lay with the applicant (i.e. the local authority). It must be shown on the balance of probabilities that some abusive act has occurred (not necessarily a criminal offence) *and* that this is likely to lead to harm. 'Likely' in this context is described as 'a real possibility that it is not sensible to ignore given the feared harm in a given case'.

It is the experience of the authors who both currently work in the civil court arena that where thorough expert assessments are undertaken it is often possible for cases to be mounted which pass these 'threshold criteria'. In our view, it is necessary to undertake thorough assessments at an early stage in the management of a case and, more importantly, to act on the conclusions. We are mindful here also of the need to avoid delay in care cases and would refer the reader to the Protocol for Judicial Case Management in Public Law Children Act Cases (Lord Chancellor's Department 2003) and to the Code of Guidance for those who act as expert witnesses in family proceedings. Intervention will need to be commensurate (i.e. proportionate and necessary as discussed above) with the risk identified. On occasions it may not be possible to seek orders in the court. In such cases it may be possible to intervene to protect a child or children on the basis of registration of the child on the 'at risk' register as outlined in the document *Working Together* (Home Office *et al.* 1999).

It is worthwhile to pause here to comment on the spirit of *Working Together*. The government departments which collaborated to produce this document (Health and Education, the Home Office, and the National Assembly for Wales) emphasise that 'promoting children's well-being and safeguarding them from significant harm, depends crucially upon effective informal sharing, collaboration and understanding between agencies and professionals'. It is advised that 'all agencies and professionals' should be alert to potential indicators of risk and 'be alert to the risks which individual abusers, or potential abusers, may pose to children'. Whilst the focus of *Working Together* is the well-being and protection of children, the philosophy of inter-agency working to monitor and manage risk to vulnerable individuals is just as applicable to the protection of vulnerable adults in our communities.

The issue of registration on the Child Protection Register is also discussed at length in Briggs *et al.* 1998.

OTHER INITIATIVES

There are a number of initiatives that, at the time of writing, are in the pipeline e.g. the Home Office (Home Office and Department of Health 2004) is piloting a project in a number of prisons and special hospitals aimed at improving the management, including treatment, of people who are diagnosed as having a dangerous severe personality disorder (DSPD).

There are a number of pieces of legislation which are aimed at minimising the risk of unsuitable people securing employment or abusing positions of trust with children and vulnerable adults. The Police Act 1997 (Home Office 2001) required the provision of a certificate relating to previous convictions for those applying to work in a paid or unpaid capacity with children. The Protection of Children Act 1999 (Parliament 2000), when enacted, will extend that provision and will replace the current Department of Education Consultancy Service Index (known as 'List 99'). This Act requires the Secretary of State to keep a list of persons who are unsuitable to work with children. This list will relate not only to persons who have been convicted but those who 'have been dismissed, or transferred from a child care position, resigned or retired' because of 'misconduct which has harmed or put at risk a child whether or not this misconduct occurred in the course of employment'. It will be possible for information to be put on the list subsequent to the individual's departure from an organisation. Self employed or agency workers may be entered on the list if an organisation has 'refused to do further business' with them in the above circumstances. Inclusion on this list will be able to be mentioned on certificates issued under the Police Act 1997.

The Care Standards Act (Department of Health 2000) establishes a 'Care Standards Commission'. This will work within extensive rules for the regulation and registration of institutions and individuals who work with children and vulnerable adults. The regulation and registration requirements apply to the following: children's homes, hospitals, clinics, care homes, residential family centres, fostering agencies and foster carers, social and residential care workers, registered child minders, boarding schools and colleges, and employment agencies providing staff in this field.

POLYGRAPHY

The polygraph is a device which measures physiological changes (heart rate, breathing and galvanic skin response) in a subject, in response to specific questions. If a subject reacts by showing increased anxiety, the most likely explanation is that the subject is lying. However, a small but significant number of subjects exhibit an anxiety reaction whilst telling the truth. As such, it is more useful in enabling subjects to be more open about their behaviour than it is purely as a 'lie detector'. A pilot study is being operated in some probation areas in England to test its effectiveness as an adjunct to treatment. For a review of evidence and preliminary results of the pilot study, readers are referred to Grubin *et al.* (2004).

At the first examination, 31 of 32 subjects (97%) disclosed an average of 2.45 high risk behaviours which were previously unknown to supervisors (by far the most common being masturbation to deviant fantasies). At the time of the second test, 21 subjects returned and 71 per cent disclosed an average of 1.57 risk behaviours, a significant decrease. These offenders also appeared to be more honest with supervisors. The authors suggested that those motivated not to reoffend found polygraphy useful, whilst those less motivated sought to avoid it. The pilot has been expanded although involvement remains voluntary.

CONCLUDING REMARKS

It is essential that action on all of the above is undertaken in an inter-agency, multi-disciplinary context, in compliance with local protocols and guidelines. It is clear that treatment is only one part of a wide range of measures to manage men who sexually abuse.

Grubin (1998) has argued that

> The likelihood of a sex offender re-offending will vary over time, depending on his mental state, social circumstances, and general well-being; many benefit from knowing there are explicit external controls around them. There will therefore need to be ongoing reassessment of risk, visible monitoring, and appropriate interventions at times of increased risk. Those involved in the management of sex offenders will need to know how to evaluate risk and how to intervene and reduce it. At times this may involve treatment, at times social support and at times community notification. The science, and the art, is in knowing when to do which. (p.43)

CHAPTER 3

Staffing Issues

Working with men who sexually abuse is intellectually and emotionally demanding. It is essential that appropriate staff are selected to do the work and that they are properly trained and supported. There is a duty of care on those who manage programmes. The obligation is to reduce the risk to staff of being overwhelmed and damaged by the experience of working with sexual abusers, to ensure that assessments, decision making and management strategies are as sound as possible, and that those who work with abusers do so professionally, in the fullest sense of that word.

The potential adverse effects on staff working in the field of sexual abuse are well documented (e.g. Beech *et al.* 1998; Clarke 2004; Erooga 1994; Menzies 1970; Morrison 1990, 1998; Salter 1988). The areas of concern are outlined below.

DEMANDS UPON THE WORKER

Salter (1988) has described some of the tensions for therapists inherent in this work. These tensions include uncertainty about treatment efficacy, the imposition of goals upon the therapists, the setting of limits in relation to behaviour and confidentiality, the difficulty in trusting sexual offenders, the potential for therapist narcissm, the balance between respect and collusion, and the need to confront offenders.

Erooga (1994) describes other tensions. Working with sexual abusers involves exposure to powerful emotions and necessitates dealing with high levels of distortion about human sexual behaviours. Workers may adopt defence mechanisms in order to protect themselves from the emotional impact of the work. Erooga has described individual factors which he believes are particular to work with sexual abusers. These reflect the fact that sex and sexuality are a constant feature of the work. Any sexual problems which the worker experiences or has experienced may be highlighted. Any victimisation the worker may have experienced may be restimulated. Descriptions of abusive sexual behaviour or responses may intrude on a worker's private thoughts.

Issues of 'identification and fear of contamination' are outlined by Erooga. These issues may be evident, for example, in male workers working with men who have abused adults, where abuser behaviour is motivated by power, dominance and hostility. Some male workers may have held beliefs which are hostile to women and may hold 'rape support-ive' beliefs. In turn, female workers may have experienced behaviours in a domestic, social or work context which reflect the abusive practices of their abuser clients. Such factors may impinge heavily on the quality of interac-tions between abusers and workers and between co-workers.

The context of this work can add other pressures. Gordon and Hover (1998), for example, in commenting on prison based treatment programmes, note that some prison staff may view sexual abusers nega-tively, may equate treatment with 'softness' on crime, and may sabotage the efforts of their treatment colleagues.

Notwithstanding the above, there is an expectation within some parts of society that work with sexual abusers will rid society of such behaviour and that no abuser will ever repeat his behaviour. The second author here had regular contact with the media by virtue of his office within the National Organisation for the Treatment of Abusers (NOTA). Frequently, questions from journalists were framed in terms of seeking 'guarantees' that behaviours would never be repeated, an expectation shared by many members of the public. These expectations of workers to provide a 'cure' are clearly unrealistic, but they can represent a particular source of stress.

The issue of resources available to do the work is an associated source of potential stress. There has been pressure on all public services to deliver 'more for less'. We frequently observe situations where workers are expected to undertake risk assessments without proper training or support, without proper time to undertake the work, or proper supervision and management oversight of the work. Time for planning and debriefing may be seen as a 'luxury'. This is not conducive to good assessment, decision making or planning. Nor is it conducive to the welfare and safety of workers. Quite simply, it does not promote child or public protection.

EFFECTS UPON WORKERS

Given our comments above, it is clear this work has potential to impact negatively on workers. Such effects may include feelings of being deskilled, overwhelmed or 'burnt out'. Workers sometimes, unsurprisingly, report feelings of revulsion about general or specific aspects of work they are undertaking. This may take the form of feeling 'tarnished' or dirty in a physical sense. Colleagues have described to us the need to go straight home and shower immediately after group sessions, for example.

Workers in this field have also reported feeling victimised. This may represent a resurgence of a past experience or a countertransference reaction. However, it may also be a result of direct (overt or implicit) behaviour by an abuser or abusers towards the worker experienced in one-to-one or group work contexts. Similarly, workers may feel intimidated for similar reasons. Abusers who are motivated by the abuse of power and by hostility are unlikely to reserve such behaviour for their 'own' victims. Such behaviour towards workers can be activated particularly when abusers feel threatened or are seeking to reassert dominance.

A number of workers have reported experiencing intrusive thoughts or images relating to aspects of their work with abusers. Our experience is that it is difficult to predict which aspects of the work (if any) will cause distress, under what circumstances, and to whom. Sometimes reading victim statements will provoke intrusive thoughts. The experience of being surrounded by distasteful information (e.g. in a group or court setting) may aggravate the propensity for intrusive thoughts to occur.

Effects on sexual arousal may also be reported. These may include disinterest in sexual activity or may result in short or long-term sexual dysfunction. Reports of increased arousal also exist.

Workers who have children have reported cautiousness in their relationships with children because of the way that intimate contact may be interpreted. They have also reported 'hyper caution' about letting their children interact with adults. Particular feelings, for instance, of anger and revulsion have been reported, where abuse described by clients has been towards children who are described as similar in age or in other characteristics to the worker's children.

Workers, more commonly female workers, have reported fears of becoming part of an abuser's sexual fantasies. This of course does occur sometimes. The abuser may choose to disclose such fantasies so as to disempower or attempt to abuse the worker. Other workers, more commonly male workers, have reported feeling guilty or ashamed about traditional male attitudes to women and children, sometimes aggravated by difficulties accepting 'feminist' views of the causes of sexual abuse.

Mothersole (2000) elegantly reviews these issues in a paper which addresses clinical supervision and forensic work. He categorises the problems clinicians may experience in respect of their reactions to offenders under three headings: the experiences of repulsion, helplessness and 'voyeuristic motivation'. He emphasises the need for clinical supervision to address these issues, including supervision for qualified and experienced staff. He draws a clear distinction between clinical and management supervision, as well as between clinical supervision and other activities such as consultancy, counselling and other psychotherapeutic support to staff.

In outlining these potential effects on workers we stress that they are common across gender (although some will apply more to men than to women and vice versa) and varying disciplines. It is often forgotten, for instance, that secretarial staff are exposed to offensive material and may have very little support (Home Office 1998b). These effects are a function of the work that is undertaken with sexual abusers. They are not fundamentally caused by weakness in individual workers. The effects may be aggravated or mitigated by organisational structures and other pressures. They may also be aggravated for particular individual workers in the light of personal experiences at different times and in different situations.

Clarke's (2004) study indicates that workers are more likely to suffer distress early in their careers working with sex offenders. This supports Farrenkopf's (1992) findings that workers progress through distinct 'phases of impact' eventually reaching an 'adaptation' phase. This indicates the necessity for high levels of support, training and supervision for those early in their careers. It should *not* be assumed, conversely, that experienced workers do not need proper support. Ennis and Horne (2003) reviewed literature and conducted their own study. They found that peer support was an important factor in preventing psychological distress.

The professional accommodation syndrome

Morrison (1990) has described how the atmosphere within an organisation can contribute to problems workers may have or assist in resolving them. He adapted the work of Summitt (1983) who had described the 'child abuse accommodation syndrome'. Morrison describes a process which he calls the 'professional accommodation syndrome'.

Workers who have a problem may not be able to tell anyone because of the culture of their organisation. For example, there may be a fear of appearing weak in an organisation that prides itself on its expertise and hard work. Continued *secrecy* may lead to feelings of *helplessness* and negative self attributions such as a perception of an inability to cope, or feelings of shame. In such a structure or atmosphere, workers feel *trapped* and may *accommodate the thoughts and feelings*. They blame themselves. Any *disclosure may be delayed or unconvincing*. The disclosure may then be *retracted* with the worker dismissing it as the result of situational pressures (e.g. 'it was a bad day', 'it was nothing to do with work really').

With the above in mind, employers, managers and staff are urged to create an organisation where openness is encouraged, and where it is expected that it will be difficult to cope sometimes. Openness is to be rewarded and promoted as a strength. Disclosures are to be welcomed and believed. Retractions are to be questioned.

STRATEGIES FOR HEALTHY AND POSITIVE OUTCOMES

It is clear that organisations should have a policy and strategy in relation to work with sexual abusers. This should relate to the aims of work with sexual abusers within that organisation, the management structures to support that work and personnel strategies, including policies such as staff selection to develop the work. It should ensure proper training and support for staff (which will vary depending on their specific role) and outline structures and frameworks for conducting assessments, delivering and evaluating treatment and implementing risk management strategies. For example, Beech *et al.* (1998) recommend that group leaders (tutors) should not run two treatment groups in a row so as to avoid burn-out.

It is essential that no worker (however 'expert' he or she is perceived to be) should be left unsupervised to make decisions, undertake treatment or implement risk management strategies alone. Such structural deficits may lead to serious misjudgements even by experienced practitioners, resulting in consequent difficulties or even tragedy (e.g. Aberdeen City Council 1998).

Deployment

It is suggested that workers should only be employed to work with sexual abusers if they have expressed a willingness to do so. There are clearly reasons why an individual may have difficulty undertaking work with sexual abusers. These reasons may relate to prior victimisation experiences, current experiences close to them, or religious reasons whereby it would be inappropriate to discuss explicit sexual matters with another adult. It should not be necessary for individuals to have to disclose in detail such matters to managers in order to avoid exposure to material which may cause distress or embarrassment. In addition, it is not in an organisation's interests to have workers in positions where these difficulties might provoke reactions which are unhelpful to the proper undertaking of the task. Reactions might include avoidant or collusive behaviour or overly punitive attitudes. In the ideal world, organisations should have a policy allowing workers to opt in to this work.

Difficulties of course may emerge at a later date, once staff are engaged in the work. Staff should have the option of withdrawing should disabling circumstances arise. An organisation which ignores these factors may not be 'getting the job done right' and may be damaging the health and welfare of staff. In certain circumstances it may be rendering the organisation susceptible to legal proceedings for emotional damage.

Staff attitudes and behaviour

Staff should not be appointed to the work who display attitudes supportive of abuse of whatever sort, including sexist attitudes. There is little room in this work for those whose attitudes to sexual abusers are collusive at one extreme or overly punitive at the other. Such attitudes may be detrimental to the worker's ability to conduct objective assessments or to work adequately in a group or individual treatment context.

Marshall *et al.* (2003) have studied the characteristics and behaviours of therapists which were most likely to effect change in sex offender groups run by the Prison Service. They found that a confrontational style correlated with negative outcomes. Those characteristics of therapists which correlated with change on a number of indices included the traits of warmth, empathy, directiveness and an ability to reward progress. Marshall *et al.* regard these as being 'cardinal virtues' of therapists. (The specific application of these factors to treatment is examined further in Chapter 5).

Selection

The appointment of staff to work with sexual abusers is clearly an important process, given the above. There are diverse roles to fulfil, e.g. assessor, treatment provider (individual or group based), evaluator, researcher, surveillance officer and supervisor/s. It may be that the skills required for these roles are quite distinct, though in our experience it is not unusual for the assumption to be made that a worker has transferable skills that meet all needs. There may be a need for specialisms to develop in this area.

Before staff are appointed to job roles with sexual abusers, the principles of good selection should be followed. A 'job analysis' should be conducted of the role, with determination of the essential knowledge, skills, abilities and traits required. Robust and reliable assessment methods should be determined to evidence competencies which match the above. Multiple assessment methods are likely to enhance reliability.

Those who will make the assessment decision should be appropriately trained to evaluate and assess the competencies using appropriate methods. Sources of bias and decision error in the selection process should be identified and strategies to compensate or deal with them put in place. The selection process itself should be subject to evaluation and follow-up. Those who enter the process should receive proper support and feedback.

Perhaps controversially we advise that those who are selected for job roles in this area should be subject to re-selection procedures after three to five years. It would be erroneous to assume that the worker's skills and outlook continue to match the job requirements across time. Workers change (for good or bad) and job requirements change.

Training

It is essential that workers in any field are trained to do the job required of them. Stress is a function of the distance between that workload required of an individual and the individual's ability to perform the task. Clearly, it is detrimental to an individual worker to be asked to perform tasks in which they are not given adequate training. It also compromises the quality of outcomes which an organisation can expect. If the assessment and management of abusers is based on an inadequate understanding of theory and research, and undertaken by workers who have not been trained in relevant skills, this may well compromise the safety of vulnerable people and bring criticism upon the organisation providing the assessments.

There is an argument here for a full training needs analysis to be conducted in respect of staff members, for each staff member to have a personal development and training plan, and for such a plan to be reviewed at least annually, e.g. as part of a formal appraisal.

Supervision

Line management supervision is the primary vehicle via which workers are held to account by their agency. It is an opportunity to monitor the quality and quantity of what a worker is doing on behalf of the agency. Good line management supervision should also ensure that staff are working within policies agreed by the organisation. This protects agencies and individuals within them. Responsibility for decisions is thereby shared and 'owned' by agencies.

Good line management supervision will also identify development needs and offer support. All of the above applies to any working situation but is particularly important in the sexual abuse field because of the stresses identified, and because of the danger of individuals making poor judgements if left unsupervised.

Managing the 'expert' practitioner

A particular situation which may challenge line management is that of the 'expert' practitioner who believes they cannot or should not be managed by someone who does not have an equivalent level of skill or expertise in work with sex offenders. This is not an unusual situation. Sometimes those who manage expert practitioners may have comparatively little history of working with this client group direct, their appointment to management being based on the principle that management skills can be generalised across situations. A manager who is effective in his or her support and guidance of staff does not necessarily rely on specialist knowledge of sex offenders.

The 'expert' practitioner in this context can present challenges to the manager, for example, attempting to undermine the manager's position through professing greater knowledge or skills base, in their lack of pre-paredness to learn, or their avoidance of critical reflection. This may lead to authority clashes with the manager where authority is deemed to be something drawn from practice expertise. It may raise concerns as to fos-silisation of practice (with the worker assuming that he or she 'knows what there is to know in this area') and may serve to disempower both the manager and less expert colleagues.

In considering tactics to manage this phenomenon we would advise that the dynamic is 'named', i.e. that the manager challenges the practition-er with his or her perceived resistance to supervision. We advise that the manager draw a distinction between the person-management task and the case-management task, reminding the expert practitioner that manage-ment is often about resource allocation, boundary setting, service delivery, oversight, quality assurance and public accountability. The manager in turn should ensure the pursuit of broader human resource strategies to ensure the development of other staff and manage turnover. Wherever necessary the manager should attend training to develop his or her own management skills but should also encourage both the expert and non expert practitioner to continue to learn and develop through the utilisation of appropriate training opportunities. Questions the manager might ask of the expert practitioner within sessions may include the following:

- What were the objectives for the session or piece of work?
- How do these relate to the supervision plan?
- What techniques did you consider using to meet the objective before choosing a particular technique (in effect, why was the technique used)?
- Have you reviewed your work?
- Have you integrated current thinking, research and professional knowledge into your practice?
- What have you learnt from doing this work recently?

The authors have experience of a number of cases where individuals claim expertise but are resistant to new experiences or challenges. In the long term this supposed expertise has been found to be based on a false premise. Genuine 'experts' will relish the opportunity not only to share their practice but will be open to ideas from whatever source and will be appropriately self critical.

Managing the targeted practitioner

Occasionally workers will bring to supervision information which suggests they may be at risk from the abuser. As indicated above, for example, they may indicate that the abuser has disclosed sexual or violent fantasies about them. Supervision should clearly serve to protect the worker. A clear and explicit risk assessment of the situation should be conducted. It will be necessary to explore:

- What (in detail) was said by the abuser to the worker which raises concerns?
- What was the worker's reaction to the abuser's comments? (Is it possible on the basis of what is known about the abuser to determine whether the worker's reaction will have reduced or exacerbated risk?)
- What was the perceived motivation on the part of the abuser in making disclosure of fantasies about the worker?
- Are there other acute risk factors present which suggest the abuser is entering a more dangerous phase?
- Is the detail of disclosure here consistent with the detail of the pattern of the abuser's previous assaultive/abusive behaviour?

It will also be necessary to explore the options for resolution of the situation, respecting throughout the concerns and needs of the worker. Options may include:

- removing the worker from the case, permanently or short term
- assigning or reallocating a co-worker
- advising the staff member to re-schedule client appointments, e.g. so that the client is not seen at the end of the day, so that the manager is always present in the building, so that appropriate office space is available and the like
- exploring with the worker whether it is advisable to confront the issue with the abuser and in a way which encourages the abuser to reflect on his motivations for disclosure, the appropriateness of such and strategies for promoting healthy respect for the worker
- advising the Multi-Agency Public Protection Panel of developments in the case
- increasing the frequency of supervision.

There is no easy solution to this situation but, as we have said above, protection of the worker is paramount here.

Consultancy

External consultancy is considered useful by some, although others argue that it is not generally necessary if good management and training is available (Home Office 1998b). Consultancy is not a substitute for line management supervision, training or counselling. Indeed, there is a danger that agencies may abdicate their responsibilities to a consultant.

Both authors have experiences of 'consultancy' where they have been used as an 'insurance policy', such that managers have been able to promote the worth of their programmes whilst not necessarily taking leadership of management decisions. Similarly, we have had exposure to management structures and activities which have served to directly undermine the work of consultancy. Morrison (1998), adapting the work of Hay (1992), suggested a balanced, triangular relationship between agency, staff and consultant, but also neatly illustrated how these triangular relationships may become skewed (see Figure 3.1).

Morrison (1998) defines consultancy as:

> A structured negotiated organisational process involving two or more staff in which one person, the consultant, is identified as having some expertise, either subject or process expertise or both, which is used to facilitate a developmental or problem solving process regarding a work-related issue with the consultee(s). (p.13)

Morrison describes the aim of the consultation process in this context as being 'to promote and support the effective management of sexual abusers so as to control and reduce the risk they pose to others'. Consultancy is relationship based and consultants offer a range of approaches to the work.

Heron (1989) has described six styles of 'facilitation' which consultants use:

- prescriptive (giving advice, being directive)
- informative (teaching, being instructive)
- confrontative (being challenging, giving direct feedback)
- cathartic (helping to release tension, sharing feelings)
- catalytic (encouraging reflection, self-directed problem solving)
- supporting (approving, validating, conforming).

Morrison also reflects on characteristics of consultancy style and focus. He outlines a matrix whereby consultancy may be used for organisations, teams or individuals, and directed at targets ranging on a continuum from 'hard', measurable outcomes, e.g. the production of a programme manual, to 'soft', e.g. improved working relationships.

If consultancy is adopted to assist with the management of sexual abusers, it is important to be clear about the basis on which the consultant is engaged. It should be a contracted activity with clear lines of accountability, management and review. Consultancy is unlikely to be productive if supervisory and support structures are weak and proper training of staff has not been undertaken.

Consultant and agency perceived as out to get the consultees

Consultant (invited as rescuer but seen as persecutor)

Consultee
(victim)

Agency (seen by consultees as persecutor)

Consultant and consultees perceived as out to get the agency or manager

Consultant

Agency/
manager

Consultees

Agency and consultees perceived as out to get the consultant

Agency/manager (persecutor)

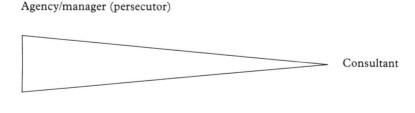

Consultant

Consultees

Figure 3.1*: Triangular Consultancy Relationship Model*

The consultancy contract should specify:

- the purpose of consultancy
- the provider and recipients
- the frequency/duration of consultancy
- what form consultancy will take (e.g. informative, catalytic)
- lines of accountability, including detail of the reporting and review structures
- the responsibilities of the consultant towards the consultees, to their manager(s) and the organisation
- details of record keeping
- the limits of confidentiality
- under what circumstances consultancy will be suspended/terminated
- the costs (professional fees)
- the process by which changes to the contact will be made.

Counselling

Many organisations offer confidential counselling for staff (often not just those working with sexual abusers). However, in our experience some staff are reluctant to use the service because someone in the line management structure must know that they have used the service, and there is a fear that this is perceived as weakness and held against them. Tutors on the Prison Service's Sex Offender Treatment Programme and facilitators in the Probation Service Accredited Programmes are required to meet a counsellor periodically. This avoids the problem of attendance being perceived as weakness but may mean that the contact becomes routinised.

Noteworthy here is feedback from staff engaged in running sex offender treatment groups in prisons (Beech et al. 1998). Staff have suggested that in addition to personal counselling core programme tutor training should refer to the psychological impact of working with sexual abusers. It is suggested that experienced group leaders could share their experiences of the impact of the work and the coping strategies they used to deal with such.

It is our belief that all engaged in this work should have opportunity to discuss the impact of this work on them, and that this be a requirement of work in this area.

Co-working

Co-working is the norm for group working with sexual abusers. We would recommend its adoption more routinely for work with individual abusers.

Colleagues may comment that this is a luxury when resources are tight. It could be argued however that co-work is cost effective. Indeed a *Thematic Inspection of Work with Sex Offenders* undertaken by the Probation Service (Home Office 1998) indicated that supervision solely by individual probation officers resulted in significantly poorer work being undertaken than where co-work and group work was involved (Table 3.1).

Table 3.1: Quality of work related to nature of intervention
(Source: Home Office 1998)

Nature of intervention	Quality of work (%)			
	Very good	Satisfactory	Unsatisfactory	Very poor
				–
Group work and supervision	58%	33%	9%	–
Co-work	39%	51%	9%	
Individual	22%	56%	18%	4%

Co-working, of course, need not imply paired working from within the same agency. Indeed, good practice might dictate a need for co-working across professional disciplines. Further, the co-working dyad might change according to the stage of the work. It may be unnecessary often for the same two workers to pursue the work from start to finish.

Hodge (1985) identified a number of benefits of co-leadership which accord with our experiences in working in and consulting to programmes. These include:

- the enrichment of leadership resources available
- the sharing of tasks
- the modelling of social and interactional skills to group members
- the modelling of respectful, positive gender roles
- the provision of mutual support between co-workers
- different perspectives being brought to address a problem
- the maintenance of focus (if one leader becomes temporarily confused or out of touch the other leader may take over to retain direction)
- the provision of opportunity for experienced workers to train less experienced colleagues.

There are of course potential tensions in a co-working relationship. It is essential that co-workers plan properly ahead of sessions in order to address these problems. Indeed, co-worker tensions are frequently discussed in consultation. Tensions identified by Hodge which are again supported by our experiences include:

- irreconcilable differences in theoretical or ideological orientation
- differences about valid techniques
- clashes of leadership style
- leaders slipping into competitive roles
- agency related tensions impinging on co-work relationships
- inadequate planning
- co-leaders acting out group members' fantasies about their relationship
- co-leaders succumbing to 'splitting techniques' used by members
- co-leaders being flooded with negative feelings being referred from members
- vulnerability to group process.

It is essential therefore that proper planning time is allowed to address practical application of tasks, content issues and process issues. Equally important is that debriefing should be scheduled as an integral part of a session, be that following group or individual work. Failure to debrief may mean that thoughts, feelings and behaviours relating to sessions are not properly processed. This may be detrimental to the emotional well-being of workers. In addition, failure to debrief may lead to the perpetuation of co-work disturbances in future sessions or the avoidance of difficult group content.

Debriefing need not be an unduly complex process. The Northumbria Probation Service Sex Offender Team evolved a simple, straightforward and effective debriefing checklist (published in Morrison 1998, p.63). The outline is as follows:

- gathering together
- winding down and desensitisation
- reviewing sessions
- reviewing relevant process issues
- evaluation of each group member
- discussion of co-work processes

- reviewing residual feelings workers may have
- determining action points.

Professional networking

Barbaree and colleagues (1998) have commented on the difficulties in recruiting qualified staff to treatment programmes. Beech *et al.* (1998) make particular reference to the shortage of female tutors in some prisons, commenting that 'female tutors are important in maintaining healthy, non-sexist values and attitudes within progammes'.

It could be argued that to recruit and maintain staff within highly specialised programmes they must not feel disenfranchised and cut off from their mainstream professional community. A sense of isolation from mainstream colleagues can be mitigated if staff are provided with opportunities for meeting with and sharing views with other colleagues engaged in this work, including being provided with opportunities to attend specialist conferences and being supported in application to relevant cross-professional bodies. The National Organisation for the Treatment of Abusers (NOTA) is the only organisation in the UK and Ireland which provides services specifically to professionals working in the field of sexual abuse. Since 1991 it has provided the largest professional conference in the UK for professionals working with sexual abusers. It provides numerous other valuable services to members such as training, access to research, a journal and newsletter (details can be found at www.nota.co.uk). Other organisations and resources available for professionals to access support are identified in Chapter 14.

McGrath and colleagues (McGrath, Cumming and Holt 2002) have commented specifically on issues pertaining to collaboration among sex offender treatment providers, probation and parole officers. They see a shortage of sex offender treatment providers internationally. Within this context they advise ongoing collaboration across disciplines, frequent and substantive two-way communication about risk management, and consideration of probation officers who are not currently treatment providers personally visiting treatment groups. McGrath and colleagues invite those who are involved in collaboration across disciplines to consider crucial questions. If community safety is the *primary* goal of intervention with sex offenders, does this conflict with professional ethics for any discipline? Do multiple relationships with the abuser (e.g. the worker who is both treatment provider and agent of the court) constitute unethical behaviour in the context of sex offender treatment? Do collaborative models of sex offender intervention require us to think about the delivery of treatment and supervision in new ways?

Physical safety

Finally, we return to the issue of the physical safety of staff. Many men who sexually abuse are superficially compliant. Any potential negative effects for workers from such clients relate predominantly to those emotional pressures outlined above. However, some men may pose a direct physical threat to staff. It may be useful to refer to Thornton 2000 (described in Chapter 2 of this volume) to identify sexual abusers who may be particularly likely to pose a risk of assaulting staff.

We suggest that a number of factors may be taken into account and which should signal concerns. This list is not exhaustive however and if any concerns are raised staff should err on the side of caution. Risk factors include:

- abusers who have sexually assaulted adults
- abusers whose sexually assaultive behaviour has been characterised by 'extra' or gratuitous violence or who have a record of physical aggression
- abusers with a history of 'hands off' as well as 'hands on' offending
- abusers whose behaviour appears to be motivated by vindictiveness, anger and hostility
- abusers with a history of 'stalking' or harassing.

Where any such risk factors are identified it is essential that staff consult managers, refer to their agency's protocols on dealing with dangerous offenders and staff safety, and ensure that procedures are rigorously applied.

CHAPTER 4

Working with Difference

We describe throughout this book how a consensus appears to be developing that men who sexually abuse should be managed via a combination of treatment (at present best based on a cognitive-behavioural model with particular attention paid to relapse prevention) and control strategies (based in criminal justice and child protection legislation, and including incarceration). A tendency to orthodoxy however may not acknowledge that the management of abusers from some social groups may require the adaptation of conventional approaches.

There have been concerns about how or even whether a model based in 'white' Western psychology is applicable to different racial and ethnic groups (e.g. Cowburn 1996; Gahir and Garrett 1999; Hopkinson 1995; Lewis 1999; Morrison, Erooga and Beckett 1994).

Some writers (Atkinson, Worsfold and Fisher 1998; Briggs 1994) signal problems inherent in the objectives of some programmes which appear heterosexist in bias or embrace homophobic assumptions, both of which may inhibit the effective engagement of gay men in sex offender treatment.

It has long been widely recognised (e.g. Bowden 1994; Briggs 1994; Doyle and Gooch 1995; Langevin, Marentette and Rosati 1996) that models need to be adapted for abusers with a learning difficulty and some developments in this field are noted elsewhere in this text.

The area of work with abusers who have a physical or sensory disability appears in the main to be neglected.

It is sometimes easier to describe how and why the management of sexual abusers may be exclusive, however, than to propose ways forward. Indeed, some practitioners have been inhibited by the fear of 'getting things wrong'. Others have been fearful that they need to become expert in understanding the culture and norms of every minority group. This is clearly not possible. From personal experience the author is aware that the interpreter service in Newcastle upon Tyne, for example, has interpreters available for 20 languages. In Lewis' book *Cultural Diversity in Sexual Abuse Treatment* (1999) there are chapters describing work with seven different ethnic groups.

ANTI-OPPRESSIVE PRACTICE

It is outside the scope of this book to present a 'how to' list to cover differing abuser groups as a function of their racial background, ethnicity, gender preference or physical/sensory/mental abilities. However, there has been some useful recent work that outlines principles which can readily be adapted to guide our approach to minority groups, and those who may suffer discrimination.

The term 'anti-oppressive practice' has been adopted mainly within social work and probation training to acknowledge that to progress our work it is necessary to identify and work with difference and to acknowledge that there are power differentials within and between groups which must be addressed. There are in addition the inevitable power differentials which exist between a professional and a sexual abuser.

Hackett (2000) proposes a model of anti-oppressive practice outlined below. This is based on a definition of oppression provided by Dominelli and colleagues (1995), as follows:

> the systematic exclusion of people from the public domain by denying them
>
> - access to full citizenship rights
> - participation in society's decision making structures
> - access to socio-economic and political power
> - access to resources
> - the value of their contribution to society.

NOTA (1999) used a definition of oppression as 'unfair or unequal action against another person or group of people (including) on the basis of age, colour, gender, religious belief, sexuality, sexual orientation, nationality, cultural background, disability, age or class'.

NOTA and others have acknowledged that work with men who sexually abuse can itself be oppressive and reaffirms a number of key beliefs which we and others support:

- abusers should not be defined solely by their actions but should be assessed and addressed as a 'whole person'
- assessments, particularly where these have implications for highly intrusive intervention in people's lives, should be based on comprehensive knowledge of each individual, and grounded in a thorough understanding of the theory and research relevant to each case

- a motivational, respectful style of intervention is likely to be more effective in helping abusers control their behaviour in future than an aggressive, confrontational style

- the conditions under which abusers are expected to engage in programmes of work, and the implications for failure to engage should be clear and relevant to the behaviour being addressed.

Further, we are mindful that work with sexual abusers is undertaken within the context of interventions offered to people (abusers) who oppress others (victims). It is essential therefore to reaffirm that the primary aim of work with all abusers is to prevent a recurrence of their behaviour towards potential victims.

The fulcrum model

To help workers retain the balance between the needs of the abuser and the need to maintain public protection as a primary focus, Hackett (2000) has conceptualised a 'fulcrum' model whereby both 'over liberal' and 'pathological' approaches may be avoided. This is a development of an original idea by Ahmad (1992) and is illustrated in Figure 4.1.

Oppressive over liberal

Oppressive pathological

THE ANTI-OPPRESSIVE FULCRUM

- Collusion
- Risk understated
- Problems over-simplified
- Over-optimism

- Labelling
- Possibility of change understated
- Strengths denied
- Over-pessimism

Acknowledgement of an individual's experience of oppression and its impact upon that person's abusive behaviour.

Sensitivity to the individual's specific needs.

Positive use of difference in overcoming abusing behaviour without collusion or promoting distorted responsibility.

Figure 4.1: The fulcrum model of anti-oppressive practice (Source: Hackett 2000, reproduced with permission)

Hackett gives examples of how over liberal and pathological views of minority groups may lead to work which does not effectively address their needs; this is adapted in Figure 4.2.

	OPPRESSIVE OVER LIBERAL	OPPRESSIVE PATHOLOGICAL
Black people who sexually abuse	• Offence explained away or 'understood' merely as a consequence of racism • The myth of the cultural acceptability of sexual abuse within black communities • Treatment not applicable to black people – excuse to offer no services • Fear of being seen as racist leads to inaction • Cultural paranoia, framed as cultural sensitivity, leads to inaction (Ahmad 1992) • Responsibility 'overload' for family/community to control and change person's behaviour.	• Oppressive myth of dangerous black (male) sexuality • Individual's potential for change is minimised; i.e. 'he can't help it' • Family strengths denied • Person's cultural identity is seen as part of the problem • Person's and family's race is seen as problematic to white dominated service providers • Specific cultural needs seen as evidence of problematic presentation of the individual, awkwardness and lack of cooperation • Responsibility 'underload' for family to control and change person's behaviour.
People with learning disabilities who sexually abuse	• Not intentional abuse: 'they do not know any better' • Sexual aggression is simply a reflection of missed opportunity and lack of education • Behaviour always easy to identify • Behaviour always opportunistic and unplanned • Not serious to victims • 'They are only like infants anyway' • If we leave it, it will go away • Sexually abusive behaviour is seen only as 'acting out' without abusive intent or meaning • Disbelief about (extent of) abuse due to myth that people with learning disabilities are asexual.	• Nothing can be done • All sexual opportunities need to be limited • No right to sexual expression • No control of penis • Not responsive to treatment • 'Sexual defectives' who cannot experience healthy sexual relationships.
People who are gay or lesbian who sexually abuse	• Offences are just a reflection of sexual confusion • Offences would not have happened if the person had had access to other channels to express sexuality • Re young people the fault of parents, non-acceptance of gay identity	• Ongoing identification as gay means ongoing risk • Consensual sexual experiences seen as person abusing • Homosexual sexual feelings seen as evidence of lack of control • Person denied right to healthy same-sex sexual experiences • Treatment aims to counsel person into heterosexuality • Positive gay identity confused with paedophilia.

Figure 4.2: *Oppressive perspectives upon sexual abusers (Source: Hackett 2000, adapted with permission)*

Cultural competencies

Another approach which is helpful in outlining principles to deal with difference is based on the concept of 'cultural competence'. Cross *et al.* (1989) outlined how a culturally competent system of care would better address the needs of 'emotionally handicapped children and their families'. The principles however can be generalised to work with men who sexually abuse, and are principles which cross areas of difference beyond those of race and ethnicity.

Cultural competence is defined as a 'set of congruent behaviours, attitudes and policies that come together in a system, agency or profession' and which enables work to be undertaken effectively in cross-cultural situations. Culture implies 'the integrated pattern of human behaviours that includes thoughts, communications, actions, customs, beliefs, values and institutions of a racial, ethnic, religious or social group'. Cross *et al.* (1989) argue that practice can be sited on a continuum ranging from 'cultural destructiveness' through 'cultural incapacity' to 'cultural precompetence', moving to 'cultural competence and proficiency' (p.3).

NOTA (1999) used the work of Cross *et al.* (1989) to develop a set of principles as follows. In moving to culturally competent practice professionals will need to examine themselves and their organisations with regard to their assumptions, biases, attitudes, values and behaviour. These are rooted in their historical and cultural influences. NOTA advise:

- The family as defined within each culture and other support systems experienced throughout an individual's life will need to be understood. This will have implications for the individual's learned behaviour, attitudes, concepts of authority, concepts of therapy etc. and consequently will affect the basis of interventions.

- It is necessary to acknowledge that individuals within minority groups must function within at least two cultural or social groupings. This creates a unique set of pressures to which services need to respond. These pressures may result in dissonance and stresses. Service providers must understand where an individual may perceive their major support systems to be, which will have implications for intervention.

- Individuals and families may make choices based on cultural forces which need to be understood by service providers. This will have implications for what are perceived to be 'rational' choices, the mutual perceptions of worker and client, and the motivation of clients.

- Inherent in cross-cultural interactions are dynamics that must be acknowledged, adjusted to and worked with.

- Agencies must sanction and in some cases mandate the incorporation of cultural knowledge into practice and policy making through training, consultancy, partnerships, shared experiences and recruitment.
- Practitioners and their agencies should work in conjunction with natural, formal and informal support and helping networks. The aim should be for the relationship to be mutual and consultative, acknowledging however that the law applies to all and that child protection concerns will remain paramount.
- Practitioners and their agencies should assume that problems are best addressed when communities themselves come to own and recognise the problem, and develop their own solutions. Workers can assist in this understanding by offering training, consultancy, support and networking opportunities.
- Agencies should develop their own understanding of services to minority groups by ensuring involvement of such groups at employer, manager and practitioner levels.
- Agencies should adapt provisions in order to provide interventions that are relevant to communities and individuals whatever their varying needs. This might involve the adaptation of services to facilitate the involvement of individuals in groups, attempts by neighbouring agencies to pool resources to provide a bigger catchment area for services, or provision of individualised programmes in certain cases.

Professional training

As indicated above, it is suggested that agencies incorporate cultural knowledge into practice and policy making through training as well as other activities. Extrapolating from discussions of a working group of trainers in clinical psychology, Clare, Scaife and Buchan (2002) offer principles for developing awareness of diversity. They suggest:

- the profession and its members need to show respect for and be open to learning about all people (clients and colleagues), their different characteristics, beliefs and values
- the culture of the profession, and the enculturation of new recruits into associated values and beliefs, benefits from a continuous process of change
- the issue of diversity must encompass all elements of, and all participants in training. This includes course team members and supervisors. An integrated approach is required.

- diversity needs to be addressed on a continuous basis for awareness to develop and be maintained
- didactic teaching is insufficient alone as a means of helping people to learn about diversity. While some didactic teaching related to diversity may be helpful, opportunities for experiential learning are essential.

We believe these principles are sensible and of relevance to the specialist training of all professionals working with sexual abusers.

IMPLICATIONS

There are a number of practical implications which derive from the above. Hackett (2000), again developing the work of Ahmad (1992), suggests that workers begin by:

- examining their values and perceptions regarding those who sexually abuse others, with specific regard to those from minority groups
- distinguishing between an abuser's possible control of personal problems and external constraints beyond his control
- clarifying that an assessment is not restricted because of assumptions that resources are not available for a person simply as a result of their difference or minority status
- ensuring that the assessment of an abuser's behaviour is located within a clear child protection framework, where the needs of victims and potential victims are paramount
- being sensitive to cultural implications without collusion
- identifying and if necessary challenging deficits in the policies of institutions or practice of the professionals involved.

Jones *et al.* (1999) argue that workers should not assume that 'what works for us should work for you' (p.32) and warns that treatment models have been delivered to minorities on the untested and unstated assumptions that they will be similarly effective. They also argue however that culturally competent practice usually calls for 'an expansion, rather than a complete revision of existing treatment models, processes and goals' and that 'the challenge is to identify and keep the aspects of existing treatment approaches that have good utility with minority clients, while also extending into new and sometimes unfamiliar territory' (p.6). To do so will require professionals to address issues at varying levels.

SPECIALIST TEXTS

Readers are referred to specialist texts for further reading about issues relating to particular groups. Matters concerning sexual abusers from specific ethnic and racial groups have been addressed for instance by Cowburn (1996), Gahir and Garrett (1999), Jones *et al.* (1999) and Lewis (1999).

Further, Marshall *et al.* (1998) provide examples of treatment programmes for ethnic populations and diverse populations including intellectually disabled, deaf, female and adolescent abusers, alongside descriptions of work with 'professional' abusers, including clergy offenders.

CONSIDERATIONS

It is possible to derive from the foregoing discussion a number of points which should be addressed before engaging in assessment or treatment and which may affect other management strategies.

Workers need to understand the abuser's social and historical contexts. If an abuser has suffered racism (either on an individual basis or as part of the collective experience of a minority group), homophobia, or in the case of an abuser with learning disabilities has experienced a history of over-control (at one extreme) or collusion (at the other extreme) from authority figures, that experience will inevitably influence their perceptions about their current workers.

It is important that practical arrangements are made to allow abusers access to programmes. This may necessitate programmes being delivered on an individual rather than group basis. It is noteworthy here that whilst efforts have been made throughout Britain to standardise aspects of sex offender treatment via accreditation of programmes, some abusers are excluded from these programmes. Typically, offenders who have active mental health problems, those who show chaotic substance misuse, and those who may need an interpreter are excluded. The Northumbria programme offers constructive suggestions for inclusion of clients with particular difficulties by reference to other programmes or through individual work (National Probation Service 2001).

The Prison Service runs an adapted programme for offenders who have a low IQ and/or learning disabilities. This programme is showing clinical changes in participants measured on psychometric scales (Mann 2003). It is hoped that these will translate into long-term reductions in offending in this population. To date the Probation Service's accredited programmes exclude offenders who have low IQ/learning disabilities. The second author is at the time of writing in discussions with the National

Probation Directorate about the development of a community-based programme for this population of abusers.

Some 'adaptations' are clear: the use of interpreters or 'signers' to facilitate communication, the adaptation of written material into graphic or visual forms or audio tapes, the adaptation of buildings for disabled access, the adaptation of written material to include minority experiences are obvious considerations.

Developing the above, it is suggested that the following practical issues are considered:

1. When working with third parties such as interpreters and signers it is important that they are properly trained and supported. Jones et al. (1999) identify difficulties in using interpreters because of 'the non equivalencies and nuances in word meanings and tonality' (p.22) which may lead to misunderstandings. If an interpreter is not familiar with the content of work with sex abusers, the interpreter's emotional responses may in turn influence the response of the abuser. It is essential that interpreters are properly trained in order that the effect of them mediating what is said by the worker or the abuser is minimised. The effect of this work on professionals as outlined in Chapter 3 should not be neglected when considering the welfare of third parties.

2. Jones et al. (1999) have suggested that people in minority groups or who suffer discrimination may suffer adverse effects on their self-esteem. Embarrassment at being unable to understand tasks or being unable physically to participate in written exercises and role plays may also impair self-esteem. Self-esteem is thought to be important in influencing dynamic risk factors such as cognitive distortions and arousal (Marshall et al. 1999), and changes in self-esteem have been associated with relapse (Hanson 2000; Pithers 1993).

3. Body language and eye contact may be interpreted very differently depending on an individual's life experience. (This is not of course confined to minority groups.) It is important to be aware in any exercise involving physical contact that such contact may be difficult for some, for example, because of an abusive experience. Similarly, different conventions between males and females or between different positions in a social hierarchy affect our appreciation of touch. Workers should check their assumptions about concepts such as 'personal space'.

4. A number of common factors which have importance in the assessment and treatment of sexual abusers may be of questionable validity outside of 'white' Western heterosexual psychology:

- Some psychometric tests are normed in such a way that caution is necessary in applying them across cultural and ethnic groups.

- The use of highly intrusive assessment techniques such as the penile plethysmograph or polygraph, as well as the use of explicit stimulus material, may be regarded as particularly invasive.

5. The concept of empathy is widely regarded as a key factor in the assessment and treatment of men who sexually abuse (for a detailed discussion, see Chapter 9 of this text). It cannot be assumed that empathy is conceptualised in the same way amongst all cultural groups. The conceptualisation will be influenced for example by how much a person's cultural experience emphasises collective responsibility as opposed to individualism, and how much a person identifies strongly with a cultural group to protect themselves against racism or homophobia.

6. Stresses may emanate from cross-cultural tensions. In turn, stress may inhibit engagement in treatment. Similarly, it may be relevant to relapse prevention. As noted earlier in this chapter, Cross et al. (1989) commented on how people in minority groups need to survive in at least two cultures. Such stress may lead to strong feelings such as anger and resentment (Jones et al. 1999), which in turn needs to be acknowledged and managed.

7. The concept of 'locus of control' is also regarded as an important variable in the assessment and treatment of sexual abusers (Beech et al. 1998). Abusers with learning disabilities may have had a lifetime experience of control by families or within institutions and may suddenly be under pressure to take responsibility for their actions. Further, it is important to acknowledge how much control individuals are expected to have over their lives across (and indeed within) different cultural groups.

8. Impulsivity is a factor which many sexual abusers need to address (Thornton 1999). Jones et al. (1999) argue that impulsive traits may be aggravated where there has been an experience of poverty and oppression with which a 'present orientated time perspective, impulsive decision making and a desire for immediate gratification and low frustration tolerance' (p.19) is associated.

9. It is important to understand who are the major influences in an abuser's life. This will be influenced by gender roles, attachment to major support systems, and possibly the involvement of powerful individuals such as religious or community leaders or

support groups in communities. In the same way that such influences will vary in white Western cultures, differences within all ethnic and social groups should be examined.

10. We have often heard it stated that there may be taboos in some cultures about discussion of very intimate sexual details related either to religion, gender roles or social embarrassment. Again, there is often an assumption that discussion of personal sexual details is general in white, Western, secular culture; an assumption which is not universally valid. These are only discussed with abusers because it is they who have breached cultural norms. Assumptions should not be made about the attitudes of individuals from any background in relation to these issues.

11. There is a general view in the UK that therapy is a less favoured option than it is in the USA, although this may owe more to popular film culture than validated research. Jones *et al.* (1999) and Lewis (1999) remind us that in some cultures therapy is regarded as an alien concept. Difficulties may be overcome here by enlisting spiritual or religious authority figures or other support groups within communities to promote treatment. Of course, this may be a double-edged sword in as much as it may be necessary to 'neutralise' the influence of those members of an abuser's family or network who may undermine the work.

CO-WORKING

When treating sexually abusive males via co-working arrangements the dynamics of the co-working partnership are clearly crucial. Mistry and Brown (1991) have written about the significance of race and ethnicity in the co-working of groups and the relevance of race and ethnicity to the co-working relationship, to group behaviour and group dynamics. They offer practical guidelines.

1. First, they suggest clear decisions must be taken as to whether co-working should include two or three workers, whether a black/white pairing is appropriate, and whether a particular pair of black and white colleagues are personally compatible with working together. They suggest a readiness and ability to talk about the race dimension within the co-working relationship as a prerequisite.

2. Second, they suggest 'preparation' for co-working. Included here are the ground rules to be employed on racism such as how it will be responded to in the group, and explicit agreement that issues of race will be discussed regularly.

3. Third, they refer to issues of consultancy and the need for frank discussions about the choice of consultant, 'where choice exists'. They indicate 'in black/white co-working two factors arise. The first is whether a black or white consultant is preferred, and the second is whether in addition to consultancy for the co-worker pair, individual consultancy, probably from another consultant, is needed for one or both of the workers'.

4. Fourth, they suggest that co-workers have responsibility for helping group members understand rules regarding the unacceptability of anyone in the group being treated in a derogatory or discriminatory way because of personal characteristics.

5. Fifth, they advise that co-workers arrange to share group tasks on an equal basis, carrying equal responsibility, assuming that both workers have roughly equivalent levels of experience and ability. Mistry and Brown talk here of the need for the modelling of an effective black/white co-working relationship.

The authors have also noted situations where individuals have been assumed to be an 'expert' on issues within 'their culture' and where cases have been referred on the basis of naive stereotypes (e.g. a professional complained that because of his skin colour he was allocated offenders who were actually from a neighbouring country to his, a country which had a different religion and language and with whom his country had been on the brink of war for 50 years).

CONCLUDING COMMENTS

There is a danger of workers becoming daunted by the challenge of being entirely correct in every move they make in order to work 'anti-oppressively' with men who sexually abuse. Fortunately, the literature is growing, a literature from which we can gain guidance and support. An increasing number of workers have experience which can be drawn upon when trying to ensure that the best possible service is delivered to men from all backgrounds who sexually abuse, and in order to minimise the risk of repetition of their behaviour.

PART II
TREATMENT OF MEN WHO SEXUALLY ABUSE

CHAPTER 5

Sex Offender Treatment

What Works with Whom?

'Does treatment work?' is a simple enough question. Unfortunately, the answer in relation to men who sexually abuse is somewhat complex, not least because individuals will have their own views on what the question means.

Laws (1997) and Marshall, Anderson and Fernandez (1999) have argued that delaying the onset of recidivism is valuable, given that some abusers offend at high rates with behaviour that is extremely harmful. Any delay in the onset of behaviour means that there are fewer victims.

To others the cost-effectiveness of treatment is likely to be a concern, particularly for politicians, employers and managers, and particularly where it may be perceived that resources are being provided for services to offenders at the expense of services to victims and survivors. Marshall (1999) and Prentky and Burgess (1990) have both argued that even very small reductions in recidivism are financially cost-effective. Clearly, the emotional costs for every victim are not calculable merely in financial terms. However, the cost to public funds in respect of each victim associated with investigating the crime, subsequent criminal and/or civil proceedings, and ongoing therapeutic services is tremendous. When asked how many crimes a sex offender treatment project needed to prevent so as to make it cost-effective Grubin (1996) replied 'not many'.

EVALUATION CRITERIA

The most common criterion for assessing whether treatment works is whether the recidivism rate of treated offenders is significantly lower than it would have been if they had not been treated. Even this apparently simple measure requires careful consideration, however. When recidivism rates are quoted it is important that the following questions are addressed in order for them to be meaningful.

- Is the sample large enough for the figures to be statistically significant? Clearly, if a sample is very small (e.g. a single report of one delivery of a small group) then any results could be explained by chance. This has prompted the use of the statistical procedure of 'meta-analysis', that is, the amalgamation of smaller studies to build up large sample sizes, in evaluation of sex offender treatment.

- Is there a good control group, i.e. a group of offenders who did not receive treatment and who are matched on important variables with the treated group? This is not easy to achieve, not least for ethical reasons. For instance, it would not be ethical for a probation service to refuse to allocate an abuser to a treatment group purely for research purposes, especially if it is believed that his chances of re-offending could be reduced by his attending the group. Some institutions who house more abusers than they have treatment places for will randomly assign offenders who are eligible and motivated for treatment into a treated or non treated cohort. Even this may not guarantee a matched control group, however. For instance, Marques (1999) reported a longitudinal study where by chance more abusers with some higher risk characteristics (previous treatment drop out, mental disorder) were randomly assigned to the treatment group.

- Is the follow-up period long enough? The proportion of sex offenders re-offending will increase over time (Hanson 1997; Thornton 1998). Marshall et al. (1999) therefore argue that a follow-up period of less than four years will yield results of very limited value.

- Is the conclusion of one study applicable to other groups of offenders in other treatment programmes? For instance, if the treatment given to a certain group of offenders is poorly framed or insufficient for that group, then it is not proper to generalise the failure of that programme to other groups.

The debate about the effectiveness of sex offender treatment became more rigorous after Furby, Weinott and Blackshaw (1989) argued that there was no evidence that sex offender treatment reduced recidivism. However, this was not to say that future treatment programmes could not reduce recidivism. Indeed, Furby et al. acknowledged that many of the treatment programmes they had studied were very old and included treatment strategies that were no longer utilised. In the UK, Beckett et al. (1994) had pointed out that early programmes gave insufficient attention to the needs of some sex offenders (notably rapists), that the programmes studied tended to neglect relapse prevention, and that they were often not long enough.

NEGATIVE OUTCOMES

The Marques (1999) study referred to above indicated little change through treatment, but it was subsequently argued that the treatment group contained higher risk offenders than the untreated group. Other studies showing negative outcomes (Hanson, Steffy and Gauthier 1993; Quinsey, Khanna and Malcolm 1998; Rice, Harris and Quinsey 1993) have been criticised by Marshall et al. (1999) for failing to have relevant control groups, or for generalising outcomes of inadequate treatment programmes to all sex offender treatment.

OTHER OUTCOMES

More optimistic conclusions were drawn by Hall (1995) in a meta-analysis of 1300 sex offenders followed up for an average of seven years. He found a reduction in recidivism from 27 per cent for untreated offenders in comparison with a recidivism figure of 19 per cent for treated offenders. Outcomes were better for drug treatment and cognitive-behavioural treatments, with the latter being more successful when delivered on an out-patient basis. However, Harris, Rice and Quinsey (1998) have criticised this study for failing to take account of a disproportionate number of 'treatment failures' in the untreated group, rendering them higher risk.

Hedderman and Sugg (1996) found that those treated in programmes in the Beckett et al. (1994) report were less likely to be re-convicted of a sexual offence (5% compared with 9%) and none of those assessed as 'significantly treated' was reconvicted. This study had only a two year follow-up, however.

Marshall et al. (1999), as well as identifying (and criticising) studies with negative outcomes, cite a number of studies with more positive outcomes (p.155).

- Marshall and Barbaree (1988) report reductions in recidivism from 43 per cent to 18 per cent for child molesters with female victims, and 43 per cent to 13 per cent for those with male victims. Recidivism of incest offenders was reduced from 22 per cent to 8 per cent.

- Nicholaichuk et al. (1998) are quoted as having found reductions in recidivism averaging from 42 per cent to 14 per cent for rapists and from 62 per cent to 18 per cent for child molesters.

- McGrath, Hoke and Vojtisek (1998) quoted a recidivism rate of 1 per cent compared with 16 per cent or 11 per cent (depending on which of two control groups was used).
- Bakker *et al.* (1998) described a reduction in recidivism from 21 per cent to 8 per cent for child molesters.
- Proulx *et al.* (1998b) show reductions from 67 per cent to 33 per cent for child molesters and from 71 per cent to 39 per cent for rapists.

In a meta-analysis which post-dates Marshall *et al.*'s (1999) review, Gallagher *et al.* (1999) indicate a reduction in recidivism rates of around 10 per cent although limitations of this study have been noted (Hanson *et al.* 2002).

The most rigorous treatment review to date appears to be that sponsored by ATSA (Association for the Treatment of Sexual Abusers) and undertaken by a team of researchers led by Karl Hanson (Hanson *et al.* 2002). This analysis examined a range of studies to ensure that the treatment methodologies met current criteria for satisfactory treatment. The number sample size was 9000 and follow-up was four years. Hanson *et al.* conclude that sex offence recidivism was reduced from 17 per cent (untreated) to 10 per cent (treated). This represents a 40 per cent reduction, with some programmes reporting reductions in the region of 50 per cent. In addition, there was a significant reduction in non sex offence recidivism.

Different protagonists within the treatment effectiveness debate form different conclusions. Harris *et al.* (1998) conclude: 'To say that treatments have not thus far been conclusively evaluated is not to say that they do not work nor to assert that different therapeutic approaches are of equal efficacy.' They argue that the best option is to use treatments that fit with what is known about the treatment of offenders in general, to use treatments which are based on a convincing theoretical rationale motivated by what we know about the characteristics of sex offenders, and to use the treatments which have shown proximal changes in theoretically relevant measures. They argue for treatments which are feasible in terms of acceptability, cost and ethical standards, treatments which are described in detail so they can be measured, and treatments which can be integrated into institutional regimes and supervisory procedures.

Marshall *et al.* (1999) conclude that 'treatment can be effective and the balance of the evidence weighs in favour of positive treatment outcome'.

We share the view of Grubin (1998) that treatment gains appear to be 'modest' and reassert the view that treatment should always be one part of an inter-agency, multi-disciplinary, risk management strategy.

We also suggest that it is necessary to look behind simple outcome data at the more complex picture which is emerging from the research. For example, it appears that many sexual abusers will not recidivate whether they are treated or not, although it is difficult to be confident about which offenders these may be. The current authors have sometimes accepted apparently 'low risk' offenders into groups in order to assess them more thoroughly. At the other extreme there appear to be offenders who may be highly resistant to treatment. This points strongly therefore to the need for good assessment in order to best target resources where they are likely to be most effective, and to maximise benefit to the public.

TREATMENT RESISTANT ABUSERS

It appears from the research outlined below that there are groups of sexual abusers who may be resistant to treatment, and therefore must be considered carefully prior to being assessed as suitable for treatment. These are as follows:

- highly deviant sexual abusers (as defined by Beech, Fisher and Beckett 1998)
- previous treatment drop outs
- mentally disordered offenders
- psychopaths.

Deviance

Concerning 'highly deviant sexual abusers', Beech, Fisher and Beckett (1998) had argued that indicators of successful treatment could be found via a range of psychometric tests. In their research they had measured denial, pro-offending attitudes, predisposing personality factors and relapse prevention skills.

'High deviance' individuals were those characterised by psychometric evidence of low social competence, high cognitive distortions, high levels of emotional congruence to children, high levels of deficits in empathy for victims and high levels of emotional loneliness.

On the basis of psychometric test results, abusers were classified into three groups as follows:

1. low deviancy-low denial: these abusers showed an overall treatment effect both in short and long groups

2. low deviancy-high denial offenders: these abusers did better in longer groups, i.e. on measures of pro-offending attitudes and overall treatment effects

3.   high deviancy men: these abusers also showed significant
      reduction in pro-offending attitudes in longer groups, but even
      in those longer groups showed little overall treatment effect.

Similar findings were made by Allam (1998) in her study of the West
Midlands Probation Programme.

Psychopathy

The issue of psychopathy features highly with regard to treatment
outcomes. Psychopathy is widely regarded as an aggravating factor in
assessing risk (Quinsey *et al.* 1998; Thornton in Grubin 1998). Hare
(1994) has argued that those scoring highly on his Psychopathy Check List
– Revised are not treatable. Thornton (1999) has argued that treating psychopaths may increase their risk of recidivism.

Treatment of rapists

The treatment of rapists requires particular comment. Alexander (1999)
separated treatment outcome by offender types and found little difference
in recidivism rates for treated and non treated rapists. Further, Marshall
(1993), Pithers (1993) and Beckett *et al.* (1994) have all argued that cognitive-behavioural treatment is limited with this group. It is argued that
rapists in comparison to child abusers tend to be:

- younger
- more likely to be psychopathic
- less motivated
- too 'macho' to engage in treatment
- characterised by general, pro-offending attitudes
- more hostile and angry
- fearful of intimacy
- more criminal in their lifestyles
- more impulsive
- more likely to abuse drugs and alcohol
- more likely to deny their offences
- excessively high or low in their self-esteem.

The motivations of rapists are complex. Knight and Prentky (1990) identified a typology of rapists. They described 'opportunistic' rapists as having
a general history of poor impulse control, rape being a further manifestation of this problem. 'Pervasively angry' rapists were said to have a general
history of uncontrolled aggression (to both males and females) and
general lifestyle impulsivity. The primary motivation of pervasively angry

rapists is extreme, gratuitous rage. 'Sadistic sexual' rapists were said to have erotic and sadistic thoughts and fantasies. Extensive planning and acting out of violent fantasies characterised their offending. 'Sexually motivated' rapists were said to have distorted attitudes to women alongside extensive sexual fantasising. Offending for the sexually motivated rapist was not characterised by gratuitous aggression, furthermore aggression was not apparent in other domains in their lives. 'Vindictive' rapists tend to have good impulse control. The rapes of the vindictive rapist were said to be motivated by a desire to harm, humiliate and degrade.

Treatment needs to take such factors into account. Early treatment programmes may not have given sufficient emphasis to some of these factors characterising general criminality (Beckett *et al.* 1994). Studies of more recent programmes which target general criminality yield more optimistic findings about treatment outcome with rapists (e.g. Allam 1998).

Drop out

Marques (1999), reviewing a longitudinal study in California, found that offenders who had dropped out of previous treatment programmes fared worse in their programme, which is consistent with other research findings (Hanson and Bussiere 1998). Treatment drop out is a long-term risk factor.

It is clear that scarce treatment resources should be targeted on those offenders who are most likely to benefit. Having offenders drop out of groups is a waste of resources and may be disruptive to those group members who wish to benefit. It is not clear however whether short periods of treatment cause heightened risk, or whether those who drop out had other risk factors in any event. It is therefore essential that a thorough assessment of suitability for attendance at programmes is undertaken.

WHAT CONSTITUTES GOOD TREATMENT?

Good treatment, whether it is delivered in a group or individually, should always be set in the wider context of a risk management programme and supported by adequate resources. A number of provisions for the risk management of sexual abusers are outlined in Chapter 2.

Staff delivering treatment should not have primary responsibility for the management of cases. A manager detached from the case should have final responsibility for coordinating decision making and risk management plans. Further, the risk management and therapist roles at practitioner level should not rest with one person. Various phenomena may impair the judgement of an individual therapist. These include the so-called 'Stockholm syndrome' (Goddard and Carew 1988), a concept originally used to describe the way that captives often begin to identify with their captors, and the 'rule of optimism' (Blom-Cooper 1987; Parton 1986), whereby some of those in the caring professions repeatedly view clients in an unduly good light. Salter (1997) also identifies the concept of 'therapist narcissism', arguing that those in high status, high profile, specialised posts may develop an inflated view of the effectiveness of their interventions.

Risk managers should always take account of a wide variety of opinions in planning and implementing risk management strategies. They should actively include those who are in a position to provide evidence based on observed behaviours. This will include workers in residential settings (such as hostels, prison wings and hospital wards) and day centres, where abusers may spend much time. 'Chaperones' and appropriate family members may also be able to provide useful information.

Professional judgements should be anchored by research relating to actuarial assessments of risk accommodating both static and dynamic predictors, and with due respect for the modest impact of therapeutic interventions, particularly with certain types of offender as noted above.

Against this background it has been argued (Underdown 1998) that treatment programmes work best when they fulfil certain criteria. These criteria have been adopted by the Joint Prison/Probation Accreditation Panel (Perry 1998) and include:

- an explicit, empirically based model of change
- the targeting of relevant dynamic risk factors (also known as 'criminogenic factors')
- responsivity to the needs of those in treatment
- a cognitive-behavioural theoretical base
- a skills orientated approach
- a range of relevant targets
- a 'dose' (i.e. length of programme) relevant to the deviancy levels of group attendees
- links between work offered in custody (where applicable) and post-custody supervision
- ongoing monitoring of supporting conditions, programme integrity and evaluation.

The Home Office document *Effective Practice Initiative Pathfinder Project: Initial Assessment Checklist* (Perry 1998) asserts that an *explicit, empirically based model of change* should identify who the programme is for, what is to be achieved during each major phase of the programme and, drawing on relevant theory and research, should explain why the combination of targets and methods has been identified.

Perry (1998), based on the work of Underdown (1998) and Gendreau, Little and Goggin (1996), identifies a list of dynamic risk factors for *general offending*. They include:

- poor cognitive skills
- anti-social attitudes and feelings
- strong ties to and identification with anti-social/criminal models
- weak social ties and identification with pro-social/non-criminal models
- difficulty with self management, decision making and pro-social interpersonal skills
- dependency on drugs and alcohol
- some adverse social or family circumstances
- psychopathic personality
- unemployment
- literacy and numeracy difficulties.

Dynamic risk factors related more *specifically to sexual offending* are identified as:

- deviant sexual interests – offence related interests, especially arousal problems, and excessive sexual preoccupation
- weak commitment to avoid reoffending
- cognitive support for offending – distorted thinking used to justify offending
- empathy deficits (particularly in relation to victims)
- impulsive, anti-social lifestyle
- difficulty generating appropriate coping skills for relevant risk factors
- deficits in interpersonal, self management or problem solving skills
- social support for sexual offending
- absence of social support for relapse prevention strategies.

These lists are consistent with other writers who describe effective programme content; they also note that within programmes these factors are clustered into groups ('modules' or 'menus') which have similar features (Beech *et al.* 1998; Marshall *et al.* 1999; Middleton 2002). In addition, it is necessary either within groups or via individual work supporting groups to address *associated factors* which, though not directly correlated with recidivism, are necessary to address for treatment to be effective. Important examples are motivation, denial, locus of control and self-esteem (Beech *et al.* 1998; National Probation Service 2001).

Any programme should be delivered in a manner which is *responsive* to the needs of the participants. The programme should successfully engage participants. Methods should address the learning styles of participants, should address issues such as literacy and comprehension levels, and give attention to problems such as anxiety levels. Participants should be adequately motivated to change and a motivational style of delivery should predominate (Jenkins 1990b; Miller and Rollnick 1991). Briggs *et al.* (1998) argue that learning occurs best in an atmosphere of 'high support and high challenge'. Beech *et al.* (1998) found that group cohesion correlates with good treatment outcome.

Learning in whatever context should be reinforced in the community, e.g. in hostels, in work with individual supervisors or, if appropriate, with family members.

Programme design should address anti-discriminatory practice issues including being responsive to cultural, ethnic and racial issues. It should take account of the varying age of offenders. In addition, issues of gender preference or physical disability may also need to be addressed. Some abusers with learning disabilities may be able to be accommodated with others in groups, but others may need to be dealt with separately. This will depend on an assessment of the nature and severity of their disability. (We deal with issues of 'working with difference' more comprehensively in Chapter 4.)

Perry (1998) identifies effective methods as those based within a *cognitive-behavioural* framework. This is consistent with research described above which identifies cognitive-behavioural techniques as the most effective therapeutic method for reducing sex offenders' recidivism at this point in time. Methods included here are cognitive restructuring, training in self monitoring, problem solving, encouragement of role-reversal and role rotation, modelling, role play, graduated practice, contingency management, behaviour therapy, and behaviour modification. These and other treatment methods are described in Part II of this book.

It is argued that a *skills orientated* approach is important. These skills should be specifically relevant to the aim of avoiding criminal activity and successfully engaging in legitimate activity.

The length of time an abuser is in a programme, i.e. 'the dosage', should reflect the level of deviance of that abuser. The Home Office Thematic Inspection (Home Office 1998) identified inconsistencies in the length of Probation Service led programmes, some of which may be unnecessarily long for low deviancy abusers, but some of which were clearly too short. Beech *et al.* (1998) also identified the necessity for programme length to relate to levels of deviancy and denial. Allam (1998) found that changes in offenders based on psychometric measures related to length of attendance.

Hanson (2000) has warned against putting low risk offenders through long treatment programmes, noting from the work of Andrews and Bonta (1998) in general criminal populations that this has the potential to increase their recidivism rate. Indeed, one study of sex offenders found that low risk offenders reoffended at a significantly higher rate than a matched sample of untreated offenders: 11 per cent vs 3 per cent (Nicholaichuk 1996). Whilst the evidence is not conclusive, Hanson (2000) argues sensibly that the possibility of negative iatrogenic effects 'cannot be dismissed', for example, by giving low risk offenders the opportunity to meet other sex offenders, to learn information about sex crime, and to ruminate about sex offending.

The relevance of programmes to individual offenders should build on their previous treatment experience. This is particularly important in respect of abusers who may have undertaken a sex offender treatment programme in custody. The Northumbria Sex Offender Groupwork Programme (Doyle *et al.* 1998; Grubin 2000b) has adopted a system whereby individuals are assessed prior to release from custody, to examine what elements of the programme they need to undertake after release. They may be required to repeat a core cognitive-behavioural group work programme, or alternatively may be allocated directly to the relapse prevention group. Alternatively, an individualised programme may be offered. This assessment is undertaken by a forensic psychologist and psychiatrist, both of whom have specialist expertise in sex offender work, by probation officers specialising in sex offender work and probation service colleagues from the field. Prison staff are also invited to assessment meetings. These meetings also make recommendations about risk management plans.

It is important that programmes are delivered consistently with their stated aims and content. Thus *programme integrity and treatment integrity* are essential. There are a number of important factors in relation to programme and treatment integrity which include:

- staff continuity
- a clear timetable
- consistent selection criteria
- good attendance
- a workable size of group
- proper planning
- proper debriefing
- consistency between what is delivered and what is described in the programme manual

- competent staff to deliver the programme
- a focused approach
- management of group attendance
- engagement of group members
- challenges to anti-social behaviours
- the setting of relevant objectives for programmes and for individuals within programmes
- proper recording.

Programme and treatment integrity may be monitored by the use of written records, debriefing, videoing of sessions or live observation. It is equally important that programmes offered to abusers on an individual basis have integrity and attention should be given to this in supervision. Some issues may best be delivered on an individual basis (for example, work on arousal and fantasy or addressing the abuser's own victimisation experiences). Aspects of the programme delivered individually should also be appropriately monitored.

THERAPEUTIC ENVIRONMENT

It has been well established in group therapy that the therapeutic environment must be conducive to promoting change. Most of the early work relating to this was undertaken with patients or clients who attended treatment voluntarily, and who were therefore likely to have acknowledged at least some of their problems (e.g. Rogers 1951; Yalom 1975). Marshall *et al.* (1999), however, criticised early writers for being 'preoccupied with therapeutic process almost to the exclusion of procedure', although they also noted the opposite tendency in some therapists with a background in behaviourism. As noted in Chapter 3, Salter (1988) described tensions in working with sex offenders that do not apply to other therapeutic settings, including the often mandatory nature of their attendance, persistent suspicion about whether group members are always truthful, and the fact that confidentiality in group work with sex offenders is limited by public protection concerns.

Whilst caution therefore has been expressed about transferring uncritically early insights about group dynamics to sex offender work, research has demonstrated the need for cohesion and a supportive group atmosphere if treatment with sex offenders is to be successful. The STEP research team (Beckett *et al.* 1994) identified a subset of offenders in group work programmes who developed more negative attitudes towards victims during treatment. This appeared to relate to the punitive attitudes of workers and the premature exposure of offenders to emotionally charged victim empathy work. Beech and Fordham (1997) and Beech *et al.* (1998)

noted that group cohesion, as measured by the Group Environment Scale (Moos 1986), correlated well with positive outcomes. Indeed, Marshall *et al.* (1999) argue that the group environment itself can be nurturing and promote change in some dynamic risk factors, notably those which related to intimacy and relationship skills.

Another area that Marshall *et al.* (1999) examine is that of leadership style. They support arguments that an overly punitive style may be serving the needs of the group leaders rather than members, by allowing them to express their disgust at the offences members have committed. This has been called 'legitimised nonce bashing' by Sheath (1990). Marshall *et al.* (1999) warn against therapist styles that mirror the abusive behaviours in which sex offenders themselves have indulged in the past. They argue, for example, that a programme is unlikely to promote empathy if the leaders are not seen to be empathic.

Marshall *et al.* (2003) observed videotapes from group work sessions in the HM Prison Sex Offender Treatment Programme and therapists were rated on a number of features. A confrontational style was found to correlate with negative outcomes. Interestingly, they found that apparently contradictory features such as directiveness and the ability to ask open-ended questions both correlated with a positive outcome. They argue that therapists need the flexibility and ability to know when appropriate interventions are relevant. Marshall *et al.* report that of 11 characteristics which correlate with positive outcomes there are four important characteristics which show the most effect, being:

- warm
- empathic
- rewarding
- directive.

They suggest that 'increasing the role of the therapist, by reducing strict adherence to detailed procedural manuals, may increase the effectiveness of such treatment'.

Briggs (Briggs *et al.* 1998), drawing on insights from occupational psychology, has suggested that people generally achieve most in an atmosphere where there is a good balance between 'support' and 'challenge'. In that earlier text he proposed a grid that illustrates the responses that might be expected from group members where there is an imbalance between these factors.

Briggs (Briggs *et al.* 1998) describes examples of supportive behaviour as: praising clients when appropriate, asking about and acknowledging their feelings, helping them to express feelings, acknowledging client strengths and clear contracting. Examples of challenging behaviours are:

being truthful when information is disbelieved, sticking with difficult subject matter, honesty about how a client's behaviour made a worker feel, identifying discrepancies in a client's presentation, and pointing out barriers to progress that a client is presenting. Staff are crucial to the determination of therapeutic environment. Issues relating to staffing are discussed in Chapter 3.

RISK MANAGEMENT

We have stressed that 'treatment' should be rooted within a risk management strategy. Roberts (1991) proposes that intervention should be multi-factoral. He identifies four components to intervention.

Specific offending behaviour components relate to the targeting of criminogenic factors via group or individual interventions as described above.

Community reintegration components are designed to strengthen a non criminal lifestyle and provide reintegration opportunities within the community. Examples may include work on adult education, leisure, housing and employment.

Offending associated behaviour components may include anger control, alcohol abuse and other addictive problems. Such work will be particularly important with those who have problems with impulse control and have more generally 'criminal' lifestyles. These issues may relate closely to the identification of relapse prevention strategies (described later).

Presenting problems brought by abusers will involve tackling interrelated factors of environmental stress and disadvantage such as unemployment, housing problems, poverty, relationship breakdown, isolation and the loss of social influences.

Concerning those presenting problems described above, sexual abusers have committed acts which often anger and repulse even highly experienced practitioners. It is therefore tempting to discuss some of the above as consequences rightly bestowed on an abuser for his actions. However, the primary aim in working with sexual abusers is to reduce the likelihood of them committing further abuse. If immediate and presenting issues are not addressed or at least acknowledged, then this may pose a block to addressing other dynamic risk factors.

Roberts' four components are not independent of each other. For example, work on the factors described is likely to have a direct impact on dynamic risk factors and associated factors such as low self-esteem and social competence. More regular contact with adults, albeit in non-sexual contexts, may address the problem identified by Finkelhor *et al.* (1986) and Beech *et al.* (1998), whereby many child sexual abusers are identified as having a high degree of emotional 'congruence' with children.

OTHER EVALUATIONS

Finally, Kafka (2002) has reminded us of the importance when evaluating sexual abusers of exploring psychiatric disorders that may be associated with paraphilic sex offending. He believes that the appropriate 'diagnosis, psycho-education and pharmacological treatment' of these associated disorders will enhance compliance with the psycho-therapeutic treatment of the sexually abusive behaviour. He suggests that

> Most paraphilic sex offenders have at least one, but usually several lifetime psychiatric diagnoses. The most common psychiatric diagnoses may be mood disorders (especially low grade depression, major depression or bi-polar spectrum disorders), anxiety disorders (social phobia, post traumatic stress disorder), psychoactive substance abuse (alcohol abuse, cocaine abuse), and impulsivity disorders (attention deficit hyperactivity disorder, conduct disorder). (Kafka 2002, p.2)

Of these, he believes that mood disorder, substance abuse disorder and attention deficit hyperactivity disorder are most often overlooked.

Kafka suggests that treatment which combines psychotherapy with psycho-pharmacology can yield better treatment outcomes for these sorts of disorders, and expresses optimism for improvements in psychological treatment outcomes and the prevention of recidivism.

NEXT STEPS

We have noted that to date the cognitive-behavioural treatment of sex offenders in well structured programmes appears to reduce recidivism by some 40 per cent over about four years. The question arises as to whether we can improve on those figures in the future.

Preliminary findings (Allam 1998) also give cause for optimism that focusing on relevant dynamic risk factors in a particularly difficult target group (i.e. rapists) will generate positive treatment outcomes. As indicated above, this population has previously shown less good treatment effects.

Creativity and therapeutic ingenuity is not lacking as we continue in our endeavours. Marshall and Bryce (1996), for example, have described work specifically targeting intimacy deficits in sexual offenders. In some cases these deficits need addressing via intensive, long-term work. Often such deficits are a function of chronic, poor attachment experiences.

Another example of developing work is that of Mann (2003). She has described work aimed at helping offenders identify and manage the effects of 'schemas'. This is a concept used to describe the way that individuals process facts and shape their 'view of the world'. In abusers such schemas may relate directly to their offending. Examples include a belief that 'women are deceitful' or that one is 'always cast as the victim'.

Intimacy deficits and schemas are addressed in the Prison Service's extended programme which appears to be showing significant clinical gains on psychometric measures (Mann 2003). It remains to be seen whether these translate into long-term reductions in recidivism rates.

Relapse prevention has long been promoted as an integral part of any comprehensive sex offender treatment programme (e.g. Beckett *et al.* 1994). The limitations of the 'orthodox model' of relapse prevention have been documented (Hanson 2000; Ward and Hudson 2000) and an alternative 'self-regulation model' based on the pursuit of goals (approach or avoidant) by offenders has been proposed (Hudson and Ward 2000). Work has been undertaken to develop the practical application of the self-regulation model (Bickley and Beech 2003), which appears to support its use. Relapse prevention and self-regulation are discussed in detail in Chapter 12.

Ward (2002) has proposed a 'good lives theory', arguing that in addition to focusing on identified deficits (i.e. dynamic risk factors) abusers need to be enabled to develop the capacity to live fulfilling, independent lives.

This is the underlying principle reflected in the most recent programme developed by HM Prison Service (2004). The programme manual quotes Ward and Mann (2004) as saying that

> Treatment based on removing deficits or risk factors is unlikely to sufficiently motivate offenders and also does not pay enough attention to the issues of psychological agency and personal identity.

They go on to state that relapse prevention should be 'embedded within a more constructive, strength based capabilities approach'. Risk factors are viewed as obstacles to an individual's capacity to lead a more fulfilling life. Treatment targets in the 'Better Lives Booster Programme' include the setting of personal goals, recognising and building on strengths, strategies to feel more comfortable in adult relationships, healthy sexual attitudes and practices, examining the role of sex for the individual, and identifying support networks. We wait to see whether these promising developments, all of which have face validity, translate into further reductions in recidivism rates for abusers who have engaged in treatment.

COMMENT

'Treatment' of sexual abusers can reduce recidivism for a significant number. However, it is essential that treatment programmes are part of an effective risk management strategy. To this end, a range of agencies and disciplines should be involved in the ongoing assessment and management of sexual abusers. Account should be taken not only of apparent progress in treatment, but of objective observation of behaviour and a thorough understanding of research into what types of treatment are likely to make a significant impact on what types of offenders.

CHAPTER 6

Managing Client Motivation to Change

It is something of an accepted wisdom in most fields of counselling and verbal therapy that motivation is an essential prerequisite for successful treatment. If the client is not motivated to change how will that client mobilise the emotional, cognitive and intellectual energies required of the therapy concerned? The assumption that motivation is crucial to success-ful treatment is found in our work with sexual abusers too. Whilst we lack treatment outcome studies relating measures of motivation to extent of change in sexual abusers, motivation is widely referred to in the treatment literature. Kennington *et al.* (2001) refer to it as an 'associated risk factor' in the Northumbria Probation Accredited Groupwork Programme, drawing on previous work by Fisher and Beech (1998).

In our previous book (Briggs *et al.* 1998), we reviewed what we regarded to be a pivotal model developed by Prochaska and DiClemente (1982) which addresses how a client's motivation is likely to vary depend-ing on which stage of change they are currently undergoing. The stages are identified as follows:

- *Precontemplation*, in which no problem is acknowledged. At this stage motivational work is required.

- *Contemplation*, when a client may begin to acknowledge that there is a problem. Motivational work continues and some action is indicated.

- *Action* is the phase where work is undertaken to change or manage the factors which have motivated and maintained abuse.

- *Maintenance* is the phase in which it is necessary to reinforce changes made and prevent reversion to previous behaviours.

- *Relapse* represents a reversion to previous behaviours. In the case of sexual abuse this is likely (if known to the authorities) to be referred for further investigation.

Ward and Hudson (2000) identified how individuals generally have differential motivation in relation to different aspects of their lives and relate this model to sexually abusive behaviour and work by individuals to regulate it. They argue that individuals seek goals in ways which are acquisitional (or approach orientated) or inhibitory (or avoidant). Individuals who are approach orientated will have a history of success in achieving their goals, so initial failures will be reviewed in the light of this general success. Those with avoidant goals, in contrast, will generally try to avoid behaviours and failure is likely to reinforce a perception of inadequacy.

As applied to offending it is argued that some offenders will wish to stop but fail, either because of lack of coping skills (avoidant passive) or the use of inappropriate coping strategies (avoidant active). Approach orientated offenders are thought to lack any real desire to avoid offending and may either revert to habitual lifestyles (approach automatic) or deliberately seek to reoffend (approach explicit).

It is argued that treatment should be presented as the opportunity for a new, purposeful offence-free lifestyle rather than merely an avoidant experience. This model and its practical application is discussed elsewhere in this text, notably in Chapter 11.

Marques (1999), in her report of California's Sex Offender Treatment and Evaluation Project (SOTEP), notes that early treatment drop outs have the highest rate of reoffending, endorsing her earlier, similar findings (Marques et al. 1994). Treatment drop out here may be an indicator of motivation (though could also, of course, relate to other factors).

Beech et al. (1998) found that therapeutic outcome (at least as measured by psychometric tests) appeared to relate to levels of cohesiveness in the sex offender treatment groups they studied: '...members' involvement, commitment and concern, and friendship they showed for each other are strongly related to a positive therapeutic outcome'. Group cohesion here may directly influence motivation.

Further, Marques et al. (2000) report on a study conducted towards the end of the SOTEP's treatment phase. Three rapists and six child molesters who had reoffended were interviewed. All reported having been motivated to change at the outset of treatment but could not sustain motivation across time. Some believed that it was 'useless to struggle against their long-standing deviant interests'. Marques et al. comment that these men failed to avoid critical high risk behaviours following treatment, reporting that 'these individuals clearly did not "get" the program that we provided'.

In an associated area of professional activity, Daly et al. (2001) have reported on predictors of men attending domestic violence programmes. Their research suggests that less educated men, men who were unemployed at intake, those not court ordered to attend and those with a history of alcohol-related problems completed fewer sessions. Further, they suggest the results of their research are consistent with psychotherapy research linking social factors such as instability and class status with programme attendance. By inference, similar factors may be associated with motivation in sexual abusers to complete treatment. Replication of this study focusing on sexual abusers' treatment attendance would be welcome.

CONCEPTUALISATIONS

We have to be careful how we conceptualise motivation. It might be too simplistic to consider motivation as something simply fixed or not 'within' the abuser. Motivation is about energy and effort. In the context of sexual abusers and their treatment, this refers to the ongoing energy on the part of the abuser to achieve and sustain an abuse-free lifestyle.

As stated, motivation is not a static phenomenon. It will be influenced by the abuser's belief about his capacity to change, by the belief that his offending behaviour is undesirable, by external factors which model and promote change, by the particular 'chemistry' of the relationship between the abuser and worker(s), by the abuser's general emotional strength and stamina, and by statutory levers and mandates (e.g. the requirements of a community order, licence or care plan, including knowledge of the sanctions likely in the event of a failure to cooperate).

Within this context, issues of ethnicity and culture cannot be ignored. Cowburn (1996) has commented, for example, that sexual offenders from ethnic minorities might not be prepared to enter treatment programmes because of difficulties in engaging with white staff or fear of sacrificing support in an inherently racist environment. Gahir and Garrett (1999) similarly comment that sexual offenders from ethnic minorities might be unwilling to attend a white dominated group programme for fear of scapegoating, of marginalisation or isolation in a dominant white group.

Levels of motivation may change across time. It is rare that an abuser in counselling will sustain steady motivation throughout. More often, motivation follows periods of increased emotional energy and drive, but with interceding periods of low energy and de-motivation.

External influences are of relevance here, including the quality of social supports. Borduin *et al.* (1990) have commented, for example, on the failure of some adolescents in treatment programmes, linking motivation with levels of familial support and supervision. We can extrapolate from this to consider whether motivation to change is similarly linked to familial support factors in men who sexually abuse.

The skilled worker will recognise the abuser's periods of low energy and de-motivation as inevitable in their work. Rather than something to become angered or irritated about, the worker might consider helping the abuser to reflect on their low motivation, and thereby invite a collaborative approach to re-motivation. Further, often that which motivated a client early in the work will be different to what motivates him later in treatment.

Marques *et al.* (2000) comment that offenders who have not developed their own sources of motivation might be vulnerable to relapse when they leave structured treatment settings. Further, motivation to change based on punishment should be treated with caution, e.g. motivation to change based on a desire to avoid future punishment or social/family rejection might be flawed: 'More intrinsic and internal rewards for success must be developed if motivation is going to be sustained.'

Jenkins (1990a) has established a philosophical and pragmatic approach to work with abusers. He argues persuasively for the establishment of a proper engagement style between worker and client to enable those who have abused to find motivation to change and relate to others in healthy, respectful ways. He implies that well intentioned workers may paradoxically fail to enhance the motivation of their young abusers though the process of assessment, categorisation and intervention, and indeed may have more motivation than their clients. He argues the need for clients to establish their own intervention goals and to develop their own motivation to achieve them. He describes a model of 'engagement' with clients based on invitations to the client to develop an alternative sense of identity to that of the 'sexual abuser', one which highlights the concept of choice in intervention, and one based on the principles of responsibility, accountability and respect (i.e. 'respectful to those who have abused and must promote and enhance respect of self and others').

Motivation and denial

Motivation to avoid offending in some abusers may be considered independent of the concept of denial of past offending. Traditionally, programmes have excluded those who appear to deny totally any offending or who deny there is the potential to reabuse. However, whilst it is acknowledged that those exhibiting such forms of denial might be difficult to work with in traditional programmes, that is not to say they cannot benefit from some form of intervention, and may for example benefit from psycho-educational approaches. Denial, if a reflection of guilt and the need to protect self, does not preclude efforts to avoid reoffending.

The above debate has been re-ignited since the publication of Hanson and Bussiere's (1998) meta-analysis of factors associated with the risk of reoffending. Denial did not feature as statistically significant in predicting future risk of reoffending. Further, in the subsequent 2003 meta-analysis, Hanson and Morton-Bourgon reported that categorical denial and minimisation of offending appeared unrelated to recidivism (Hanson and

Morton-Bourgon 2004). Lund (2000) cautioned about drawing any definitive conclusions about Hanson and Bussiere's findings. He argues that the lack of definition of denial, the different times that it might be studied, and the lack of differentiation between offenders make any conclusions about the role of denial and future risk premature.

Marshall and Marshall (2000) have described how they have incorporated small numbers of men into their treatment groups and not directly challenged them about their denial of their offences. Significant numbers of men have changed their stance. Schlank and Shaw (1997) have also described how they have run groups of abusers who deny any offence, with a view to helping them to change their behaviours and move into a mainstream group. Such change occurred in about 50 per cent of their subjects.

Finally, we note a recent study which has explored the concept of engagement with treatment and its links with denial and treatment progress. Levenson and Macgowan (2004) note Macgowan's conceptualisation of engagement as a multi-dimensional construct (Macgowan 1997). Seven dimensions to engagement are described:

- attendance (attending or completing group sessions)
- contributing (speaking/participating in group sessions)
- relating to worker (showing support for the work of the leader)
- relating with others (interacting with other group members)
- contracting (adopting the group contract)
- working on own problems, and
- working on others' problems.

The results of the Levenson and Macgowan study revealed a strong correlation between engagement in sex offender group therapy and sex offender treatment progress. Denial was inversely related to treatment progress and engagement. The authors suggest that admitting to a sex crime 'is a necessary condition for progress and engagement in treatment'.

The authors suggest that strategies for increasing engagement include:

> using a positive, empathic approach that encourages and supports client ownership of change. Motivational approaches based on empathic understanding, mutual trust and acceptance may empower clients to choose to engage in the therapeutic process rather than have the intervention imposed by the therapist. (Levenson and Macgowan 2004, p.51)

We believe that the links between treatability, denial and motivation need further clarification. This is very much 'work in progress'.

Motivation and relapse

As indicated above, there is strong clinical belief that motivation is a crucial factor underpinning treatment outcome. The somewhat limited methods we have at our disposal for measuring motivation and reabuse risk (typically measures of reconviction), not surprisingly, do not indicate a strong link between expressed motivation for treatment and recidivism. e.g. Hanson (2000).

Theoretically, motivation has been linked to likelihood of lapse and relapse in the traditional relapse prevention literature via the concept of the 'abstinence violence effect'. Clients at risk of relapse were those who, having made a commitment not to engage in behaviours which placed them at risk of reoffending, breached this self-imposed rule. Awareness of this internal rule breaking was thought to create dissonance, self attributions of failure and a perceived loss of control. In turn these factors could lead to relapse. More recently the relevance (and indeed validity) of the concept of abstinence violation as applied to sexual abusers has been challenged (Hanson 2000). Hanson comments that 'many (?most) sex offenders have low motivation to change'. He expresses surprise that there has been 'little attention to other methods of motivating offenders' given George and Marlatt's (1989) comment that relapse prevention as a treatment technology 'offers little promise for the unmotivated offender and cannot induce motivation'.

Precursors to change

Hanna (2002) has written about variables which he believes are conducive to psychotherapeutic change, variables which he draws from psychotherapy research. He terms these variables 'precursors to change', and describes them as 'client specific' factors, that is those factors the client brings to treatment. He argues that each has empirical validation. If these precursors are present in an individual then therapeutic change is possible. He believes that in the absence of these precursors, however, change is unlikely. Indeed, if even one of the precursors is missing, the process of therapy is likely to be inhibited. Clients who resist therapy lack precursors to change according to his theory. Conversely, change is more likely to occur in a client the more the precursors are present.

Hanna describes these seven precursors as follows:

A sense of necessity is that sense on the part of the client that change must take place.

A willingness or readiness to experience anxiety or difficulty is the client's willingness to feel the discomfort that comes with change. ('Defensiveness', the opposite to this precursor, is about the client's attempts to avoid discomfort or anxiety.)

Awareness is the understanding the client has of the nature of the problem or issue and the behaviours, feelings and thoughts associated with it. (Awareness in this context is the opposite of denial or obliviousness.)

Confronting the problem is described by Hanna (2002) as

> the steady and deliberate attending to and observing of anything that is intimidating, painful, or confusing, in spite of the inclination to avoid, shun, or act out. It is operative when a client is looking at a problem squarely and directly and continues to observe, explore or investigate it until he or she grasps its essence. (p.32)

Effort or will towards change is about the expending of energy, making a commitment, coming to a decision and initiating action. It can be seen in the client changing his thoughts and attitudes, and in the real world in coping with real life situations.

Hope for change refers to the client's expectation of change occurring, that change can and will occur.

Finally, *social support for change* relates to the client having supportive relationships dedicated to him, his well-being and improvement.

Hanna suggests that with difficult clients it is important first to reflect on the seven precursors above and establish those which are deficient or missing, and then address these before attempting more traditional therapeutic activities. He believes that therapy with difficult clients may involve a different set of therapeutic skills than those used with motivated and involved clients. He believes this work calls for workers who have particularly effective relationship and empathic skills. Hanna offers optimism that clients can learn the skills of therapeutic change.

The reader is referred to Hanna's excellent text for further discussion of those issues and clinical applications, including techniques and practices for the establishment and enhancement of the precursors.

OBJECTIVES FOR INTERVENTION

Whilst accepting that it will be necessary to keep a continuous focus on motivation throughout work with the client, we suggest some preliminary targets for clients in treatment as follows. (The numerical targets in brackets below are set from our experience. Other workers may choose to set differing targets on the basis of their experience and the client group they are dealing with.)

- Following intervention the client will be able to generate at least (six) reasons why it is important to undertake work to address his abusive behaviour.

- Following intervention the client will have identified at least (three) people, other than his therapist, who can assist him to change. (For each, the client will be able to specify the person by name, how that person can be accessed, the nature of the help these individuals can provide, the action to be taken by the client to ensure that help is available, and the information that person needs about the client and his treatment to ensure the help is relevant and customised to the client.)

- Following intervention the client will have identified at least (three) people who might hinder his attempts to change. (For each, the client will be able to specify the person by name, will identify clearly how that person would serve to undermine their efforts to change, and would have identified at least two strategies to counter each undermining tactic.)

- Following intervention the client will be able to explain what the worker might do to facilitate his, the client's, learning and development. Further, following intervention the client will be able to explain what the worker might do to hinder the client's learning and development. (As part of any subsequent contract for work with the client, the worker will make clear his/her contribution to facilitating client development, reflecting information gathered as part of his objective.)

- Following intervention the client will be able to specify issues that might get in the way of their regular attendance at sessions (e.g. shift patterns, travel difficulties, competing demands on their time) and have an action plan in place to address these issues.

- Following intervention the client will be able to describe those issues which he most fears talking about in the group, and why, and will have explored with the worker how best to tackle these issues. The client will be reminded of 'why' there is a need to be open and direct in this work.

- Following intervention the client will be able to articulate an image of himself as a non-offender so as to encourage a future perspective and to encourage change.

- Following intervention the client will identify a situation in the past in which he has managed to control sexual urges to abuse, thereby reminding himself that he has skills which can be built upon.

EXAMPLES OF INTERVENTION
Motivational interviewing
It has long been argued that people are more likely to be motivated to change if they subscribe to ideas that they have developed themselves, and that there is tendency to resist arguments that are imposed by others.

Miller and Rollnick (1995) promoted a technique called 'motivational interviewing' whereby clients were encouraged to question the validity of their own position by the use of open questions and comparing their statements with different realities. This promotes 'cognitive dissonance', a mind state in which the client begins to be aware of contradictions in their own position. This causes psychological tension. It is the task of the therapist to help the client to develop a new, more pro-social set of ideas, rather than revert to the 'comfort zone' offered by habitual thought patterns.

It would be inappropriate within this text to attempt to prescribe the activities underpinning motivational interviewing. The second edition of Miller and Rollnick's text is now published and readers are referred to this for further information (Miller and Rollnick 2002).

Socratic questioning

Mann, from her work with the Prison Service Sex Offender Treatment Programme (Mann 2000), expresses empirical support for the technique of so-called 'Socratic questioning'. This is a method in which the questioner promotes dissonance in the client by withholding their own expertise and acting as the 'naïve examiner'. For instance, 'Help me, John. I don't understand how a six-year-old girl knows what an erect penis looks like.'

Fernandez et al. (2001) have described Socratic questioning as the use of 'thought provoking, non hostile questions that assist the recipient in thinking something out for himself'. They believe that through the process of reflecting on the questions and generating a response there is opportunity for cognitive restructuring. They make clear that Socratic questioning is not the same as information gathering, involving questions such as 'How did you feel?'.

Guidance is offered as to the sorts of questions to be avoided, questions that are not Socratic in style and hence unlikely to lead to cognitive change, for example:

- assumptive questions ('When you masturbated to deviant fantasy...')
- closed questions
- leading questions ('Can you see that...?')
- confrontational questioning ('Can't you see that...?').

The style in which Socratic questioning is undertaken is crucial we would argue. The tone of voice and pace of questioning can be inherently confrontational if care is not taken to understand the client's position and perspective. We would return to the importance of a balance being achieved here between the support and challenge of the client.

Reasons for change

Ideally, if clients are to generate reasons for addressing their offending behaviour these should reflect their particular situation and they should have 'ownership' of them. Some clients struggle to generate reasons. It might be useful in such circumstances to present the client with a set of 'reasons' (for example, printed on cards) and invite the client to choose examples from these which may have relevance to him. Alternatively, he could rank the statements from 'most relevant' to him through to 'least relevant'. In discussing his selection the client should be encouraged to reflect on the balance of motivating factors between those which lead to positive outcomes (e.g. 'If I work hard in treatment I'll learn to respect myself') as opposed to those which reflect 'negative outcomes' (e.g. 'If I don't get treatment I'll end up in prison again'). The client might also be encouraged to reflect on such a list at various stages of treatment to examine any shifts in such factors.

Example of such 'motivating statements' here might include:

- 'I must tackle my sex offending to make sure I don't harm the people I care about.'
- 'If I work hard in treatment I'll learn to respect myself' (feel good about myself, feel in control of my life, feel part of society again, feel worthwhile, feel strong, etc.).
- 'If I address my sex offending this will be a way of showing my victims that I am sorry for what I did to them.'
- 'If I don't address my offending behaviour I'll always feel I'm a victim.'

Clearly, the list is not exhaustive. As workers build experience they might be encouraged to collate such a list, adding to it as clients generate new and varied reasons.

It will be important for the worker to remember the particular motivating factors for each client, reminding the client of those at times of slippage or despondency.

Bearing in mind that motivation is an idiosyncratic state, the worker should try to avoid imposing his or her concerns upon the client, and similarly should avoid encouraging the client to 'buy into' the concerns of others (e.g. 'your wife will be relieved if you get treatment'). Our experience suggests that clients who build a set of their own motivating statements, i.e. statements which meet their own needs, are more likely to sustain these. The earlier histories of our clients are often tinged with psychological maltreatment. Offenders in their formative years often learn to please others and disregard their own needs. Treatment for the abuser has to induce a sense of personal responsibility taking and self respect.

Supports for change

It is a difficult task for some clients to identify individuals, other than immediate therapists, who can assist in the change process. Many abusers lead self-absorbed or lonely lifestyles. Some will have learnt to distrust offers of help from others.

One activity to assist the abuser to recognise potential 'supporters' would be the invitation to complete a simple questionnaire such as that described below (Figure 6.1), with the worker and client thereafter discussing the implications of the results.

Clearly the list of people suggested in Figure 6.1 is not exhaustive, rather represented here as a guide. We are interested to identify all those individuals the abuser might perceive to be a source of help (including 'questionable' individuals such as other offenders and victims). It is important to manage the abuser's use of social and emotional supports, to encourage the use of healthy influences, and to discourage the use of potentially 'risky' influences.

Once individuals are identified who might assist the abuser to sustain motivation to change, the worker and abuser might consider how best to engage those individuals in the change process. (Sadly, there is no substantive history of developing techniques for the recruitment and training of 'sponsors' in the UK and many community programmes are not resourced to deal with this issue.)

Evaluation

In considering the abuser and his motivation to change, there are various factors which may help the clinician evaluate such motivation. Some of these are *historical*, for example:

- a history of beginning a sex offender treatment programme but failing to complete it
- a history of beginning other offending treatment programmes but failing to complete them
- a history of uncooperative behaviour during previous treatment e.g. past failure to comply with homework requests, a history of lateness, 'group tourist' behaviour (i.e. moving in and out of group treatment programmes with no evidence of completion), breaking contracts and not adhering to boundaries and access rules
- a history of substance misuse during prior treatment
- behavioural incongruence during previous treatment, i.e. a history of 'talk the talk' but not 'walk the walk' behaviour, including here 'intelligence' reports of ongoing abusive behaviour during past treatment.

Think about the people below. Can they help you in any way to stop sexually abusing others? If you think they might help, try to explain *how* they might help.

Person	Name	Can't help me	Not sure	Can help me	How they can help me
Partner					
Former partner					
Partner/grandparents					
Former carers					
Sisters or brothers (include 'step' and 'half' brothers and sisters)					
Children (include 'step' children)					
Personal or family friends					
Neighbours					
Other offenders					
Victim(s)					
Church leaders					
Colleagues at work					
GP					
Other professional people *not* involved in my treatment					
etc.					

Figure 6.1: *Who Can Help Me?*

Some factors are *contemporary,* for example:

- ongoing alcohol/substance misuse
- exposure to models of non-cooperation with treatment (including family members, other sexual offenders and significant others who believe that treatment is irrelevant or unnecessary etc.)
- acute stressors which disinhibit attention and concentration on therapeutic targets (e.g. absence from residence, bereavement, relationship collapse)
- mental health factors which destabilise attention and concentration on therapeutic targets (e.g. depression, psychotic breakdown)
- pervasive and/or instrumental anger
- ongoing evidence of behavioural incongruence ('talk the talk' but not 'walk the walk' behaviour)
- evidence of the offender having rehearsed statements to the effect that treatment will not work and of his inability to change
- psychopathy (a factor which may exclude clients from group work).

Motivation might also be evaluated via *assessment tasks* and *activities*:

- the offender's response to the Programme Expectations Questionnaire (Figure 6.2)
- the offender's response to the Decision Matrix (Figure 6.3)
- the offender's preparedness to complete a detailed Personal Diary (Figure 6.4)
- the offender's response to the Disclosure Ranking Exercise (Figure 6.5)
- the offender's preparedness to name significant others who could be contacted by programme leaders to support the work, i.e. by completing the Contact Sheet (Figure 6.6).

Other materials which may be of assistance in promoting change include the simple questionnaire 'Learning from my Past (Figure 6.7) and 'The Change Contract' (Figure 6.8).

Why do you need to attend
this Programme?

What do you hope to achieve
from the Programme?

How can the staff team assist
you to achieve your goals?

How can other people assist
you to achieve your goals?

What do you need to do to
achieve your goals?

What would get in the way
of you achieving what you hope?

The process will require honesty –
how can we tell when you are not
being honest?

Have you done this sort of work   Yes/No
before?
If 'Yes', what did you gain?

What work was left to do?

Who wants you to stop
reoffending?

What worries you about
the thought of working on
your sex offending?

Figure 6.2: *The Programme Expectations Questionnaire*

	Decision to reoffend	Decision not to reoffend
Positive consequences		
Negative consequences		

Figure 6.3: *The Decision Matrix*

✓

Day: _____ Date: ___/___/___

	Non-sexual activity	Sexual activity	Who in contact with	Mood/ feelings	Place
Morning					
Afternoon					
Evening					
Night					

Figure 6.4: *Personal Diary*

This exercise is designed to help you identify when your motivation to change may need the support of others. Rank the following statements in order of what you would find easiest to undertake (1) and what would be most difficult (12):

	Disclose within treatment that you continue to have fantasies of sexual offending.
	Give an account of your current offence to a probation officer.
	Tell your adult partner about your deviant sexual fantasies.
	Describe to your parents/brother/sister etc. the sexually aggressive behaviour which led to your conviction.
	Attend the police station to sign the Sex Offenders Register.
	Help your partner to understand your Schedule One status.
	Fill in a job application form, declaring your conviction(s).
	Tell the probation receptionist that you have come to attend the treatment group.
	Tell your group leader that you are angry and do not agree with their instruction.
	Share information about your offending with your group peers.
	Explain to a neighbour that you cannot baby-sit.
	Tell a prospective friend that you are in treatment for offences against children.

Figure 6.5: *Disclosure Ranking Exercise*

✓

Name:

Address:

- Who do you live with? (List all people in the household.)

- Who do you socialise with at work? (List all.)

- Who do you socialise with away from work? (List all.)

- Who could offer you support? (List all.)

- Do you have a mentor to support you?

- Please mark with an asterisk all those above we might contact to support this work, indicating also their telephone number/contact address.

- Who would you contact in an emergency?

- How can we contact you in an emergency?

Figure 6.6: Contact Sheet

There have been times in the past when I have felt like offending but haven't done so. When I have reflected on these times, it seems there may be things that I can use to keep myself safe in the future.

The thoughts that I have had which might keep me safe should I want to reoffend in future include:

The things I might do to keep me safe and which have worked well for me in the past include:

Date: ___/___/___

Figure 6.7: *Learning from my Past*

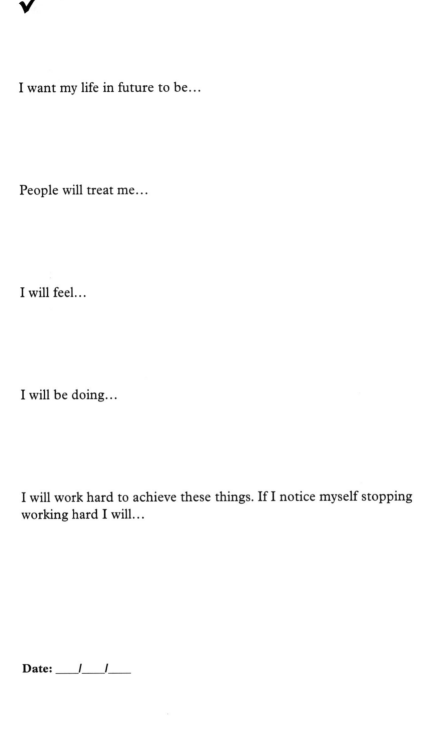

I want my life in future to be...

People will treat me...

I will feel...

I will be doing...

I will work hard to achieve these things. If I notice myself stopping working hard I will...

Date: ___/___/___

Figure 6.8: *The Change Contract*

David Briggs and Carol Morton had coordinated these evaluations as part of an assessment tool for the West Yorkshire Probation Service. The data typically would be recorded as in Figure 6.9.

Stage One (Historical)	Yes	No
History of failure to complete sex offender treatment programme	☐	☐
History of failure to complete other treatment/counselling programme (of any sort)	☐	☐
History of uncooperative behaviour during previous treatment/counselling of whatever sort	☐	☐
History of substance misuse during prior treatment/counselling of whatever sort	☐	☐
Suspicion of ongoing lapse/offending behaviour during previous counselling/treatment	☐	☐

Stage Two (Contemporary)	Yes	No
Evidence of ongoing alcohol misuse	☐	☐
Evidence of ongoing substance/drug misuse	☐	☐
Exposure to models of non cooperation with treatment	☐	☐
Presence of acute stressors	☐	☐
Presence of destabilising mental health factors	☐	☐
Evidence of pervasive or instrumental anger	☐	☐
Evidence of ongoing lapse/offending related behaviour	☐	☐
Evidence of offender rehearsing/articulating negative statements about the value of treatment	☐	☐
Evidence of psychopathy	☐	☐

Stage Three (Process)	Yes	No
Client has completed the Programme Expectations Questionnaire	☐	☐
Client has completed the Decision Matrix	☐	☐
Client has completed a Personal Diary	☐	☐
Client has completed the Disclosure Ranking Exercise	☐	☐
Client has named significant others to sponsor the work	☐	☐

Figure 6.9: *Assessment Summary Sheet*

TIPS AND HINTS

Often, workers develop contracts with clients at the outset of the work. For example, those attending group treatment programmes will often enter contracts about matters such as confidentiality, attendance, homework requirements and the use of recording equipment. In turn, the workers may signal within such initial contracts the overall aims of the programme and the areas to be covered within the programme. The use of contracting as an activity can be a powerful motivator. To sustain and enhance motivation it may be useful to use 'sequential contracting', i.e. contracting with the client at each major stage of the work (for example, such as before each module to be entered into). This provides the client with an opportunity to be reminded of the particular content of the next phase of the work, but also for the contract to be customised to reflect any particular concerns which have arisen from the preceding module. Therefore the client in treatment has a sense of a developing contract throughout treatment, not simply one at the outset.

Honesty goes a long way with most people. If the worker is concerned about a client's poor or lessened motivation it is appropriate to make a disclosure of that concern to the client. This provides a useful opportunity for the worker to model openness, for the worker and client to explore perceptions about change, and for the client to practise problem solving.

As clients hopefully grow and develop within treatment the quality of the relationship they experience with the worker(s) may also change. The relationship may strengthen and grow. Sometimes, however, because of a fundamental difference in style the relationship may grow stale and may inhibit the learning of the client. For example, whilst an externally controlling, possibly authoritarian, worker style might have secured an ambivalent client's attendance and activity in the early stages of the work, as the client's resolve to engage in the work strengthens a more 'democratic', client-determining worker style might be useful. We know very little of the 'who works' agenda in this respect, as opposed to the 'what works' agenda. If resources permit, sometimes changing workers, especially when the client-worker dynamic is acknowledged to be uncomfortable (with an honest explanation of why the substitution is occurring), can be a very enabling tactic for the client.

Whilst this chapter has focused on the motivation of the client within treatment, we cannot neglect the motivation of the worker. We should not assume that as workers our energy and effort levels in providing support and guidance to clients will always be high. We have to be careful not to indulge in the hypocrisy of being critical of our clients for appearing less than optimally motivated on occasions whilst our own motivation fluctuates.

Lest it be thought that the tone of the above is too idealistic, it must be remembered that there will be occasions when it will be necessary to issue threats of sanctions (and be prepared to carry out those threats) to sustain motivation, particularly in statutory work.

Some abusers will observe that there is 'nothing in it' for them. In some cases, for example, notwithstanding the level of effort and commitment the abuser makes to treatment and to sustaining change, he may never achieve family reunification or find a mutually satisfying relationship. Therapists should not seek to persuade clients to engage by giving unrealistic messages. However, in our experience some abusers may be able to achieve a more worthwhile, abuse-free lifestyle by engaging in treatment than if they had not, irrespective of whether they subsequently develop what in some cases may be idealised relationships.

A final thought is one which stems from 'industry'. To quote Rich Teerlink, former Chief Executive Officer and Chair of Harley-Davidson: '...in the absence of crisis, people rarely commit to a program that is imposed on them. But they will willingly commit to a program they help create' (Teerlink 2000). This presents a challenge to the prescriptions for programme delivery which are being encouraged by some agencies in the UK at the present time. A particular challenge here for those who run treatment programmes is the active consolidation of 'consumer' expectations and satisfaction. Simple 'quality assurance' measures here – for example, of our clients' expectations and satisfaction with services – are appropriate. Clients' expectations as to what they should receive from treatment, how long they expect to be in treatment and the level of effort required should be managed. Motivation to remain in treatment may decrease as the client perceives improvement and develops a sense of control. Gothard et al. (2000) have commented on these issues in developing treatment programmes for maltreated children; their recommendation for the development of programmes have immediate relevance to our work in managing sexual abusers.

CHAPTER 7

Managing Cognitive Distortions

WHY ADDRESS COGNITIVE DISTORTIONS?

The nature of cognition and its relevance to sexual abuse has long been explored (Nelson and Jackson 1989; Segal and Stermac 1990). Attempts have been made to delineate different cognitive events and to relate these to theories of offending and relapse (Keenan and Ward 2003; Mann and Beech 2003).

Whilst writers differ somewhat in the terminology they use, the thoughts that abusers have which support their abusive behaviour are identified as 'dynamic risk factors' in a number of empirical studies of sexual abusers. Thornton (2000), adapted by Mann *et al.* (2002), clustered dynamic risk factors into four 'domains'. One domain is concerned with 'distorted attitudes' in which Thornton found that the following factors were associated with increased risk: callous and adversarial attitudes, sexual entitlement, beliefs that children are sexual, and other justifications and beliefs that women want or deserve rape or that they are deceitful. This is consistent with the work of Hanson and Harris (2000) who also found that attitudes supportive of offending related to higher risk, and Beech *et al.* (1998) who identified 'global distortions' (about children and sexual abuse) as a factor in their psychometric evaluation of 'high deviancy' offenders.

It is also consistent with older models such as those of Finkelhor (1984), who described rationalising cognitions as a way in which child abusers 'overcome internal inhibitors' to offend, and a study of rapists by Malamuth *et al.* (1993), which identified attitudes supportive of rape, acceptance of 'rape myths' and hostility to women as one set of factors which were distinguishing features of sexually aggressive men. Cognitive distortion also represents a key stage in the cycle of offending models developed by Wolf (1988) and Ryan *et al.* (1987), as reviewed in Briggs *et al.* (1998).

A useful starting point for those wishing to refresh or update their understanding of the role of cognitive factors in relapse prevention is that of Langton and Marshall (2000).

Terminology

Murphy (1990) illustrated the terminologies and concepts used to describe the role of cognitions in sexual abuse. He suggests cognitive distortions to be those 'self statements made by offenders that allow them to deny, minimise, justify and rationalise their behaviour'. Such mental events are not believed to cause offending but rather justify and maintain offending.

Finkelhor (1984) has suggested that those men who are motivated to sexually abuse children may justify or rationalise their interests and behaviours so as to overcome any internal inhibitions which might otherwise restrain their actions. These special 'rationalising cognitions' serve to disinhibit, but do not fundamentally cause the abusive behaviour.

The excuses of abusers are familiar to those who work in this area, e.g. the commentary of the incest perpetrator who says 'I was only teaching my daughter about sex', the exhibitionist who says 'It happened to me and it didn't do me any harm', the rapist who asserts 'She wanted it rough really', and the extra-familial abuser who argues that seven-year-old boys can be sexual and flirt with adults.

Cognitive distortions (sometimes referred to as 'thinking errors') will be the focus of methods referred to later in this chapter. That is not to suggest, however, that other mental events do not have relevance to sexual abuse. 'Beliefs', for example, are an important area of interest.

Murphy (1990) has commented on beliefs and identifies an approach to cognitive factors 'from a more feminist perspective', particularly concerning the act of rape. He notes the relevance of the abuser's acceptance of myths about rape, of gender and sex role stereotyping, the acceptance of violence towards women and adversarial sexual beliefs. He suggests that the literature associated with these concepts implies such beliefs may have causal significance in sexual aggression.

Marshall et al. (1999) attempt to explore the roots of cognitive distortions. They introduced Ward's concept (in press at that time) of so called 'implicit theories'. Ward reflected on the way abusers perceive their world and interpret information about it. Ward had suggested that our perceptions and interpretations are guided by underlying theories and 'schemata', typically, assumptions about people, 'theories' about women and children or particular beliefs about victims (see Keenan and Ward 2003).

In turn, Mann and Hollin (2001) offer an overview of cognitive factors in sexual offending:

- cognitive distortions
- excuses and justifications
- offence supportive attitudes
- schemas/implicit theories
- surface cognitions.

'Schemas' are described here as 'beliefs, rules and assumptions about how the world is and how other people should be'. Mann and Hollin give an example of such rules concerning 'power and control', e.g. 'I must control others, others should submit to me, others must be controlled or else they will threaten me, I can't stand to have others dictate to me'. They suggest various schemas have received attention in sexual offending research, including the concepts of hostile masculinity, suspiciousness, sexual entitlement, a perceived hostile world and motivations to dominate and humiliate.

In turn 'implicit theories' are said to be 'used to explain other people's behaviours and make predictions about the world'. An implicit theory of a rapist for example may be that the male sex drive is uncontrollable, or that because the world is so dangerous you either have to control or be controlled. An implicit theory of a child abuser might be that children are inherently sexual beings.

A person's interpretations of life events will be influenced by schemas which in turn have their roots in developmental experiences, some of the most powerful of these being early attachment experiences.

Mann and Hollin rightly conclude from their tentative steps into this area that the concept of the schema has relevance to our understanding of sexual abuse but is hampered by problems of definition.

WHAT DOES THE ABUSER NEED TO KNOW?

At a pragmatic level we suggest that abusers should understand the following:

- If abusive behaviour is to be controlled then the relationship between thoughts, feelings and behaviour has to be recognised.
- Early life events, particularly our experiences of maltreatment and trauma, can influence the way we view the world; some early life experiences condition us to switch on automatic feelings and thoughts when faced with situations that remind us of those early life experiences.
- We can learn to control our thoughts, which will allow us then to control our feelings and behaviour.

- Sexual abusers have thoughts which allow them to abuse others (these thoughts have been given labels such as 'cognitive distortions').

- One goal for the sexual abuser should be to recognise the thoughts (excuses) he has used in the past which helped him target, groom and abuse others and then to develop strategies to counter these thoughts (and indeed other unhealthy thoughts) if they reoccur.

- Abusers may need to link work on cognitive distortions with other dynamic risk factors. For instance abusers may revert to habitual ways of thinking if they are in certain mood states or a high state of sexual arousal.

We can look forward to further research and theorising about various mental events and their relevance to the assessment and maintenance of sexual offending. As we are in subtle territory which is often difficult to evidence, there is a danger that the practitioner who is not particularly sophisticated in cognitive psychology will feel alienated from such work. Fortunately, there are some useful texts/manuals which help clinicians make a bridge between practice and theory; one we would commend in this area is Morin and Levenson's manual designed for sexual offenders in treatment (Morin and Levenson 2002).

DENIAL

The excuses of abusers not only serve to disinhibit the abuser who is motivated to abuse, but subsequent to abuse may serve to protect the abuser from psychological acceptance of what he has perpetrated and the essential harmful nature of his actions. This is when the abuser may use the defence mechanism of 'denial'. The abuser when denying may not face or accept readily the fundamental nature of his actions. This may be because of the shame that acceptance of his behaviour may evoke. At its most dramatic there can be denial of abuse having been perpetrated, sometimes even in the face of overwhelming evidence. The abuser may simply assert, 'I didn't do it'. This may be accompanied by extensive arguments, e.g. 'I was somewhere else at the time'.

Alternatively, the abuser may argue 'technical evidence' as to mismatches between the detail of the allegations and his presentation/actions. This form of denial is often referred to as categorical or 'absolute' denial. A different manifestation of denial is that of denial of responsibility for the abuse. This may include elements of victim blaming such as 'she asked for it', circumstantial excuses such as 'he stumbled in on me when I was masturbating', and excuses of loss of control, 'I was drunk and couldn't help myself'.

A third manifestation of denial is that of denial of victimisation, e.g. 'she wasn't harmed', 'he's grown up and had children of his own now and never complained'. Denial in child sexual abusers is often signalled by the implicit or explicit expression of the belief that children can be sexual and consent to sexual acts, e.g. 'she didn't say no', 'he knew what he was doing', or alternatively the belief that victimisation only equates with physical harm or overt signs of distress, e.g. 'he didn't bleed', 'she didn't scream'. For those abusers recently charged/convicted and approaching sentencing, there may be the acceptance of the commission of abusive acts, often minimised in frequency and intensity, but accompanied by the denial of future risk of reabusing, e.g. 'I'll never do it again, I've learnt my lesson'.

Salter (1988), Kennedy and Grubin (1992) and Marshall *et al.* (1999) present similar frameworks for describing denial and minimisation. Marshall identifies seven elements to this: complete denial (alleging false accusation, memory loss or an alternative abuser), partial denial (the behaviour wasn't really sexual abuse or was not representative of a significant problem), minimisation of the offence (e.g. in terms of frequency, use of coercion or degree of intrusion), minimisation of responsibility (including elements of victim blaming or loss of control through intoxication), denying/minimising harm, denying/minimising planning, and denying/minimising fantasising.

Levenson and Morin (2001a) describe five types of denial: 'denial of the facts', denial of awareness, denial of responsibility, denial of impact and denial of the need for treatment. They do not view such denial, however, as being the sole prerogative of the abuser, rather they suggest that examples of each form of denial here may be manifest in the abusers, the non-offending parent and child. Indeed, in their work with non-abusing partners they emphasise the need for the partner as well as abuser to explore and understand the forms denial took within the family unit.

Notwithstanding the above, at this point in time our approaches to the theorising, evaluation and management of cognitive distortions and attitudes towards offending are limited. As Langton and Marshall (2000) suggest

> the approaches to treatment have been characterised by rather vague descriptions of procedures aimed at changing these dysfunctional cognitions. Not surprisingly there is little in the way of support for any particular technique. These limitations in the literature have prevented the development of understanding cognitive distortions as they are manifest by sexual offenders, and this has impeded the effectiveness of our attempts to modify these cognitions. (p.183)

We have to be clear as to what is meant by 'distorted attitudes' and 'beliefs', and associated concepts such as 'denial' and 'minimisation'. The risk assessment literature can appear confusing. The literature suggests that distorted attitudes and beliefs may link to risk. However 'denial' did not appear to be a predictor of risk in Hanson and Bussiere's classic 1998 study or the subsequent meta-analysis of Hanson and Morton-Bourgon (2004). The work of Thornton and others prompts us to explore and understand the predictive role of distorted beliefs in assessing risk.

LINKS TO VICTIM AWARENESS

An emerging debate of note concerns the distinction between offence/victim specific cognitive distortions, e.g. of the sort 'my victim was..., my victim did..., my victim felt...', and broader cognitive schema, e.g. 'women are devious', 'children can control sexual situations'. We await empirical research which indicates the relative value of challenging (own) victim-specific distorted thinking as opposed to general cognitive schemas (Polaschek 2003).

Unsurprisingly, many programmes which aim to provide comprehensive treatment for sexual abusers include targets for work with denial and the excuse-making of abusers. Targets can also be found for work with non-abusing partners, sometimes referred to as 'caretakers'.

Levenson and Morin (2001b), for example, advocate a competency based approach to treatment. Their clients are expected to demonstrate the ability to put into practice their learning from treatment before they are considered 'successful completers'. Of relevance to the subject matter of this chapter they suggest the following 'safety objectives':

- the caretaker and offender both acknowledge that abuse occurred and that it was not the child's fault
- the caretaker acknowledges the offender's potential for future abuse
- the caretaker can name the five types of denial
- the caretaker can spontaneously recognise denial in self, offender and others
- the caretaker can describe her partner's offence pattern, grooming behaviours, high risk situations, thoughts, feelings and behaviours.

OBJECTIVES FOR INTERVENTION

Examples of objectives to be worked towards here include that the abuser should be able to:

- explain the difference between a thought and a feeling
- explain what is meant by distorted thinking and why it is important to explore this issue
- explain the role of distorted thinking in the development and maintenance of his offending behaviour
- give examples of both appropriate and inappropriate sexual thoughts
- offer examples of at least three distorted thoughts he used previously to justify or excuse his offending
- explain the assumptions underpinning each distorted thought and offer counter responses to neutralise the distortion
- identify distorted thoughts from the dialogue or scripts of other abusers attempting to explain their behaviour
- explain how a change in thinking can lead to change in behaviour, giving an example from his past life (not involving sexual behaviour)
- define 'consent'
- explain to his non-abusing partner or significant other details of the above objectives and their attainment or otherwise of these
- offer a description of his past offence which is free from distorted thinking or excuses.

EXAMPLES OF INTERVENTIONS

Clearly, the first step in helping an abuser address distorted thinking is for the abuser to understand properly what is meant by such. To begin the process the client must be aware of the distinction between thoughts, feelings and behaviour. To assist here the client could be encouraged to think of examples of thoughts, feelings and behaviour, putting these within separate columns on a flip chart. Alternatively, if the client struggles with this, examples could be given on 'post it' notes with the request that the client consider each and place the sticker under the appropriate heading.

The client may be invited to watch brief sequences of popular television dramas, with the request that for each sequence they not only describe the behaviour viewed but determine the likely thoughts and also feelings the characters are experiencing. (In treatment groups, clients may be asked to watch scripted role plays and conduct a similar analysis.)

The client may be encouraged to keep a critical incident diary in which they record highly significant events. The client should record details of the incident (e.g. an argument at work) alongside their behaviour before, during and after, their feelings before, during and after, and also their thoughts before, during and after the event.

Inevitably, any intervention will have an educational component. Many workers find it easy to introduce the topic of distorted thinking by inviting clients to consider behaviours other than sexual offences that they are embarrassed or ashamed about. An essential point is made to the abuser that it is part of normal behaviour in Western society to try to make oneself comfortable when faced with embarrassment, shame or guilt. A very straightforward way of achieving such self protection is by pretending that the problem behaviour was less worrisome than might have been thought, that others might have been responsible for the problem, or that there is no real harm to be done as many people share the behaviour.

Group work is the currently preferred medium for the treatment of sexual abusers (Proeve 2003) and in this context a range of exercises may be used to address cognitive distortions. These include guided discussion and role play to promote perspective taking, including the viewing of issues from the victim perspective. There tends to be a high degree of overlap with exercises aimed at promoting victim empathy, as perspective taking is an important component of empathy (see Chapter 9). These exercises tend to be extremely powerful and should only be undertaken after proper training and within good support systems, taking into account the psychological well-being of staff and group members. Particular exercises to address cognitive distortions are described below.

Clients can be invited to recall as many situations in which they have behaved inappropriately in the past, felt bad about doing so and then tried to convince themselves that the situation was not as bad as it at first seemed. The client can then be asked to consider the 'pros and cons' of using such distorted thoughts. The 'pros' inevitably relate to the client feeling better. 'Cons' to be explored include the proposition that such thinking errors tend to take away from the seriousness of the situation and therefore might make it more likely that the client will be less troubled about repeating the behaviour in the future.

Once examples of distorted thoughts from everyday situations have been identified and the pros and cons of using such have been outlined, the client might then be invited to reflect upon his sexually abusive behaviour and identify the particular thinking errors used to sustain that. Again, the pros and cons underpinning the use of distorted thinking might be determined with the client being encouraged to draw similarities between this list of pros and cons and that drafted for everyday problem behaviour, i.e. to show that there is nothing particularly or inherently special about distorted thoughts and that they serve the purpose of protecting oneself. What does change is the nature of the words used for the particular behaviour concerned.

One suggested objective described above was that of the abuser offering examples of (at least three) distorted thoughts he had used previously to justify or excuse his offending. There are various questionnaires which help the clinician evaluate the abuser's attitudes towards their potential victims and past abusive behaviour. For example, in his 'Kids and Sex Questionnaire' Beckett et al. (1994) invites the respondent to rate various statements using a simple scale ('very true', 'somewhat true', 'somewhat untrue', 'very untrue', 'don't know'). These statements include items such as 'children like to talk about sex', 'children know a lot about sex', 'children want sexual contact with children' and 'there is nothing wrong with sexual contact between children and adults'. Similarly, Patton and Mannison (1995) in their 'Revised Attitudes Toward Sexuality Inventory' use a six point rating scale (ranging from 'strongly agree' to 'strongly disagree') to invite respondents to evaluate statements such as 'a woman cannot be forced to have intercourse against her will', 'it doesn't hurt children to have a little bit of sex play with their older relatives', 'a girl should give in to a guy's advances so as not to hurt his feelings' and 'if the couple have dated a long time, it's only natural for the guy to pressure her for sex'.

One exercise therefore to help the abuser disclose the distorted thoughts he used previously might be that of inviting the abuser to reflect on such questionnaires but to complete them in the past tense, i.e. invite them to respond as if they were completing them at the time they perpetrated their abuses. These instructions also help with the client's natural defensiveness when feeling that their attitudes are subject to criticism. The invitation to complete 'in the past tense' draws an implicit distinction between 'then and now', affording the client the opportunity to believe that attitudes can change.

Other questionnaires that might be of help to the clinician here include the 'Rape Supportive Attitude Scale' (Lottes, reported in Davis et al. 1998) and the Abel and Becker 'Cognitions Scale' (Abel et al. 1984).

In addition to using questionnaires to prompt review of the distorted thinking that was used to support offending, the client who has engaged in ongoing repetitive offending may be invited to consider his offending cycle (Lane 1997) or offence chain (Morin and Levenson 2002), considering at each stage of the cycle or chain the thoughts that he had and which allowed the development of his offending.

One further exercise that has encouraged the abuser to explore common excuses used to justify offending and the assumptions underlying these is described below.

The abuser is helped to understand that the excuses used by offenders to facilitate their offending are based on faulty beliefs about themselves or their victims. Knowledge of the flaws underpinning these excuses can help inoculate against the use of these thinking errors in the future. The offender is offered the 'Excuses and Assumptions: Example' sheet (below) to demonstrate the range of assumptions which may underpin a thinking error and counter arguments to these assumptions. The offender is then asked to work through the 'Excuses and Assumptions Worksheet' also reproduced below.

The worker may choose to draft scenarios to approximate the offender's offence scripts in this instance, i.e. supplying the excuses the offender himself has used.

TIPS AND HINTS

When discussing cognitive distortions the use of examples may be difficult for 'concrete thinkers'. Non sex offence specific examples may not be helpful. For instance, a therapist asking an abuser to imagine that he is speeding on a motorway to encourage him to think about the excuses he may use to justify his behaviour may be met by the reaction 'I don't drive'.

Cognitive distortions may be deeply ingrained. Belief systems and schemas are by definition resistant to change. Thus therapists should ensure that they consider a wide variety of sources of information when assessing whether change has occurred. This should go beyond the abuser's reply to specific questions. It will not be difficult for an abuser to spot that when asked 'So do you think that when you buy a woman a drink that entitles you to have sex with her?' that the answer should be 'no'.

The worker should be alert to the client who is simply learning to 'talk the talk' not 'walk the walk'. Examples of potentially incongruent behaviour here include the client who has learnt to express appropriate attitudes and statements in treatment but when not 'under the spotlight' behaves in a way that does not match what he says. For example, the client may endorse in treatment that a child cannot consent to sexual activity with an adult by virtue of their developmental immaturity, yet away from treatment may behave towards children as if they were much older and more sophisticated in their outlook. For example, the client may say in treatment that he values equality in his interactions with men and women yet may be dismissive of his partner's wishes and needs in his dealings with her (assuming, of course, a female partner here).

Great care must be taken not to coerce the client into offering socially desirable responses. Confrontational challenges to distorted thinking are likely to lead to only transitory shifts in distorted thinking.

Video-taped or audio-taped feedback to the client may be useful. For example, one target here is that of the abuser offering an excuse-free description of his offence, an account free of statements which may give evidence of distorted beliefs. Often the first few versions the client

Excuses and Assumptions: Example	
Scenario	A father who has committed an offence of incest against his daughter.
Excuse	'I only did it to teach my daughter about sex.'
Assumptions	1. that people learn about sex by having sex 2. that people learn about sex by having sex with adults 3. that a daughter should learn about sex from her father 4. that a father should teach his daughter about sex 5. that an adult can commit an offence in the pursuit of education/teaching a child 6. that the sole purpose of the act was for the daughter's benefit.
Counter arguments	1. It is possible to learn about something without experiencing it. 2. The child who has sex with an adult may well feel frightened, unsure, helpless etc., emotions which do not help the child learn about healthy intimacy. 3. A father has to teach a child proper sexual boundaries and the encouragement of consensual acts – by having sex with his daughter a father models *inappropriate* boundaries/responsibility. 4. The power relationship between a child and her father is such that the child might be unable to say 'no' to her father. 5. There are other ways for a father to ensure that his daughter learns about sex, other than by him having sex with her. 6. The sex act met needs in the abuser/was pleasurable at some level.

Excuses and Assumptions Worksheet

Scenario One

A rapist who says that his victim deserved to have sex forced on her because she invited him back to her home, kissed and petted with him, but then changed her mind about sex.

Excuse

Assumptions

Counter arguments

Excuses and Assumptions Worksheet

Scenario Two

An exhibitionist who says that the children he exposed himself to weren't harmed because they knew him and he paid them afterwards.

Excuse

Assumptions

Counter arguments

Excuses and Assumptions Worksheet
Scenario Three An abuser of children who, whilst baby-sitting, said that the children were already sexually aware as they had seen pornography on the internet and were curious therefore about sex.
Excuse
Assumptions
Counter arguments

attempts will contain distorted thinking. The client can be invited to review video or audio recordings of their offence accounts and to identify for themselves evidence of cognitive distortions in their narrative. The worker only assists when the abuser obviously misses crucial examples. The client can hear/see evidence of their progress in this area as successive attempts (hopefully) produce narratives that are excuse free.

Limited disclosure on the part of the worker may also be of benefit here. For example, the worker may choose to reveal examples of how distorted thinking on their part has previously served to justify behaviour they wished to change (e.g. smoking, overeating) and how changing the way they think about such issues helped them change that behaviour.

Whilst it is tempting to institutionalise work on addressing cognitive distortions within a particular 'module' in a sex offender treatment programme, it is work that is a constant and long-term activity throughout treatment. Examples of faulty thinking should be challenged as an inappropriate manner when they arise.

Cognitive restructuring is a skill. Thoughts are unlikely to change unless the client practises doing so. The worker should not aim for a 'quick fix'. The best evidence of changed thinking will be changed behaviour in the longer term.

We reiterate that dynamic risk factors have an effect on one another. It will be important for abusers to rehearse strategies to avoid reverting to habitual, damaging thoughts when experiencing for example destabilising moods or states of arousal.

When working with an abuser who is denying significant aspects (or any) of their abusive behaviour, workers will be aware that denial can manifest itself in different forms and be a result of different causes, as described above. For some abusers denial may be a rational choice (i.e. straightforward lying) to avoid negative consequences relating to legal processes. Workers need to be clear with clients what the consequences of disclosure might be. In some circumstances new information will need to be passed to the prosecuting authorities, in others it may not and abusers may be unnecessarily inhibited from disclosure by an unwarranted fear of prosecution. It is not possible to give definitive advice here as the circumstances vary from case to case. Workers need to be aware of the policies of their agencies and projects in relation to disclosure. Public protection should always be the paramount consideration in decision making. Common situations encountered by the current authors include:

- disclosure that an abuser has abused his victim more times than he admitted to in court

- disclosure that a more serious offence (e.g. rape or incest) did actually occur after a 'plea' bargain where a plea of guilty to a lesser offence was accepted and a 'not guilty' verdict entered on the more serious offence, or an acquittal on a more serious offence and conviction on a lesser offence

- disclosure of past abuse where it has not been possible to identify any victim or precise circumstances

- disclosure of past abuse where it has been possible to identify victims or circumstances

- the need to discuss in civil proceedings behaviour which resulted in a decision not to prosecute, or an acquittal in criminal proceedings.

CHAPTER 8

Managing Deviant Sexual Interest

WHY ADDRESS DEVIANT SEXUAL INTEREST?

To state the obvious, sexual abuse involves sex. It is not surprising therefore that most major theoretical models of sexual abuse identify deviant
sexual interest in some form as an important dynamic risk factor.
Finkelhor (1984) identified 'sexual arousal to inappropriate stimuli' as a
motivating factor for child sexual abusers. Malamuth *et al.* (1993) identified arousal to rape depictions as a variable distinguishing samples of
rapists. Groth and Birnbaum (1979) identified how rape represents the
use of sex to fulfil other emotional needs. This work was developed by
Knight and Prentky (1990), who developed a typology of rapists based on
different motivating factors: i.e. sex (sadistic or non-sadistic), vindictiveness, anger and opportunism. Practitioners (e.g. Grubin *et al.* 2000) have
argued that some child abusers are motivated by similar factors. This view
has received empirical support, e.g. from Smallbone and Milne (2000).
Cortoni and Marshall (2001) have identified how sexual abusers tend to
use sexual outlets to cope with negative emotional states.

Hanson and Bussiere (1998), in their meta-analysis of risk factors,
identified deviant sexual preference (as measured by the penile
plethysmograph) as the biggest single predictor of reoffending. It achieves
less prominence in a recent revision of that analysis (Hanson and
Morton-Bourgon 2004), but remains an important factor. Two important, empirically informed, risk assessment tools identify categories of risk
factors relating to sexual interest. Hanson and Harris (2000) call the
category 'sexual self-regulation'. In Thornton's (2000) Structured Risk
Assessment (adapted by Mann *et al.* 2002a) he identifies one 'domain' as
being concerned with deviant sexual interest.

It could be argued therefore that sexual abuse ultimately involves
elements of sexual arousal in some form or other, even if the client does not
recognise being aroused either at the time or subsequently. Sexual abuse
may satisfy other motivations on the part of the abuser, for example, in

meeting needs for emotional intimacy or power. Ultimately, however, these needs are channelled through to the abusive sexual act.

Anecdotally, many clients tell us that they were aware of heightened states of sexual tension prior to the abusive acts they perpetrated, and that either during or subsequent to these acts they satisfied genital arousal through ejaculation. Those clients in treatment who are able to describe high risk situations often report being aware of various states of sexual arousal leading to specific sexual urges in high risk situations and seek from us techniques to intervene to reduce or contain their arousal.

Unsurprisingly, British researchers have therefore commented on the importance of treatment programmes for sexual abusers containing interventions designed to contain factors such as fantasy modification work to complement traditional work such as challenging excuse making, working with the patterns or 'cycles' of offending, developing personal/intimacy skills and the like (Beckett *et al.* 1994). Beckett and colleagues recommended the training of some probation officers by psychologists in fantasy modification techniques, in effect to make such techniques more readily available.

WHAT IS AROUSAL?

One key aspect of deviant sexual interest is that of sexual arousal. We have found it useful to define sexual arousal by reference to three domains:

- behaviour
- physical state
- cognitive/mental events.

The *behaviour* associated with sexual arousal can be sexual activity such as masturbation, scanning a child, or other behaviour designed to lead to genital satisfaction. The *physical signs* of sexual arousal include the obvious (erectile changes), as well as the less obvious (changes in heart rate, respiration rate, blood pressure and pupillary response). The *mental* changes associated with sexual arousal we consider to include sexual thoughts, sexual fantasies and sexual images. These domains are represented in Figure 8.1.

Practitioners sometimes become confused as to the distinction between sexual fantasy and sexual arousal. In the definition and Figure 8.1 it can be seen that sexual fantasy is considered to be just *one* of those mental changes that might be associated with sexual arousal. Other mental changes might occur; for example, the person might have thoughts of sex, but not experience the images of a fantasy. Behaviour, physical change and mental events are closely related and interreact. For example, sexual fantasies might trigger physiological changes which in turn might stimulate

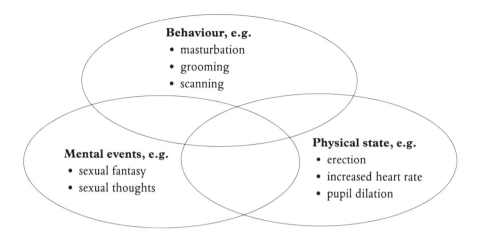

Figure 8.1*: Essential elements of sexual arousal*

other mental changes (such as sexual thoughts), which in turn might stimulate behaviour. In this example, sexual fantasy might be considered as a trigger to sexual arousal. Following sexual activity, for example post ejaculation, clients may continue to have sexual fantasies. The sexual fantasies used to trigger sexual arousal might be different to the sexual fantasies which accompany sexual activity such as masturbation, and which in turn may be different to those sexual fantasies the client utilises post ejaculation. In other words, the client's sexual fantasy life might evolve and change substantially across any sexual episode.

To give an example, one of our clients has a history of exposing himself to boys. He daydreams about sexual contact with boys, his daydreams featuring explicit imagery of boys (he fantasises about tight buttocks, blond hair and cheeky faces, and the activities he would like to indulge in, particularly masturbating in front of them whilst they admire him for doing so). This daydream can act as a trigger for sexual arousal. For this client, sexual arousal includes the physical changes of an erection and shallow breathing. Typically, he seeks somewhere such as a cubicle in a public lavatory where he can masturbate (i.e. behavioural change). His masturbation is associated with him sexually fantasising about buggering the boys (i.e. cognitive change). Post ejaculation, however, he will daydream of a romantic resolution, of contact with the boy and of them enjoying a friendship (Table 8.1).

Table 8.1: The evolution of fantasies across a sexual episode

Stage	Fantasy content
Trigger to sexual arousal	e.g. daydreams of genital exposure to boys
↓	
Sexual arousal	e.g. sexual fantasies of buggery
↓	
Post arousal events	e.g. daydreams of ongoing friendship with the boys

Thus the behavioural, mental and physical aspects of sexual arousal influence and interact with one another.

Triggers for sexual arousal are various. They can be mental events such as daydreams as described above, or memories of past sexual experience. Physical changes (such as waking up with an erection) may prompt sexual thoughts or behaviour (masturbation). Mood states might link to arousal, e.g. boredom might prompt an individual to seek out pornography and begin masturbation, or anger might link to fantasy of assault in rapists. Particular sights may lead to arousal, e.g. the child abuser who boards a bus full of school children may automatically scan the children and then begin to have sexual thoughts and experience physical changes such as an erection.

Different workers describe sexual arousal in different ways. We believe it is useful to describe somebody as sexually aroused if they have at least sexual thoughts and/or fantasies and some accompanying psychological changes, even if they do not have an erection. For example, we would describe somebody as sexually aroused if they were fantasising about rape, breathing more quickly and with increased heart rate, even if they did not have an erection or were not touching their genitals. Similarly, we would describe somebody as sexually aroused if they had physiological experiences including an erection but did not have a sexual fantasy. In that sense, sexual arousal seems to be a matter of degree, reflecting the combination of changes in behaviour, mental events and physiology.

OBJECTIVES FOR INTERVENTION

As with the preceding chapter, the objectives described below are suggested as possible targets for our work with abusers. They are not intended to prescribe any particular method for their achievement. As always, the client should be clear as to the objective, should understand why it is being progressed (should understand its relevance to their treatment) and should have consented to therapeutic effort to achieve the objective. The quantitative targets below are drawn from clinical experience rather than definitive outcome research.

Examples of objectives to be worked towards here include that the abuser should be able to:

- describe what is meant by sexual arousal, to include examples of behaviour, mental events and physiological changes associated with arousal
- describe why it is important to learn ways to control sexual arousal
- describe at least (one) of his previous sexually abusive acts to include a description of the nature of his sexual arousal at the time (specifying his behaviour, his thoughts, his fantasies and physiological/physical changes at the time)
- describe what is meant by the term 'sexual fantasy'
- describe how his sexual fantasies have related to his offending
- describe and will have practised at least (two) techniques for controlling sexual fantasies of abuse
- explain to his non-abusing partner (chaperone/sponsor/ supervising officer) the work he is undertaking to control sexual arousal (including fantasies) that might lead to offending and abuse
- identify the times at which his urges to offend are strong, and will be able to manage these urges using techniques such as thought stopping, self monitoring, relaxation and distraction.

EXAMPLES OF INTERVENTIONS

Clients may be encouraged to talk about sexual arousal if given examples of abusive peers describing their experiences. For example, a description of an offender's account of his abuses might be read to the client with instructions thereafter for the client to consider various questions.

Typical questions for the client having read or heard such a description might include:

- Was 'X' sexually aroused during these events?
- How do we know that he was sexually aroused?
- When did he first become sexually aroused?
- When did he stop becoming sexually aroused?
- Did he experience any other emotions as well as sexual arousal?

- What were his sexual thoughts and what were his sexual fantasies?
- What physical signs of arousal were there?
- What behaviour accompanied arousal?

Such questions are designed to encourage discussion of what is meant by sexual arousal. *A health warning* – if detailed material of abuse accounts are to be shared with clients it will be important before the close of these sessions for the client to be debriefed properly. It is important to ensure that the client does not leave the session aroused by the material he has heard. Particular instruction must be given that the client does not fantasise about the material thereafter. The client should be reminded of the nature of this work and why it is important to control arousal.

In progressing the objective of the client being able to describe why it is important to learn ways to control sexual arousal, it might be useful for the worker to adopt a psycho-educational approach. As described earlier, deviant sexual arousal appears to be one factor which relates to risk of reconviction. We can argue that a history of deviant sexual arousal might have been manifest in a variety of ways, including a history of deviant sexual fantasising, in the modus operandi of the abusive behaviour itself (including fetishistic and paraphilic practices), the use of pornography and abuse associated stimuli accompanying masturbation or lovemaking, the scanning of the environment for reminders of sexual stimuli, or the scanning of victims themselves. It might be useful to help the client to understand that ongoing practices of the sort described above can lead to the maintenance of deviant sexual arousal. Further, the client might be advised as to the research findings of meta-analytic studies in this area which relate deviant arousal to risk, and hence the need to tackle deviant arousal if we are to help the abuser keep safe and thereby protect the public.

Additional to educating the client as to behaviour which might constitute deviant arousal and how this relates to 'risk', the client may also be reminded of models which place arousal at the heart of any motivation to abuse. For example, Finkelhor (1984) places arousal at a crucial stage in the motivation of behaviour and it is central to the 'cycle' models developed by Ryan and Lane (1987) and Wolf (1985), reviewed in Briggs *et al.* (1998). Arousal is part of the pathway towards lapse and relapse described by Hudson and Ward (2000).

A third objective suggested above is that of the client describing a previous sexually abusive act, particularly to detail the sexual arousal he experienced at the time. Clients often find difficulty in offering detailed descriptions to such requests. They will often have rehearsed descriptions of their abuses, but use 'comfortable' ways of describing events which may tend to minimise purposeful activity on their part and the 'sexual' elements of their offending. Clients may be anxious about disclosure of detail here and the likely response to those who hear it. Simple structures can help the client to organise their approach to this task (see Table 8.2). Less literate clients may find it easier to draw symbols to complete the grid of Table 8.2.

Table 8.2: Structure to assist the client describing an offence

	Before the event	During the event	After the event
What I did			
What I thought			
What I fantasised about			
What I noticed about my body and how I felt			

Clearly, there are other ways of encouraging the client to talk in detail about his abusive behaviour. For example, sometimes inviting the client to read witness statements may remind them of aspects of arousal at the time of their abusing, particularly if these statements are not used in a confrontational, aggressive manner on the part of the therapist. Similarly, asking the client to re-enact the path of behaviour leading up to the abuse can sometimes trigger memories.

Concerning the objective of the client describing what is meant by the term 'sexual fantasy', the worker needs to be clear about possible responses. Clients may suggest that a sexual fantasy is 'something that lets you do things you can't do in real life' or 'helps you get ready for doing the real thing'. These are examples in effect of the function of fantasy, i.e. explanations of *why* people might fantasise. The question as to *what* is fantasy is often more difficult for clients to answer. Some clients will say 'it's like a dream', or 'it's pictures in the head'. The worker needs to ensure that when the client is using the term 'sexual fantasy' that he is referring to the same sort of mental event as the therapist.

In describing sexual fantasies we are talking of a series of mental images that are part of sexual arousal. Individual differences will occur in the nature of these images – some people will have visual images, some people will imagine smells and so forth. Some people will have clear images, some not. Once the worker has established that the client and he or she are talking about the same sort of mental event, then it might be useful to encourage the client to look at the functions of sexual fantasy. Case histories of clients displaying different sorts of imagery during fantasy and used for different purposes might be used to prompt discussion and demonstrate diversity.

There are various techniques for the control of sexual fantasy. Some are derived from the behaviour therapy literature and would require special training and supervision to administer, including techniques such as covert sensitisation, orgasmic reconditioning and masturbatory satiation (see below). Other techniques are perhaps more easily learnt and accomplished by workers and will form part of the standard therapeutic repertoire.

One of the most straightforward techniques to assist in the control of abuse related masturbatory fantasies is to manage those trigger events which predispose the client to the use of illegal fantasies. This will require the client to monitor the content of his masturbatory fantasy life and the events, moods or situations which typically precede masturbation. The client will need to monitor his masturbatory fantasy life over a realistic period if he is to determine a pattern to this, typically using some form of diary or journal to do so. (This will need careful management and encouragement on the part of the therapist as, typically, such diaries are embarrassing to keep and initial efforts can soon pale.) The client is looking for clear associations within this exercise. If it is found for example that the client often fantasises about abusing children after watching certain television programmes or after being in particular places, then such situations should be avoided. If the client fantasises about abusive acts most typically when bored, angry, listless or lonely for example then the therapist will need to help the client deal with these mood states in healthier ways. Clearly, here we are not tackling the fantasy direct, simply managing situations which might prompt the fantasy. As a short-term measure this often gives the client confidence that he can influence arousal and fantasy and that healthier ways of living can be achieved.

As an aside here it should be noted that our experience in asking clients simply to keep a detailed diary of masturbatory sexual fantasies can help reduce the frequency of abusive fantasies. It is as if the embarrassment of disclosure of fantasy content from client to worker serves to lessen the desirability of such fantasising (at least in the short term). Such self monitoring, paradoxically, may also provide a form of distraction.

On occasions, particularly if the client has concern about very high frequency of fantasies of abuse (such as in situations where a target might be identified and active mental rehearsal of grooming techniques is underway), the client might be asked to make daily contact with the worker or 'sponsor' supporting the client. The purpose of telephone contact would be for the client to rehearse why it is important not to fantasise about abuse, to receive encouragement and reward for abstinence from abuse related fantasising and to gain encouragement to rehearse healthy, non-abusive fantasies. If there are particular situations or moods which are pertinent and acting to further stimulate such fantasies, the worker or sponsor can assist with practical tips and guidance to deal with these situations or moods.

Another simple technique workers might consider to assist in fantasy control is that of distraction. The worker will need to assist the client in identifying activities which are sufficiently engaging and powerful so as to contain the desire to fantasise. A repertoire of techniques may be needed. The worker might consider reviewing potential distracters with the client on a regular basis to refresh their potency.

Allied to the above is the use of specific mental distracters. Asking clients to generate for themselves competing mental images can sometimes be of benefit. Images for example of a machine 'eating' abuse fantasies, of acid burning away the abuse related fantasy, of the fantasy of abuse being like a balloon which is slowly deflated to an empty sack, of the fantasy being exploded, of the fantasy being shaved away by sandpaper and so forth might be experimented with. These techniques can cater for the individuality of the client and allow for creativity and fun in the therapeutic process. Further, the mental effort required to complete such a task of itself serves to distract.

Thought stopping in its simple form is a technique in which clients are taught to vigorously think of the word 'stop' when unwanted thoughts occur, the mental image and 'sound' of the word stop being designed here to interrupt the thought. Whilst its use has not been proven to be particularly effective with complex mental disorders such as obsessive compulsive disorders (Penzel 2000), practitioners in the field of sex offender management report it to be a useful tool in the armoury of strategies for managing arousal. For example, the Thames Valley Sex Offender Groupwork Programme (Fisher and Faux 2001) describe a variant of thought stopping for use in controlling inappropriate sexual thoughts. They suggest that clients have a loose elastic band around their wrist which they pull when they experience an unwanted thought. They advise that this should be done so that it is uncomfortable rather than particularly painful and acts as a distractor which enables the individual to remind himself as to why the thought is a problem and to move on to thinking about other things such as the benefits of leading an offence-free life.

A variant on the elastic band here would be the offender using smelling salts, in effect using a noxious image combined with the self talk of 'STOP' to interrupt the sexual thought.

NON-ABUSING PARTNERS

Concerning the objective of sharing details of this work with the non-abusing partner or sponsor – to state the obvious, very careful preparation of the non-abusing partner or sponsor will be needed. If this objective is to be progressed it is not advised that this occurs without the worker having an established working relationship with the non-abusing partner, that work with the non-abusing partner has been contracted, and with clear consent being given on the part of the non-abusing partner to hear the detail of the abuser's fantasy/arousal life.

When sharing detail of the abuser's sexual fantasies/sexual arousal patterns with their non-abusing partners/sponsors, it has been important to prepare the non-abusing partner quite carefully in advance. In addition to explaining *why* it is necessary to enter into such detail in our work with clients, and as well as sharing models to help their understanding of abusive behaviour (e.g. the Finkelhor 'four stages', the 'cycles' model or a traditional relapse prevention model), we have found it useful to describe some of what we understand to be the diversity of the sexual fantasy life of non-sexually abusive men. Important here has been the understanding that non-abusive men can report a range of sexual fantasies during mastur-bation/lovemaking, indeed on occasions non-offending men will report having had fantasies of illegal or abusive acts. What distinguishes these men from the abusers sometimes is not the content of their sexual fantasy life but the preparedness of the abuser to act on it.

The worker will need to pace the amount of information shared by abusers to non-abusing partners in a way that does not traumatise or frighten the non-abusing partner, that does not place any blame on the non-abusing partner for the behaviour or intentions of the abuser, and that does not make the non-abusing partner feel responsible for the behaviour of the abuser in the future.

It has occasionally become apparent that abusers have engaged their partners in behaviours that are fuelling deviant sexual interests. These include asking partners to do things which make them look more childlike (e.g. shaving pubic hair, dressing in school uniform) or which involve sub-jugation and humiliation, such as bondage or anal intercourse. Anal inter-course may also be a sign of arousal to males, which is not a problem if those males are adult, but may signal caution if there have been concerns about risk to younger males.

It has been our experience that some partners, when they realise that their partner's behaviour has been motivated by deviant fantasies of their own children, have begun to question whether they wish to continue the relationship. It is entirely appropriate that partners should be empowered to make their own decisions based on full knowledge of the abuser's behaviour and its implications. They should never be influenced to stay with a partner because of concerns about him. However, it must be acknowledged that the break up of a relationship may be a destabilising factor for the abuser himself which may precipitate high risk thoughts, feelings and behaviours. Thus it is vital that attention is given to appropriate support systems and risk management strategies in these circumstances.

It will rarely be sufficient for the worker(s) to run briefing sessions with the abuser and non-abusing partner/sponsor together without offering *additional* contact to the non-abusing partner alone. The non-abusing partner/sponsor will need time to reflect on information shared and opportunity to discuss that information and its implications, often across several sessions. A more detailed programme of work with non-abusing partners is described in Chapter 12.

OTHER BEHAVIOURAL TECHNIQUES

As noted above, there are a number of techniques which are derived from the behavioural therapy literature and should be undertaken only by those specifically trained in these techniques. They include variations on the following:

- Masturbatory satiation – during which a client is encouraged first to masturbate to orgasm verbalising a legitimate fantasy out loud and then continuing to masturbate but to detailed descriptions of his illegal/paraphilic fantasies for an hour each session. This is said to produce boredom (Quinsey and Earls 1990).

- Orgasmic reconditioning – a positive conditioning procedure in which the client links legitimate sexual fantasies to masturbation and orgasm. If the client cannot achieve this readily he is advised to 'switch' the content of his fantasy to a non-abusive image immediately prior to ejaculation. Over time he is asked to introduce a legitimate fantasy earlier and earlier into the masturbatory sequence (Marquis 1990).

- Aversive therapies – during which an unpleasant sensation (usually a smell) is paired with deviant thoughts.

- Covert sensitisation – a 'covert and aversive counter-conditioning technique'. The client is encouraged to describe at length a fantasy in which his behaviour leads up to an abusive situation. Before imagining the abusive act, the client is instructed to introduce a detailed aversive consequence into the account (see Cautela and Wisocki 1971).

We have avoided a detailed account of these techniques because, as stated above, we believe special training is required to administer them. They should not be used unless a proper functional analysis has been undertaken of the abuser and his offence alongside an understanding of what might be the consequences of the technique 'failing'. For a description of these techniques we would refer the reader to McGrath (2001). For a more detailed description of the applicability and a critique of the effectiveness of these techniques readers are also referred to Marshall *et al.* (1999).

PSYCHOPHYSIOLOGICAL TESTING

There are two techniques which may be used to provide information about patterns of male sexual arousal. They are the penile plethysmograph (PPG) and measurement of visual reaction time (VRT). It is beyond the scope of this book to give a detailed critique or guidance on the use of these techniques; for a recent review, readers are referred to Letourneau (2002). With the PPG a small transducer is placed on the subject's penis and levels of tumescence in response to various stimuli are measured. The stimuli are in the form of slides, video or audio images of sexual activity involving adults or children and may include different levels of coercion. There are some ethical and practical concerns related to the use of this instrument which we outline in Briggs *et al.* (1998, p.54).

VRT measures the time that subjects spend viewing slides of different stimuli. This appears to correlate to sexual interest in some subjects (Letourneau 2002). VRT techniques are clearly less intrusive than PPG methods and these advantages may explain the recent research interest they have received.

We argued (Briggs *et al.* 1998) previously that in our view the PPG is best used to provide bio-feedback to motivated clients to illustrate issues relating to their sexual interest and to monitor change through treatment. It would appear that VRT may be able to perform a similar role.

MEDICAL INTERVENTION

In our experience there are a small number of abusers who have an extremely high libido, which they can not manage via non-abusive sexual activity, or who have persistent intrusive thoughts. Both of these factors can limit the effectiveness of cognitive-behavioural interventions. In these cases practitioners may wish to refer the abuser to a forensic psychiatrist for assessment as to whether medication may be appropriate in managing these factors, in conjunction with cognitive behavioural therapy. For a review of the role of medicine in the management of sexual abusers readers are referred to Grubin (2000a).

TIPS AND HINTS

- If the client is to articulate why it is important to learn ways to control sexual arousal it is important that they 'hear' themselves articulate this need. Recording a response as to why such control is necessary and then playing the recording back to the client can be a powerful reminder. If the client has access to a dictaphone/mini cassette then such reminders can be accessible on a more regular basis.

- The client can be encouraged to write down several reasons for the need for such control as bullet points on small cards, keeping these cards in places associated with such arousal (e.g. in the video storage unit if the client has a history of using videotaped pornography, on the car dashboard if the client regularly scans his environment via driving, in the bathroom if the client typically masturbates there when thinking about offending). Care will be needed on the part of the worker and the client to ensure that such reminders are not misused or ridiculed by others: sometimes coded reminders will be needed that are not obvious to the uninformed observer.

- We would emphasise strongly that deviant sexual interest is often a coping strategy for abusers in managing non-sexual problems. As such, it is often necessary to link work on sexual interest closely with factors related to lifestyle management, e.g mood management, anger or self-esteem.

- If distraction is to be used as a technique for managing arousal we recommend that the distracter be one that engages the client mentally if possible, e.g. a crossword puzzle. 'Passive distractors', e.g. going for a walk, may simply provide opportunity for the abuser to continue thinking about sexual stimuli.

- As mentioned above, it can be difficult for clients to describe in detail the content of their sexual fantasies or patterns of arousal. Anxiety is often an important emotion to consider here. Clinical custom and practice with clients who suffer focal anxiety is that of helping the client face their fears via desensitisation, by gradually introducing the client to the feared situation or object with reassurance along the way of coping and achievement. The same could be said of the client asked to describe the detail of sexual arousal. For example, it may be easier for the client to describe examples of their behaviour before describing the detail of their fantasy. It may be easier for the client to describe non-abuse related fantasies before describing fantasies of abuse. It may be easier for the client to describe physical states such as increased heart rate or flushing before describing an erection. The therapist can help here by asking questions designed to build information from low-anxiety associated descriptions to high-anxiety associated descriptions.

- Similarly, it will be important to reward the client for detail offered. The client's descriptions of his abusive behaviour and fantasies, when offered at the time of arrest or initial reporting, are likely to have been cautious, avoidant of detail and tentative. The therapist can help the client by explaining that such accounts given in the days surrounding disclosure/arrest/initial assessment are expected to have been modest. However, with effort these can be built on. Motivating statements encouraging the client to go beyond their previous accounts, to learn more of their abusive behaviour so as to avoid its repetition, to demonstrate to others including their victim(s) that they are serious about their efforts in treatment can help considerably here, especially if accompanied by recognition and praise of further detail given.

- In gathering information about the client's sexual fantasy life workers need to be careful about the language they use. For example, if we accept that individuals' fantasies differ in the nature of the imagery involved, prompts such as 'tell me what you see in your mind when you fantasise' might be difficult for somebody whose fantasies are not particularly 'visual'. General prompts such as 'describe what is happening in your fantasy' or 'tell me what you experience when you fantasise about...' might be more appropriate.

- If clients are asked to fill in fantasy logs or diaries the embarrassment this might cause needs to be acknowledged. Clients should be reassured that it might take more than one attempt to complete the task satisfactorily, and that it is better not to undertake the task than fake it. Both authors have seen examples of 'fantasy diaries' that have obviously been scribbled in the waiting room prior to the session.

- We would emphasise again the importance of training, supervision and expert consultancy for practitioners undertaking work with arousal and fantasy.

CHAPTER 9

Managing Victim Empathy

WHY ADDRESS VICTIM EMPATHY?

Most programmes for the treatment of sexual abusers in the UK and North America include components aimed at promoting victim empathy (Barker and Morgan 1994; Joint Prison and Probation Accreditation Panel 2000; Knopp *et al.* 1992; Middleton 2002). The assumed rationale for inclusion of victim empathy work is straightforward. If the abuser is unable to experience or anticipate the distress of the victim (and assuming that the abuser has no desire to cause suffering), then such empathy deficits may facilitate abuse in a motivated abuser. Without empathy there is one less factor to retard the offender's progression to abuse. Conversely, promoting empathy is thought to inhibit abusive behaviour.

However, there has been little empirical support for this proposition. In particular, empathy was not shown to correlate with risk in Hanson and Busssiere's meta-analysis of risk factors (1998). For wider reviews of the evidence see Hanson (2003b) and Marshall *et al.* (1999). Hanson argues that this lack of empirical support does not negate the well established association between empathy and general anti-social behaviour (citing Miller and Eisenberg 1988). He points out that empathy is a complex phenomenon which to date has been poorly defined, and describes how it is a relatively modern concept originally used by artists early in the 20th century to describe the tendency to feel emotion when observing works of art.

We believe that the construct of empathy is a multi-faceted one and that the phrase 'victim empathy training' may mean quite differing things to different people. On the one hand, empathy may be understood as a cognitive, almost intellectual act of being able to understand the likely experience of another. For example, if an abuser is asked to articulate the likely short and long-term effects of a child being sexually victimised, this may draw on the skills of 'cognitive empathy'. The abuser may not 'feel' anything of the victim's experience, however. This may relate to a different facet of empathy, that of the vicarious replication of another person's emotional state. A further facet of empathy is behaviour, i.e. the person who is empathic behaves in a way that demonstrates understanding of the person's experience, and based upon an experience of the other person's state.

Much progress is yet to be made in understanding the phenomenology of empathy in sexual abusers and indeed how best to encourage the development of empathy so as to promote self control in the abuser and hence child and public protection. There are intriguing debates which have yet to be resolved. For example, what are the relative benefits of providing general empathy training to offenders as opposed to victim specific empathy training? Further, we do not really understand at which point in treatment or therapy victim empathy work is most likely to be effective. For example, is empathy best addressed following work which has been designed to promote the offender's understanding of the pattern or sequence of his offending? Should it follow work which addresses any abusive experience the abuser may have been exposed to (the question here being whether some abusers can only begin to develop empathy for others once recognition of their own pain and suffering as victim has been reached)? Similarly, we might question whether empathy training can or should be institutionalised into a discrete treatment module or whether there should be repeated messages throughout and across other offence focused modules.

Victim empathy work is not without its difficulties. For example, Beckett *et al.* (1994) found that about a quarter of their sample of offenders became worse in relation to victim empathy measures after treatment. One contributory factor was thought to be that offenders were being exposed to powerful messages about victim harm before they were psychologically prepared. With such research in mind, Kennington *et al.* (2001) developed an accredited treatment programme which does not address factors in modular form, but allows for themes to be developed by drawing exercises from various 'menus'.

We believe that it is important to address victim empathy in our work with sexual abusers as this may:

1.   provide skills which in turn will promote the development of social skills and intimacy

2.   reinforce work designed to counter beliefs which support offending, and

3.   help sustain motivation to engage in long-term therapy, i.e. empathising with the victim/potential victims may give a reason for continued involvement in therapy.

DEFINITIONS AND MODELS

Notwithstanding the uncertainty which surrounds this area of work, attempts have been made to refine our definitions of empathy and develop techniques for empathy training. One widely cited description of empathy has been proposed by Marshall and Fernandez (2001). They have described empathy as a 'multi-staged process' comprising four stages. Empathy here is described first as the person's ability to recognise another person's emotional state. Second, it is the ability 'to see the world as another person does'. Third, and using an interesting choice of words, empathy is described as 'the ability to experience, without effort, the same emotional state as the observed person'. Fourth, the person should 'feel impelled to act accordingly'. In this context, Marshall and Fernandez report Hudson *et al.*'s (1993) observation that sexual offenders are deficient at emotional recognition. Fernandez *et al.* (1999) cite evidence for the sexual offender's lack of skill at 'seeing things from the perspective of sexual abuse victims and at replicating the emotional distress of victims'.

Hanson (2003b) proposes a broader conceptual model of empathy (see Figure 9.1), arguing that two important factors have often been neglected, i.e. the relationship between people and the abuser's ability to cope with distress. He suggests a model of empathy which he regards as very similar to 'sympathy', i.e. compassion in response to the perceived distress of others. Key elements of the model are relationships, perspective taking and coping responses.

Relationships

It is argued that most people may react positively to the suffering of an enemy or adversary. Abusers with a history of adversarial sexual attitudes in relationships may not be inhibited by knowing that the victim is suffering because that is what he wants to happen.

Perspective taking

Hanson (and Marshall *et al.* 1999) reviewed a range of evidence relating to the ability of sex offenders to accurately assess the perspectives of victims. Most sexual offenders showed deficits in perspective taking, particularly in relation to their own victim. However, there were some findings which indicated that violent offenders showed accuracy in emotional identification. The role of perspective taking can not therefore be assumed to be the same for all offenders.

Coping with distress

Hanson suggests that for some offenders, developing an awareness of the harm their behaviour has inflicted may provoke unhelpful strategies to cope with the distress that this awareness may cause. These might include:

- anger or anxiety reactions
- victim blaming attitudes
- hostility or externalising behaviour
- sexual preoccupation.

As we strive to refine our definitions of empathy, a reminder of the note of caution struck above should be given. As stated, there is debate as to the relative value of focusing on empathy training to reduce reconviction risk in sex offenders. It may be that focusing on other domains will prove more effective. Tony Ward (in press), in reviewing three theories of child sexual abuse (Finkelhor's precondition theory, Hall and Hirschman's quadripartite theory, and Marshall and Barbaree's integrated theory) notes:

> A careful consideration of all three theories and the literature on child sexual abuse suggest that there are four clusters of problems or symptoms typically found among adults who sexually abuse children: emotional regulation problems; intimacy/social skill deficits; deviant sexual arousal; and cognitive distortions... We consider empathy deficits to be subsumed under cognitive distortions and emotional dysregulation difficulties.

At the time of writing we appear to be in a phase where our understanding of empathy and its role in sexual abusive behaviour is uncertain but developing. As we reach a more coherent and empirically validated model of empathy, we should be able to target treatment more specifically at relevant factors.

At the moment, definitions of empathy are beginning to crystallise. Our approach (see Kennington *et al.* 2001) follows that of Marshall *et al.* (1999) in regarding the cognitive aspects of empathy as 'a particular form of cognitive distortion'. The programmes we have been involved in have exercises which are also specifically targeted at generating emotional responses.

OBJECTIVES

Examples of objectives to be worked towards here include that the abuser should be able to:

- express a range of emotions, describing to others his emotional experience across a range of situations and times
- identify and describe correctly the emotional state of others
- offer examples of how different people may have differing perceptions of the same situation
- offer reasons as to why it is important to develop the skills of perspective taking

- articulate the likely short and long-term effects of sexual abuse on victims (more specifically, the client will be able to describe the psychological, health, social, emotional and behavioural consequences of abuse, referring to both adult and child victims)
- demonstrate his understanding of the short and long-term effects of his behaviour on the victim(s) of his abusive acts
- explore and describe the similarities between his experience of being victimised (psychologically, physically and/or sexually) and the experience of those he has victimised
- draft an appropriate letter (or other form of address) of apology to his victim, one which recognises explicitly the experience of his victim(s) at the time of abuse and likely response subsequent (this draft letter not to be sent)
- respond appropriately to victim's questions about the abuse
- behave appropriately in his interaction with the worker(s).

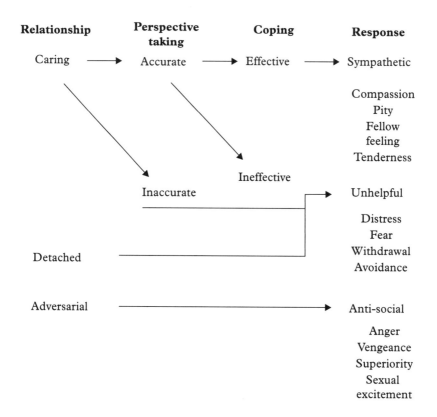

Figure 9.1: *Factors influencing sympathetic responses (Hanson 2003b)*

EXAMPLES OF INTERVENTION

Concerning interventions to develop and promote victim empathy, most texts describing sex offender treatment programmes give examples of this work. Jackie Craissati (1998), for example, has described her work with the Challenge Project in south east London. Craissati has commented that the empathy deficits of perpetrators may stem from their experiences of abuse or deprivation in childhood. She aims to develop both intellectual and emotional insight into the victimisation of children by way of exploring the perpetrators' experience of victimisation:

> In our experience, once a perpetrator has felt himself to be heard as a victim in his own right (in terms of his own early experiences), then he has a better emotional capacity for contemplating his own victim's feelings. (Craissati 1998, p.80)

Craissati describes attempts to enable offenders to develop insights as to the impact of their actions on their own victims, and in the context of understandings of 'consent' and 'compliance'. The techniques she refers to here include:

- exposing perpetrators to written or filmed materials of victims describing their experiences
- a debating session ('does the child understand what she consents to; is the child aware of the accepted sexual standards in her community; does the child appreciate the eventual, possible consequences of the decision; are the child and adult equally powerful so that no coercion influences the child's decision?')
- writing an imaginary letter as if from victim to perpetrator
- writing a victim apology letter.

Fernandez and Serran (2002) offer similar suggestions, again based on their group work experience. For example, their clients might be asked to:

- wordstorm their understandings of the concept of empathy
- describe an emotionally upsetting experience from their life, with reference to boards depicting names of emotions and drawings of the emotion (other group members giving feedback here but also commenting on their own emotional responses)
- wordstorm sexual assault victim effects, linking these to their own victim, again with other group members giving appraisal and feedback
- write a victim letter to themselves

- write a mock diary entry by the victim at different stages following the abuse
- write a 'hypothetical' letter back to the victim and then comment on how he feels subsequent to doing so.

Clients can be encouraged to express emotions via a range of techniques:

- recalling critical (memorable) incidents, positive or negative, in their lives, describing each incident and the emotions accompanying it, and by imagining the event in the 'here and now' or as if they have just re-experienced it. Clients here can be encouraged to refer to lists of 'feeling words' to extend and refine their emotional vocabulary as they recall each incident
- writing an 'emotions diary', capturing day-by-day their emotions in response to life events
- describing emotions during sessions upon signals from the therapist, the therapist here working to identify a range of emotions displayed by clients during the session and capitalising on this range accordingly
- drawing an image or identifying a symbol to represent emotions.

Whilst these techniques appear straightforward, the skill for the worker is that of enabling the client to explore, extend and refine his expression of emotion. This is difficult territory for many clients who have been exposed to psychological maltreatment and who may have learned to suppress emotion. The worker may need to sensitise the client to produce increasingly more personal and uncomfortable emotions.

Workers may need to be quite creative in their approaches to this task. One of our clients, for example, struggled to communicate emotion in sessions. He was able to express quite profound emotion in his poetry, however, and this was exploited in our work with him. Another client found he could communicate emotion by referring to music of different forms.

For some clients, as noted by Craissati, it may not be possible for them to express emotions fully until they have addressed their own victimisation experiences.

Techniques for encouraging the recognition of emotional states in others may include clients being shown photographs of facial expressions and bodily postures with coaching in the labelling of emotions. Similarly, audio tapes of prose read in different emotional tones might be used as the stimulus for coaching. Some workers may choose to play recordings of televised dramas/soap operas etc. with action frozen from time to time to provide the focus for discussion of emotion.

In association with the above, the client may be presented with vignettes of situations likely to trigger a range of emotions in the subjects featured in those vignettes. The task is for the client to anticipate or predict the emotion of the subject of those vignettes. Press cuttings may be used in a similar way, i.e. as tools to promote discussion of likely emotion.

If the work is undertaken in group, then inviting clients to identify the emotion of fellow group members, e.g. after a particularly demanding exercise, followed thereafter by feedback from the clients concerned, can serve the double purpose not only of encouraging emotional recognition but also emotional expression in group members.

Dawn Fisher (2001) has articulated a useful set of points to be elicited from clients in group work who are developing the skills of perspective taking. She advises the following learning points:

- Perspective taking is the skill of being able to see somebody else's point of view.

- Different people may have different views of the same situation.

- Individuals can have biased views of a situation, understanding other perspectives can help the individual see the whole picture.

- In turn, understanding other people's viewpoints can help you understand why they behave in certain ways.

- 'Understanding the victim's perspective helps you understand the impact and effect of your abusive behaviour.'

- 'Understanding the impact and effect can challenge the distorted thinking you used to excuse or justify abusive behaviour and this could help prevent reoffending in the future.'

Educating the client as to the short and long-term effects of abuse can be achieved straightforwardly in a didactic 'teach and tell' manner. More engaging approaches may involve quizzes, board games and the like, but care must be taken here not to trivialise the subject matter.

Questions the abuser might be invited to consider as if from their victim include:

- Why did you choose me to abuse?

- If you understood how I felt at the time, how did you manage to ignore my feelings?

- What signals did I give at the time to show I was distressed?

- What do you think has been my experience since the abuse?

- If I were to be left alone with you again, how do you think I would feel?

- Do you think I'll ever stop feeling badly about the abuse?

Some workers find it useful to show clients video tapes of victims/survivors talking of their experiences, to encourage clients to read the poetry or stories of those abused, or indeed to meet victims/survivors, victim advocates or individuals who deal with the trauma of victimisation to hear of the experiences of those abused.

With those clients who are invited to reflect on the impact of abuse on their particular victims, care should be taken to achieve a proper balance between support and challenge. It is easy for sessions to become emotionally confrontational and hence, paradoxically, inoculate the client against exploring in any depth the effect of their behaviour on their victims. A classic technique purported to encourage the development of own victim empathy is that of exposing the abuser to the witness statements of the primary and secondary victims, and to disclose the detail of medical/psychological trauma suffered by the victim, if available.

The objective of drafting a letter of apology to the victim has been referred to above. This matter is dealt with fully elsewhere (Yokley 1990), and indeed quite recently guidelines for the evaluation of victim empathy letters have been proposed (Webster 2002). It is important that the abuser is not led to believe that he has a right to forward the apology letter to the victim. (Our colleagues who work with victims too have emphasised the importance of the preparation of the victim to receive such a letter, if indeed they choose to hear from their abuser at all, and the ongoing support of the victim thereafter.)

A technique somewhat similar to the letter of apology is that of the 'empty chair'. Here, the abuser is invited to address an empty chair as if the victim were sitting in the chair, and then to offer an apology to the victim. Alternatively, the offender may be invited to assume the role of their victim, in this instance the empty chair representing them, the abuser. As 'victim' the requirement is that the abuser describes their experience of the abuse to the empty chair.

In group work sessions we have encouraged clients, subsequent to hearing an account of abuse, to draw images which capture the experience of the victim concerned and to give feedback about the reality of these images to clients.

Activity based approaches to developing own victim empathy include the use of sculpts and role play (e.g. Baim *et al.* 2002; Mann, Daniels and Marshall 2002b). Again, we would emphasise the importance of both proper preparation of the client and subsequent debriefing. As with all techniques which are likely to create discomfort in the client, it is essential that the worker is both properly trained and supervised in their administration.

The objectives above include suggestions that the client make a link between his experience as a victim of abuse and the effects of his behaviour upon those he has victimised. It is well beyond the scope of this book to suggest techniques for resolving the trauma of those abused. To signal the complexity of this work, we paraphrase here typical treatment objectives in this domain from Jongsma and Peterson (1999). Those abused might be encouraged to:

- detail their abuse history in its entirety, clarifying memories where necessary
- identify and express the feelings associated with the abuse and its effects/impact on their life
- demonstrate ability to talk openly of the abuse without feeling ashamed or responsible for the abuse
- break down the secrecy surrounding abuse by informing significant others, including those who will offer support in the recovery process
- express feelings to and about the perpetrator
- decrease verbalisation of being a victim whilst increasing self statements reflecting empowerment
- identify self as a survivor of abuse
- increase level of trust in others
- tolerate greater intimacy.

Jongsma and Peterson also add to the list above a target of the sexual abuse victim increasing their 'level of forgiveness of self, perpetrator and others connected with the abuse', and also them reporting 'increased ability to accept and initiate appropriate physical contact with others'.

We would emphasise that if the client is to make links between their own victimisation experiences and the effects of their abuse on others that this should not be done in a superficial, 'one session' manner. The dual status client, i.e. the client who is both victim and abuser, deserves our respect. Ethically, if we begin the process of helping the client explore these issues there should be adequate time allowed for matters to be dealt with fully.

There may be occasions when circumstances allow for this part of the work to be dealt with by a separate worker offering sessions in parallel with core work on victim empathy. If so, great care must be taken to ensure synchronisation between treatment providers and to check that compatible messages are given. Whilst the abuser cannot and should not be held responsible for his own victimisation, in turn this cannot be used as an excuse for his abuse of others or lack of responsibility for his behaviour in the future. Whilst it is appealing for many workers to assume they do not have the time or skills to address 'victim' resolution work here, there may be an argument for a more integrated approach to therapy with a subsequent challenge to many 'offender workers' to develop additional skills. It would not be unreasonable for a client who has built trust in those workers who address his offending behaviour problems to want the same workers to help him understand his own experiences of abuse.

TIPS AND HINTS

Whilst it may be convenient to institutionalise activities such as those described above into a discrete 'module' within a treatment programme, in effect the development of empathy is also something which should run throughout treatment. The worker has a key role to play in modelling empathic behaviour, in the labelling of emotions, in making disclosure of emotion where appropriate and continually encouraging the client to take stock of their emotions and those of others in their lives.

When focusing on own victim empathy, it has been our experience that often clients in the short term can show distress when faced with knowledge of their victim's experiences but then appear to distance themselves from this distress or sanitise that discomfort longer term. This is often achieved by them developing rationalising cognitions as to why the experience for *their* victim was perhaps not as bad as once thought. It is crucial therefore when addressing the experiences of their victims that clients are monitored beyond the initial sessions, that their cognitions are checked and realigned if self preservatory excuses are creeping in.

The countertransferences that the worker brings to this area of work will be powerful, given that it is not only the client who is facing the discomfort of the detail of their victim's experience but the worker also. These are matters for sensitive discussion and exploration in supervision, consultancy, co-work preparation and/or session debriefing.

If depositions/witness statements are to be used in treatment, then there may be an ethical obligation here to obtain the consent of those witnesses concerned for the material to be used in sessions, particularly group work sessions where other abusers may be exposed to these details. We would recommend that victim statements are not kept by the abuser but offered up to the worker for central storage.

In group based treatments in which victim experiences are described, there may be occasions when men become sexually aroused by hearing descriptions of those other client/victim experiences. Workers should regularly check for signs of sexual arousal in their clients and challenge this as appropriate. We have found, for example, that reflecting back to the client that they appear aroused is often sufficient to interrupt matters. In closing sessions we would routinely remind clients that if they find the material arousing to consider the purpose of their attending sessions, to remind them of the importance of not incorporating (and hence reinforcing) the material into masturbatory fantasy, to encourage them to use techniques of distraction and other fantasy control methods if the images continue to play on their mind. (Clearly, this is not a phenomenon encountered only in sessions on victim empathy. Wherever and whenever encountered, we urge workers to address the problem rather than ignore it.)

CHAPTER 10

Managing Social Functioning

WHY ADDRESS SOCIAL FUNCTIONING?

In this chapter we describe under the heading 'social functioning' those factors which relate to the way that abusers may behave in dealing with emotions and their capacity to manage their lives generally. As we will illustrate later, there are four main (but overlapping) reasons why these factors are important:

- for some offenders the motivation to abuse is based on factors other than sex

- dynamic risk factors influence each other and difficulties in non-sexual areas of an abuser's life may precipitate a reversion to previous habitual thoughts, feelings and behaviours related to abusive behaviour

- in particular, many abusers use sexual means to cope with non-sexual problems

- any individual attempting to manage entrenched problematic behaviour (e.g. an addiction) is more likely to succeed if other areas of their life are stable.

THE CONCEPTS

The literature has numerous references to different factors which may be categorised under the heading 'social functioning' and which may relate to offending. However, definitions and categorisations vary markedly according to different authors. It is not always clear whether exactly the same concepts are being described despite them being named similarly.

One early theory which considers social functioning factors is that of Finkelhor. In relation to motivational factors underpinning child sexual abuse, Finkelhor (1984) regarded 'emotional congruence' with children and 'blockage' in legitimate adult relationships as relevant for some of his sample of child abusers. He regarded other factors such as stress and substance use as factors which influence an abuser's ability to 'overcome internal inhibitors'.

Those who have studied rape have also considered social functioning. Knight and Prentky (1990), for example, identified pervasive anger, vindictiveness and opportunism in addition to sexual motivations (sadistic or non-sadistic) as potential motivators for rapists. They also classify rapists in relation to levels of 'social competence'. A minority of child sex abusers may also be motivated by similar factors (Smallbone and Milne 2000).

Factors relating to general anti-sociality and criminal lifestyles are also widely reported in the literature (e.g. Malamuth *et al.* 1993; Marshall 1993; Pithers 1993). Cortoni and Marshall (1998) have also identified how sexual offenders tend to use sexual outlets to cope with non-sexual emotional difficulties.

Attachment and intimacy and socialisation

The histories of men who sexually abuse are often characterised by psychological maltreatment and emotionally neglectful parenting. The concept of *attachment* has re-emerged within the professional literature as being of importance and those who work with sexual abusers have reconsidered attachment and its relevance to the development of intimacy within relationships, to the aetiology of sexually abusive behaviour and to intervention (Dodgson 2003).

The ability to develop and sustain sexual intimacy with an age-appropriate partner might be argued to inoculate against drift towards the building of relationships with inappropriate partners. Further, the particular stressors which accompany dysfunctional relationships are considered trigger events which in turn have the potential to topple events within the offence chain. Healthy attachment experience in infancy and early childhood acts as a precursor to the acceptance of intimacy in later life. The cognitive schemas and ways of viewing the world and its challenges that are developed via healthy attachment can stand the adult in good stead at times of relationship strain and dysfunction. Conversely, a perverse view of the world and dysfunctional schemas can develop from unhealthy attachment experience and be replayed in the dysfunctional behaviour of the abuser.

Much has been written about *intimacy*, not just within the field of sexual violence but also within allied specialisms, particularly domestic violence. Sonkin and Durphy (1997) note the *isolation* of men they have counselled who exhibit violence. They refer to the socialisation experiences of men who are taught to devalue discussion of emotion.

> Since our emotions may expose our more vulnerable side we hold back
> from expressing feeling for fear of what that other person may think...

That inner fear of judgement by others may be even stronger when we are feeling shame and guilt...we still want others to see us living up to our ideal male image. As a result, even our close friends may not get to know us as we really are, and we may be emotionally lonely. (p.18)

Sonkin and Durphy suggest that this type of emotional loneliness may in time cause stress, with the increased risk in effect of alienation: 'emotional isolation...causes stress, and stress can increase the risk of conflict and the feeling of not being understood'.

Johnson (2001) echoes the above, lamenting the socialisation experiences of males in the US, calling for those working in the fields of maltreatment and child protection to engineer the healthy emotional development of male youth. His recipe of activity to promote healthy masculinity has clear relevance to abusive male adults, particularly within the context of the development of healthy intimacy. He argues that as boys develop into men they need to learn to 'master emotions, not mask emotions'. To do this he believes that many males will need to learn an emotional vocabulary, i.e. will need to learn words to describe the feelings they experience. Further, he believes it is important to teach that emotions are not inherently 'bad', but how you manage emotion is crucial. He believes that boys can be socialised to be emotionally dishonest, discrediting, minimising, denying or re-labelling emotions to appear 'strong', 'non-vulnerable' or the like. He acknowledges that for some youth their early life experiences will have been experiences of pain. The emotion of the pain and the 'emotional stuckness' associated with that pain will need to be confronted if the person is to achieve this 'emotional rite of passage'.

The authors here accept the underlying assumption above that to achieve healthy intimacy it is crucial that the individual can identify and communicate emotion.

Intimacy in relationships

Van den Broucke, Vandereycken and Vertommen (1995) have reviewed the concept of marital intimacy. Whilst their work relates essentially to heterosexual, marital relationships it seems reasonable to suggest that the concepts may translate to intimacy within some non-marital, live-in relationships and relationships between same sex partners. Importantly for the subject matter of this text, the concepts may provide clues as to targets for assessment and intervention in intimacy with offenders.

Van den Broucke and colleagues suggest that to understand intimacy we must consider three levels of functioning, namely the 'dyad' (i.e. 'the degree of connectedness or interdependence between two partners'), the 'individual level', and the 'social group or network level'. When considering the marital dyad three sorts of interdependence should be explored:

1. 'affective interdependence' – described as the 'degree of emotional closeness experienced by the partners'

2. 'cognitive interdependence' – described as 'the degree to which the partners validate each other's ideas and values', and

3. 'instrumental interdependence' – described as 'the degree of implicit or explicit consensus about the rules which regulate the partners' interactions'.

The authors here suggest that these aspects of connectedness between the partners can be reflected at both an overt or covert level. For example, at the covert level these aspects are shown in the couple's emotional closeness, the 'rules' which guide their interactions and the ways they validate each other's ideas and values. Overtly these aspects of interdependence can be seen in how each partner controls the other's behaviour, how they express shared agreements and how they work together to achieve mutual outcomes.

At the individual level, Van den Broucke *et al.* suggest the need to consider two aspects:

*   'authenticity' – described as 'the ability to "be oneself" in the relationship with the partner', and

*   'openness' – described as 'the readiness to share ideas and feelings with the partner'.

Finally, Van den Broucke *et al.* suggest we consider a third level, that of the social group or network. They coin the term here 'exclusiveness', referring to 'the degree to which dyadic privacy is maintained in the relationship with others', such as friends and family.

How can Van den Broucke's ideas be used with abusers? We would suggest that the framework above implies the importance when developing an understanding of intimacy experiences of the abusers to take a history of the quality of their past relationships in terms of their experience of affective, cognitive and instrumental independence. Similarly, it might be helpful to explore what it would mean for the abuser to 'be himself' within a relationship and whether this has been achieved in past relationships. The abuser might reflect on the degree of openness expressed in past relationships. It might also be helpful to explore how the intimate quality of past relationships has been influenced by external social groups and networks.

Social and emotional functioning and risk

Empirically based efforts to identify a range of 'non sex specific' factors which have some correlation with risk of reoffending have been made. These include Mann *et al.* (2002a), who developed the work of Thornton

(2000) reviewed later in this chapter. They describe four 'domains' of dynamic risk factors. In addition to sexual interests and distorted attitudes, they identify as important the abuser's 'social and emotional functioning' – originally called 'socio affective functioning' – comprising inadequacy, distorted intimacy balance, grievance thinking and lack of intimate adult relationships. They also identify the offender's 'self management' skills or lack of them as relevant risk factors (comprising lifestyle impulsiveness, poor cognitive problem solving and poor emotional control).

Hanson and Harris (2000) identify similar factors but categorise them differently. In addition to social influences, sexual self-regulation, and attitudes tolerant of sexual abuse they identify the following relevant groups of factors: 'intimacy deficits' (comprising difficulties with partners, emotional identification with children, hostility to women, rejection and loneliness and being callous and unfeeling), 'cooperation with supervision', and 'general self-regulation' (comprising impulsive acts, poor cognitive problem solving skills, and negative emotional hostility).

Beech *et al.* (1998) developed a psychometric classification (which they called a 'deviance' classification) of child abusers in which scores on measures of social competence, emotional congruence and emotional loneliness (as well as distortions and empathy) are associated with risk of recidivism. Fisher, Beech and Browne (1998) also identified 'locus of control' as a variable related to treatment outcome.

Hudson and colleagues (1998), in reviewing treatment effects with sexual offenders in the Kia Marama programme, explored so-called stable 'dynamic risk factors', i.e. 'those variables that are changeable, but with some difficulty'. This review built on the earlier suggestions of Hanson and Harris (2000) that intimacy deficits, attitudes tolerant of sexual offending and problems with emotional/sexual self-regulation, as well as more general self-regulation showed promise as stable dynamic factors.

Hudson reviewed psychometric evidence from 219 graduates of the Kia Marama treatment programme of which 19 (8%) had been reconvicted or charged with further offences. The measures used to evaluate interpersonal competencies here included inventories to assess social self-esteem, assertion, emotional intimacy, self efficacy, social avoidance, as well as the 'interpersonal reactivity index', a self report measure of aspects of empathy.

The results of this evaluation suggested that not reoffending was associated with less distress in being assertive, as well as aspects of empathy such as the ability to identify with others and perspective taking ability.

Noteworthy from this study was that self-esteem scores did not improve over treatment 'to the acceptable range', the authors suggesting that 'offence processes may be driven by processes other than low self-esteem'. Similarly, loneliness changed relatively little.

The authors suggest that in terms of further research it may be useful to develop a scale that reflects 'self confidence' around using 'sexual safety plans'.

Thornton (2002), in commenting on a framework for dynamic risk assessment, attempts to make sense of what he calls the 'rather complex picture' of research relating to socio-affective deficits. He suggests that it is best to think of more than one syndrome when considering socio-affective deficits of sex offenders. He hypothesises four aspects of relevance:

1. inadequacy (characterised by loneliness, low self-esteem and external locus of control)

2. emotional congruence with children ('being more emotionally open to children than adults')

3. lack of emotionally intimate relationships with adults (characterised by emotional loneliness and 'shallow relationships')

4. aggressive thinking (suspiciousness, ruminating about anger, holding a sense of grievance, and 'a tendency to rehearse negative emotion').

In his study Thornton compared a group of sexual offenders who had been convicted of a sex offence against a child on one occasion with those convicted on more than one occasion. He reports: 'the repetitive sex offender also showed more socio-affective dysfunction, including both inadequacy, emotional congruence with children, emotional loneliness and the rumination of negative angry feelings'.

Self management

As noted earlier in this chapter, a number of researchers have identified factors related to self management as associated with increased risk of reoffending. Hanson and Harris (2000) argue that offenders need to self monitor and inhibit anti-social thoughts and behaviours. They describe offenders having unstable lifestyles characterised by impulsive behaviour and frequent changes of work, residence and associates. Low self control can be expressed in impulsive acts, poor cognitive problem solving, and negative emotional hostility. They argue that offenders with deficits in this area are unlikely to follow through with stated intentions and are likely to fail to avoid high risk situations. They may become overwhelmed by life events.

Thornton (2000), in the framework of dynamic risk factors referred to above, identified the domain of 'self management' as important for similar reasons. Mann *et al.* (2002a) suggest that the presence of impulsive, unstable lifestyles characterised by poor behavioural controls and superficial relationships may be of relevance. Furthermore, evidence of other criminal activity may be a significant pointer to self management problems.

Poor cognitive problem solving was again identified as an issue in this domain. In particular, offenders were more likely to act in a way which ameliorated the immediate emotional discomfort relating to the problem (e.g. by drinking or fleeing from the problem) which in the longer term avoided or aggravated the problem. Even when they were able to identify alternative options in relation to the problem they often chose options which had negative consequences.

The third factor within this domain relates to poor emotional control. This may relate to individuals who generally appear 'over controlled' and withdrawn but who have episodic outbursts of emotion which they are unable to regulate.

The importance of addressing factors relating to social functioning is also emphasised in the HM Prison Service's Sex Offender Treatment Programme (SOTP). Such factors are prevalent prior to treatment and may remain outstanding after initial treatment (HM Prison Service 2003). In the core programmme, three of the four most prevalent factors were poor cognitive problem solving, inadequacy and lack of emotionally intimate relationships (the fourth being sexual preoccupation). In the extended programme (which tends to comprise the most high risk offenders), poor cognitive problem solving and lack of emotionally intimate relationships were found to be prevalent (as well as sexual preoccupation and grievance thinking). Prevalent factors in the adapted programme (for sexual offenders with learning disabilities) were lack of emotionally intimate relationships and poor cognitive problem solving (the other two were sexual entitlement and sexual preoccupation). Offenders within the HM Prison Service SOTP may therefore be referred to a booster programme which has a strong emphasis on allowing offenders to practise and consolidate skills learned in earlier programmes.

OBJECTIVES
The first set of objectives offered below relate to the abuser determining *what might constitute a non-abusive relationship* and how his actions in the past might have contributed to dysfunctional relationships. Suggested objectives following intervention in this domain are as follows:

- the abuser will have determined what characterises a non-abusive relationship
- the abuser will have reviewed his earlier history and determined those significant relationships he experienced which might be considered abusive, and why

- the abuser will have reviewed his earlier history and determined those significant relationships he experienced which might be considered healthy, and why.

For those clients who have experienced previous *dysfunctional relationships* with age-appropriate partners the suggested objectives following intervention may be relevant:

- the abuser will have identified his behaviours that had contributed to the dysfunction within previous relationships
- the abuser will have identified the thoughts he had within previous dysfunctional relationships that had contributed to that dysfunction
- the abuser will have identified the feelings and emotions he had within previous dysfunctional relationships that had contributed to the dysfunction
- the abuser will have identified and where possible rehearsed actions to be taken to address any dysfunctional thoughts, feelings or behaviours determined from the objectives above and that might be relevant to possible relationship breakdown in the future.

Bearing in mind Thornton's hypothesis that feelings of *inadequacy* may contribute to socio-affective functioning deficits and hence risk, additional objectives following intervention might be pursued:

- the abuser will understand the concept of locus of control and its relevance to offending, change and risk management
- the abuser will be aware of thoughts which influence an external locus of control outlook
- the abuser will be able to articulate internal locus of control statements, rephrasing any external locus statements previously identified
- the abuser will have reviewed major life events in which he has influenced or changed outcomes in his life by his efforts and be aware of the importance of believing that he can effect change.

Concerning objectives for addressing *loneliness* the suggested objectives following intervention may be relevant:

- the abuser will be able to explain his understanding of the nature of loneliness and will have identified and discussed times in his life when he may have experienced loneliness
- the abuser will have considered whether loneliness is related to his sexual offending and will have explained in his own vocabulary the nature of such a link

- the abuser will have identified situations which might exacerbate his loneliness in the future
- the abuser will be able to describe, and where possible rehearse, actions that will help reduce emotional loneliness.

In considering the concept of inadequacy, Thornton suggests that this was not only characterised by loneliness and an external locus of control thinking but also by *low self-esteem*. Much has been written on self-esteem in general therapy literature (Brandon 1994; Frey and Carlock 1989; Shapiro 1993). Although self-esteem *per se* does not appear to relate statistically to a risk of reconviction in most sexual abusers (Hanson and Morton-Bourgon 2004), nevertheless Hanson (2000) has cautioned that changes in self-esteem may be a precursor to recidivism. As noted in Chapter 5, it has been regarded as an 'associated risk factor' (Beech *et al.* 1999; Kennington *et al.* 2001). Improving the client's self-esteem may well allow him then to be able to address other concerns and access therapy more efficiently. Budrionis and Jongsma (2003) have offered objectives for work with self-esteem deficits in sex offenders.

Concerning the management of *emotional congruence with children*, an over-arching goal here may be that of enabling the abuser to understand how emotional needs may be met through contact to children and the importance of regulating emotion in that context. The abuser will need to be able to identify how in the past he has used contact with children to fulfil his own emotional needs and to identify and rehearse future strategies to rectify that imbalance.

For those abusers characterised by low emotional congruence to children, it may be important to educate them to children's needs at various stages in development and how adults might meet these needs appropriately. Further, the abuser should consider ways in which he may frustrate children's needs or fail to meet these needs.

Within the context of socio-affective functioning and intimacy, for those clients who have sexual relationships with age-appropriate partners, it may be important to review the concept of *sexual intimacy*. With this in mind suggested objectives following intervention may include:

- the abuser will have discussed the concept of sexual intimacy and his previous experience of sexual intimacy
- the abuser will have discussed any history of sexual dysfunctional problems including loss of sexual interest, premature ejaculation, ejaculatory failure or erectile failure
- the abuser will have identified strategies for dealing with ongoing sexual dysfunctional problems including onward referral where necessary

- the abuser will identify any concerns or anxieties he may hold towards sexual intimacy.

Finally, and again with reference to Thornton's suggestion that *anger rumination* may be an important characteristic of socio-affective functioning, the suggested objectives following intervention may be:

- the abuser will have considered the nature of anger and the function of anger
- the abuser will have considered in what ways anger might have been considered problematic
- the abuser will have reviewed his experience of anger and angry rumination
- the abuser will have reviewed his experience of angry thoughts and identified competing or rational thoughts to counter angry rumination
- the abuser will have rehearsed competing thoughts and strategies for dealing with anger provoking situations including methods of relaxation, distraction and the like.

EXAMPLES OF INTERVENTIONS

It is beyond the scope of this book to offer a comprehensive list of exercises to address all the possible range of factors which may arise in relation to social functioning. Readers are referred to more specialised texts at the end of this chapter.

One author of this text is involved in the Northumbria Sex Offender Groupwork Programme (McGregor *et al.* 2001). That programme has a 'menu' of exercises addressing different aspects of social functioning described below for illustrative purposes. It is stressed in the manual that where abusers have pervasive problems in any sphere they may need to be referred for specialist group work, psychiatric or psychological treatment specifically for that issue. It is important that clients are given ample opportunity to practise effective coping strategies. Examples of exercises are as follows:

- *Problem solving.* Exercises involve identifying problems, options for their resolution and future plans. Worksheets are used to identify advantages and disadvantages of various options which are discussed with the group.
- *Self-esteem.* Group members are encouraged to identify positive characteristics of themselves and others.
- *Anger.* Clients identify situations which generate anger in themselves. They identify problematic aspects of anger which are then contrasted with assertiveness. Healthy responses based

on relevant thoughts, feelings and behaviour are generated and practised.

- *Mood states.* A range of moods is identified and their effects on thoughts and behaviours examined. Group members fill in a mood diary and describe coping mechanisms. These are refined through discussion within the group.

- *Relationship skills.* Exercises address practical aspects of interpersonal interactions such as listening and responding. Different types of relationships are examined, followed by discussion of the appropriateness of different types of behaviours and emotional responses within each. The concept of appropriate personal space in different relationship contexts is illustrated through role play.

- *Sexual knowledge* is addressed using a quiz format with feedback.

- *Self awareness and coping.* Group members use life maps to illustrate repeated patterns of behaviour in their lives, identifying those that have been unhelpful. They then develop and rehearse alternative strategies.

TIPS AND HINTS

Psychometric and questionnaire data can provide a useful adjunct to this work. For example, offenders may have completed instruments such as the Locus of Control questionnaire (Nowicki 1976) or measures designed to assess their emotional congruence with children such as the Children and Sex questionnaire (Beech *et al.* 1998). The client's responses to these questionnaires may provide a useful starting point for feedback to the client. They provide a springboard for discussion and with reference to responses to particular items on these questionnaires. In turn, discussing these questionnaires with clients may help de-mystify psychometric testing and encourage the offender to feel that they have a purpose in collaborative work rather than the client simply being tested for testing's sake.

As stated above, it is beyond the scope of this book to present a series of exercises to address each of the objectives above. In addition to the text by Frey and Carlock (1989) highlighted above on enhancing self-esteem, various high quality manuals and workbooks are available addressing other domains and functioning. For example, in a domain of anger control the text by McKay and Rogers (2000) is a useful resource as is *Men and Anger* by Cullen and Freeman-Longo (1995).

A useful source for reviewing the nature of child maltreatment and those actions which may be thought to undermine children's needs can be found in the *APSAC Handbook of Child Maltreatment* edited by Briere and colleagues (1996). Particular reference is made to Chapter 4 of that text written by Stuart Hart, Marler Brassard and Henry Carlson titled 'Psychological maltreatment'.

CHAPTER 11

Relapse Prevention and Self-Regulation

WHY ADDRESS RELAPSE PREVENTION AND SELF-REGULATION?

It has long been argued (e.g. Beckett *et al.* 1994) that relapse prevention should form an integral part of any treatment programme for sexual abusers. This assertion has face validity in that it is reasonable to suppose that having completed the aspects of treatment so far described, abusers need to learn long-term strategies for the management of destabilising mood states, high risk situations and urges and cravings, all of which are assumed to increase the risk of reversion to previous offending behaviour. However, the evidence that relapse prevention increases the long-term efficacy of treatment programmes is not conclusive (see e.g. Marshall and Anderson 2000). This chapter will summarise the theory and practice developments to date.

There is an extensive literature in relation to the theory and practice of relapse prevention with sex abusers. It was initially developed in the context of the treatment of addictions by Marlatt and George (1984), where high relapse rates had been noticed. Laws (1989) provides an account of the initial work of Marques and colleagues who adapted relapse prevention techniques for use with sex abusers. It is an area of work that has faced theoretical scrutiny; a critique of early relapse prevention models alongside subsequent modifications (e.g. to making such models more responsive to different coping styles) can be found in Laws, Hudson and Ward (2000).

Most sex abuser treatment groups in the UK were based initially on the so called 'orthodox model' of relapse prevention as described by Pithers *et al.* (1988) and outlined in Figure 11.1. In this model, an abuser remains in control and therefore abstains from offending until a *lifestyle imbalance* precipitates a return to earlier maladaptive thought processes and behaviours. Such imbalances may result from a number of sources, either internal or external to the abuser. A negative mood state may be triggered by an argument, the mood here triggering significant mental and behavioural changes. Not all 'internal' events may be negative. Pithers (1993), for example, noted that some rapists may be destabilised by apparently positive mood states. These are also clearly internal events.

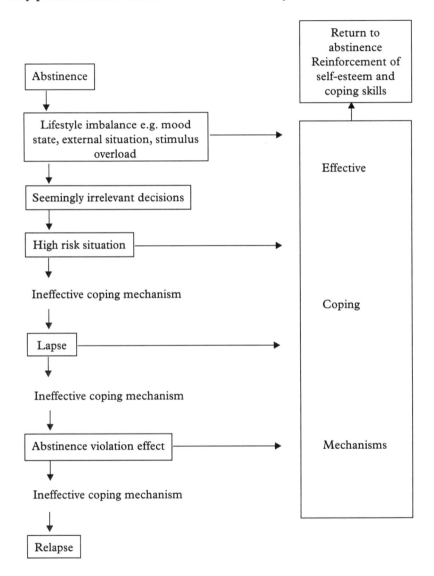

Figure 11.1: *The 'orthodox' model of relapse prevention*

Lifestyle imbalance may also follow exposure to external, unexpected stimuli, such as an item on the television news about a boys' football team, or a relative visiting unannounced with children. It was suggested that if the abuser lacks the skills to cope with these eventualities he may begin to progress through the relapse process.

The phrase 'apparently irrelevant decisions' (AIDs) was coined to describe how abusers, when destabilised, may undertake actions that might not appear to others to be linked directly with offending but which in fact move the abuser closer to high risk situations in which offending is more likely to occur. The thought processes adopted by the abuser are however consciously directed to these actions. Also called *seemingly irrelevant decisions* (SIDs), they are often presented by abusers to show how they 'could not help' being in the situation they were in. (For instance, an abuser describing how a child fell over in the park may challenge the therapist about whether he was supposed to leave the child rather than rub her knee better.)

By using this process an abuser may argue that he 'ended up in' a *high risk situation*. There are differences in the early literature about what constitutes a high risk situation. Pithers *et al.* (1988) talk in terms of increased destabilisation, whilst Steenman, Nelson and Viesti (1989) describe physical situations in which there is the potential for access to a victim. In this respect, Eldridge (1998) helpfully differentiates between 'high risk mind states' and 'high risk scenarios'. Again, in the absence of effective coping mechanisms, exposure to a high risk situation may lead to a lapse.

Lapse refers to a behaviour that is not in itself an abuse but which is part of an individual's previous pattern of offending. Examples include masturbating to an image of a child, purchasing pornography or arranging to baby-sit. It is argued that the successful use of effective coping mechanisms at this or indeed earlier stages will reinforce an abuser's sense of self efficacy. Alternatively, however, the abuser may experience what is referred to as the *abstinence violation effect*. This occurs when a lapse causes an abuser to assign negative attributes to himself (e.g. 'I'm only an old sex abuser anyway'). These negative attributes encourage him to fail, making it less likely that he will perceive there to be anything to be gained by continued resistance to offending. In such a state the likelihood of *relapse* (that is, reoffending) is increased.

Our practice experience has been that in resisting temptation some abusers have described actually feeling disappointed and cheated rather than experiencing an increase in self efficacy. This is consistent with critiques of this model described later.

Another issue that has been commented on in the 'orthodox' relapse process is the management of *urges* and *cravings*. This has been conceptualised as the *problem of immediate gratification* or the PIG. Abusers are helped to understand that indulging an urge reinforces it, abstaining from it reduces it: if you feed the PIG it gets bigger, if you don't it gets smaller.

Urges and cravings may occur at any stage of the relapse process. As sex is biologically as well as emotionally driven, it is likely that abusers will experience sexual desire at different times, and those with a high degree of arousal to inappropriate stimuli must be aware continually of the need to identify and manage their urges and cravings. Urges and cravings may be precipitated by situational factors but also by memories. Concerning the latter, we often assume that when sexual feelings are being generated that this will occur in response to positive memories. Some sex abusers however will have had life experiences where sex has been linked with unpleasant experiences (e.g. harsh punishment). It has been noted that sex abusers may be prone to use sexual activity as a way of coping with negative feelings (Marshall *et al.* 1999). It is important therefore to be aware of individual difficulties. As stated, urges and cravings can also be precipitated by external stimuli. Examples might be songs or smells which are particularly evocative, whether or not they are directly related to past abuses.

A relapse prevention programme based on this model will include exercises to identify each stage of the relapse process, with abusers identifying and rehearsing the thoughts and skills needed to develop effective coping mechanisms that will prevent them from progressing through each stage of the relapse process.

CRITICISMS OF AND MODIFICATION TO THE ORTHODOX MODEL

There have been a number of criticisms of the wholesale adoption of relapse prevention into sex abuser work. Practitioners have queried whether the model is applicable in the form described to all men. Further, what is a 'precursor' for one abuser (e.g. being outside of a newspaper shop when children were there) may be a lapse for another. It is apparent to those who work in this field that by no means all abusers are motivated to follow a 'covert pathway' to offending or indeed have a genuine commitment to stop offending. Indeed, some abusers appear to have little commitment to change, succinctly illustrated by the abuser who observed to one of the current authors that 'this stuff is alright if you want to stop, isn't it?'. In addition, in the early addiction model as related to substance abuse, a 'lapse' was conceptualised as a short-term reversion to the addictive behaviour (e.g. smoking at a party). Clearly, one reversion to sex abuse is not acceptable. Nevertheless, the model was adapted somewhat uncritically as described above.

Hanson (2000) highlighted an underlying yet often unspoken assumption in sex abuser treatment, particularly in respect of relapse prevention, namely that all sex abusers are recidivists. Studies however report variable rates of recidivism dependent on abuser characteristics (Hanson and

Bussiere 1998; Thornton 2000). Hanson argues that consistently telling low risk abusers that they are in fact high risk is unlikely to be helpful.

Other criticisms relate to the model itself. In the most detailed of these, Ward and Hudson (2000) point out that the relapse prevention process conceptualises what is essentially a negative experience, aimed primarily at avoidance. It assumes that all abusers have similar types and degrees of desire to embark on the 'covert pathway' to reoffending (although this may be an overly mechanistic interpretation of relapse prevention). They argue that while negative emotions may be associated with lapse if an abuser is motivated not to reoffend, positive feelings may lead to offending when an individual does not have this motivation. In these cases, concepts such as the *abstinence violation effect* have little relevance. Ward and Hudson put forward an alternative '*self-regulation model of relapse prevention*' that explicitly acknowledges more than one potential route to reoffending. Whether this model will have an improved treatment impact remains to be shown.

The self-regulation model is based on studies of the way in which individuals achieve goals in their lives generally. Goals may be described as either 'acquisitional' (*approach*) or 'inhibitory' (*avoidance*) in nature. In the case of approach goals, individuals are likely to have a history of success in achieving their aims, so that initial failure results in a review of what has worked in the past. In contrast, in those with avoidance goals the aim is to inhibit behaviours (not to do things rather than do them). Failure to achieve their goal reinforces what is likely to be a perception of inadequacy.

In relation to offending, it is argued that some abusers will wish to stop offending but fail, either because of a lack of coping skills (the so-called *avoidant-passive pathway*), or the use of inappropriate coping skills (the *avoidant-active pathway*). Others have no genuine desire to stop offending, and follow a route to relapse either because they do not have an awareness of a problem and seem to show a habitual reversion to previous lifestyles (the *approach-automatic pathway*), or because of a deliberate decision to carry out actions associated with reoffending (the *approach-explicit pathway*).

Ward and Hudson (2000) describe nine phases in the relapse process. These are fluid and they suggest abusers may move forward and back through the process. These phases are outlined below.

Phase 1 relates (as in the orthodox model) to a *life event* that destabilises the abuser, who until then has remained abstinent. This may cause the re-emergence of cognitions or mood states leading to Phase 2, in which there is a *desire for deviant sexual activity*. In Phase 3 *abuse related goals are established*. According to the model, it is in Phase 3 that the abuser's goal setting strategy, based either on a desire to *avoid* reoffending or on adopting behaviours to actively *approach* it, becomes relevant. At this stage, abusers with avoidant strategies are likely to experience negative emotions, whereas the emotions of those with approach strategies may be either positive or negative in nature.

In Phase 4 the *strategy is selected*. This may not occur in the form of conscious decision making, but may instead relate to the re-emergence of habitual behaviours and established 'abuse scripts'. It is at this stage that the distinction between the four pathways becomes apparent. Avoidant-passive abusers are likely to be *underregulated* and begin *covert planning* similar to the orthodox relapse pathway. Avoidant-active abusers *misregulate* their behaviour, using inappropriate strategies to avoid offending (e.g. masturbating to inappropriate stimuli to release sexual tension). Approach-automatic abusers also *underregulate*, behaving almost without thinking in accordance with previously learned behavioural scripts. Finally, approach-explicit abusers revert to *planned and deliberate strategies* in pursuit of their goal of reoffending.

Phase 5 is described as the entry into a *high risk situation*. At this stage avoidant-passive abusers may perceive themselves to be out of control, whilst avoidant-active abusers may renew their efforts but with paradoxical effects (that is, they do things that make matters worse). Approach-automatic abusers continue to engage in previous habitual behavioural patterns, but approach-explicit abusers are by now seeking out victims and planning their abuses. As in the orthodox model, an abuser may find himself in high risk situations not of his own making (although practitioners will usually need to be persuaded that this is genuinely the case).

Phase 6 is what Ward and Hudson (2000) regard as a *lapse*. They view this as the immediate precursor to the reabuse, by which time all abusers will in effect have adopted approach goals, with avoidant-passive abusers having 'given in' and avoidant-active ones feeling out of control and also 'giving in'. For Ward and Hudson however an example of a lapse is getting into bed with a child, although many would view such behaviour as being equivalent to a new abuse in itself.

Phases 7 to 9 are the *abuse, post abuse evaluation* and *subsequent attitudes to future offending* stages respectively. Following the abuse, avoidant abusers may experience the 'abstinence violation effect', resulting in the perception of a lack of self efficacy with no attempt made to curtail future offending behaviour. Men with approach goals, however, will tend to experience positive thoughts and feelings relating to their offending. In treatment programmes these phases are unlikely to be addressed directly as an abuser who had relapsed would usually be excluded from the group, even if remaining in the community. But the abuser may be referred again, perhaps with a view to a new community order, or following release from prison, or indeed if he was not prosecuted or convicted for the new abuse. Phases 7 to 9 would need to be evaluated to determine whether the abuser is appropriate for further treatment and with new information relating to the relapse incorporated into the treatment plan.

Hudson and Ward (2000) describe the practical implications of their model for intervention. They argue that for *avoidant-passive abusers* interventions closely resemble the orthodox relapse prevention approach. The main problem for these abusers is inadequate coping skills and poor awareness of the abuse process. Issues relating to social competence will need to be addressed (e.g. relationship problems, poor mood management and poor problem solving). Beliefs about poor self efficacy will need to be addressed. Bickley, Fisher and Beech (2004) have also commented on the treatment targets for avoidant-passive abusers and suggest that in addition to these abusers developing their understanding of the abuse process and developing emotional regulation skills that 'meta-cognitive control' should be developed, i.e. the abuser learning the skills of attending to and evaluating their thoughts and behaviour.

With *avoidant-active* abusers some elements of the orthodox model will also be relevant. This 'pathway' relates primarily to misregulation. Abusers are likely to attempt to regulate strong negative emotions for example but to do so in such a way as to make matters worse. It is important that these abusers develop appropriate skills to manage negative emotions early in the reabuse chain. Regulatory techniques are more difficult to implement the more difficult the problem has become (e.g. the temptation to masturbate to relieve negative emotions). Bickley, Fisher and Beech also suggest for this group the development of meta-cognitive skills, but also helping the abuser understand that their previous attempts to deal with problems have had ironic effects (made things worse rather than better). They suggest that work to disrupt cognitive distortions (victim specific distortions and justifications) may also be needed.

For *approach-automatic* abusers self-regulation is also a key issue, although for them their tendency to revert to overlearned scripts will need specific attention. These overlearned scripts may be similar to 'schemas' described in Chapter 7. The abuser is likely to revert to these behaviours without a specific awareness that he is doing so. Such schemas (e.g. entitlement, retribution) are likely to be evident in a range of 'domains' in the individual's life, such as broader relationships, leisure pursuits, accommodation and occupation. Bickley, Fisher and Beech note the importance of approach-automatic abusers developing perspective taking skills and also restructuring their distorted thoughts about victims. The reconditioning of deviant sexual interests and desires may also be important for this group. These factors are resistant to change, so external risk management is crucial for this group.

Approach-explicit abusers are thought to have core beliefs supportive of offending and to derive significant positive emotions from offending. Skill deficiencies will tend not to be apparent. Hudson and Ward argue that it is likely to be necessary to 'recondition appetitive sexual processes', a process which they acknowledge is extremely difficult. Challenging core beliefs is likely to be difficult; indeed if it does occur it may lead to a 'cognitively deconstructed state'. It may be deduced therefore that this group is likely to be the most resistant to treatment and external risk management strategies will need to be implemented. Importantly, Bickley, Fisher and Beech emphasise the importance of external monitoring, support and supervision of the approach-explicit client.

A very useful text has been prepared by Ward and colleagues (Ward *et al.* 2004), which provides an overview of the self-regulation model with case examples and suggestions for treatment.

The strength of the self-regulation model is its recognition that for relapse prevention to be effective it needs to acknowledge that differing pathways can lead to reoffending. Observing that the model implies that relapse prevention is not simply about avoidance, Mann (1998) has suggested that the relapse prevention process itself should be re-framed as a programme aimed at developing new and productive lifestyles, a concept defined as *new me*, drawing on the work of Haaven (Haaven, Little and Petre-Miller 1990) rather than focusing solely on not engaging in past activities (which presumably gave pleasure to, or at least fed some emotional need in, the abuser).

To date there have been few published studies of the empirical investigations of the self-regulation model.

Webster (2005) set out to examine the validity of the self-regulation model. He studied a UK sample of child molesters and rapists who had reoffended after having attended a prison based treatment programme. Twenty-five men were studied in total, twelve of whom were child molesters, nine were rapists and four were abusers against both adults and children. The abusers were interviewed at length using a semi-structured interview and the abuse pathway they had followed pre-treatment was ascertained as well as the pathway they had followed upon initial release from prison and when they had reoffended.

Webster found that of the 25 subjects, 11 could be allocated to a pathway both pre and post treatment. Ten of these 11 subjects had followed an approach-explicit pathway. Furthermore, ten participants could reliably be allocated a pathway at either pre or post treatment but not both. Again, the majority of these men were approach-explicit abusers. Only four participants could not be reliably allocated a pathway for either pre or post treatment abuses – these men had 'multiple concurrent pathways' running through the stages of the pathway.

Webster suggests that there is strong support for the pathways model and the reliability of attempts to classify abuses according to the pathways.

For this particular sample (of recidivists), he suggests the pathways remained stable over time and were not affected by treatment. For this group the predominant pathway was approach-explicit, which lends support to the view that those are the most difficult to treat.

That being said, clearly not all abusers could be allocated to a pathway, and as Bickley et al. (2004) comment, 'the model does not account for multiple concurrent pathways running across the nine phases'.

Yates and colleagues (Yates, Kingston and Hall 2003) also reviewed the application of the pathways model. Their sample was 33 rapists, 19 extra-familial child molesters, 24 incest abusers and 4 abusers who had multiple victim types. They found that pathways could reliably be allocated to the entire sample. Rapists were most likely to follow the approach pathway (58% approach-automatic, 36% approach-explicit). Child molesters with male victims were most likely to follow an approach-explicit pathway (83%). Child molesters with female victims however were equally likely to follow either an approach-automatic or approach-explicit pathway. Whilst half of the incest abusers followed an approach-explicit pathway, 38 per cent followed an avoidant-passive pathway to offending.

Bickley and Beech (2002) applied the Ward and Hudson model to a sample of abusers in a UK treatment facility so as to provide support for the concept of the 'four pathways'. They measured the outcome of treatment for sexual abusers against children assigned as having 'avoidant' or 'approach' goals. The *avoidant* abusers (n=15) did not show statistically significant treatment effects in relation to distortions about sexual activity with children (general or victim specific) because they held few such beliefs before treatment. *Approach* goal abusers (n=44) showed significant improvements, however, but still held distorted views which were slightly higher than those which the avoidant goal abusers held before treatment. Approach-automatic and approach-explicit abusers were not differentiated. It is also noted that in this sample some factors in the histories of the approach goal abusers correlated with those regarded as indicating high risk on actuarial measures (Hanson and Bussiere 1998; Thornton 2000), in as much as they had a higher likelihood of having no long-term relationship, of having abused extra-familial victims and male victims and of having previous sexual convictions, and previous therapy. This reinforces our view that external risk management strategies will need to be emphasised for these approach goal abusers.

THE APPLICATION OF NEW MODELS

As the above review illustrates, the theoretical basis of relapse prevention is still developing. Whilst the pathways model appears to have good face validity, it has yet to be evaluated across a range of abuser types in various settings. Further, notwithstanding the impressive efforts of Bickley and colleagues, there is only limited guidance available on how to incorporate understanding of pathways into treatment programmes.

In a review of the efficacy of relapse prevention, Marshall and Anderson (2000) concluded that 'comprehensive cognitive-behavioural programs having an internal self-management RP component that is not too elaborate appear to be the most successful'. Although they focus on 'internal self management', it is also important to note that relapse prevention may be boosted by a strong *external management* component, one which may involve family members, friends, hostel staff or, in high risk cases, the police in monitoring and supporting the abuser.

With the above in mind, the following criteria have been proposed by Kennington *et al.* (2001) for the ethos of relapse prevention programmes:

- the programme should be presented in way that makes clear to participants that whilst not all abusers pose the same risk of reoffending, a small but significant proportion of apparently low risk abusers may be convicted of a new sexual abuse (up to 10% on most actuarial measures), so vigilance is required

- the programme should be framed positively, as an opportunity for the abuser to lead a purposeful and abuse-free life, rather than focusing solely on the avoidance of past behaviours

- concepts must be framed in terms which the abusers will understand

- it should be recognised that abusers may follow different relapse pathways (or none)

- the behaviour of one abuser should not be assumed to have the same significance as similar behaviours in another abuser; likewise, abusers may progress through (or escape from) the relapse process on the basis of differing thoughts, behaviours and feelings

- while the group itself mainly addresses internal management components there must be liaison with people outside the group (some professionals, some not) in order to support and monitor the abuser and, in the most high risk cases, to carry out surveillance.

One example of relapse prevention which has been designed to meet the above criteria is the Northumbria Probation Sex Offender Groupwork Programme (Kennington *et al.* 2001). Following introductory exercises (brief because most attenders will already have experience of group work), there is a group discussion entitled 'What is relapse prevention?' to ensure that all members have a common understanding of the purpose of the relapse prevention group. Group members then identify 'strategies I have used in the past to stay in control' (based on the assumption that there have been periods in which they have not reoffended) and with the aim of helping them identify existing coping skills on which they can build. This is followed by a didactic presentation of a 'model of relapse', which in the past was based on the orthodox model of RP but which is now presented as possible stages that an abuser might go through on the route to relapse. It is emphasised that it is always possible to exit the relapse process, and that the successful generation of coping mechanisms should reinforce perceptions of self efficacy.

At this stage it is important to harness the positive thoughts and feelings that group members have about their current life in which they are not offending. To this end, the Prochaska and DiClemente (1982) model of change is presented (for a review, see Briggs *et al.* 1998). This is done in a graphic format, with each of the stages of change marked by a sheet of paper on the floor. Group members stand in turn at the different stages and discuss what these mean in terms of their own behaviour (e.g. 'precontemplation' prior to arrest, 'contemplation' whilst on remand, 'action' in the core group, and 'maintenance' indicating their current state). Members reflect on their current feelings during the maintenance phase and are then required briefly to stand at the 'precontemplation' phase. This often generates strong emotions and thoughts, and a resolve not to return to that phase of behaviour.

The essence of relapse prevention is its aim of assisting abusers not to revert to previous dysfunctional behaviour patterns. It is important therefore that group members should be aware of these patterns for every other group member. In order to achieve this, each abuser briefly presents 'my cycle' (see e.g. Briggs *et al.* 1998) or an equivalent exercise that was generated previously. The possible stages towards relapse are then addressed in turn, with each stage framed in terms of 'how would the "old me" have coped with this' and 'how will the "new me" cope?'

Both the orthodox and revised models assume that an abuser will be abstinent until he is destabilised by some life event. In group discussion, abusers identify 'things that might lead to relapse'. It is emphasised that these may be generated internally (for example, apparently spontaneous mood states) or externally (for instance, unexpectedly seeing children getting on a bus). In discussion it is important to identify a wide range of possibilities (including those that were present in the past), although it is sensible to ensure that these have a realistic connection with the abuser's circumstances, general coping style, thought processes and behaviours.

After identifying a reasonable range of possible precursors to relapse, group members are given homework tasks to begin to identify coping strategies, which are then presented to the group. In keeping with the ethos of 'support and challenge' (see Chapter 6), group members and staff may suggest alternative, more realistic strategies. To test how realistic the strategies in fact are, and to give abusers an opportunity to rehearse and reinforce them, a scenario based on the proposed strategy is role played. This may lead to further refinement. As a homework task, group members are asked to identify an example of how they have used a new coping strategy under pressure. This is presented and reviewed at the next session.

The next phase of the group is to look more closely at how the 'old me' would have coped in terms of decision making. Previously, using the orthodox model, it was illustrated how an abuser might fool himself and others into believing that he had 'ended up' in a high risk situation through a series of seemingly irrelevant decisions. This stage of the RP group has been revised to acknowledge that the decision making process (equivalent to Phase 3 'goal setting' and Phase 4 'strategy selection' in the Hudson and Ward model) is likely to vary, although it will be consistent with an individual's previous thought processes and behaviours. Pathways to relapse may involve covert planning (avoidant-passive), inappropriate coping strategies (avoidant-active), impulsivity and under-regulation (approach-automatic) or systematic planning (approach-explicit).

Abusers are initially given homework in which they are asked to consider the possible pathways in relation to their own offending. Each abuser writes up his 'pathway' and describes 'options out', i.e. ways in which the 'new me' will cope. Consistent with both the orthodox and revised models, options out include the management of thoughts, feelings and behaviours, with the abuser identifying a way of rewarding himself on successful implementation of his coping strategy. Again, the options out are discussed and refined with the help of the group, either through discussion or role play. Abusers are also asked to identify situations in which they acted differently from how they would have behaved in the past, although the exercise is not invented if no situations have arisen in the previous week.

The next stage is for abusers to learn to identify and manage *high risk situations* and *lapses*. Because of the different interpretations of what constitutes a high risk situation and a lapse, it is possible to become mired in fruitless discussion with abusers about whether a given example of behaviour was a 'precursor to a high risk situation', 'a high risk situation', or 'a lapse'. However, the aim is to encourage abusers to expect that lapses or high risk situations are likely to occur, and not to panic when they do. High risk situations and lapses are therefore discussed without assuming that a given sequence will inevitably be evident for a given abuser.

The process for dealing with lapses involves the identification of potential risky situations, discouraging the repetition of mechanistically learned coping strategies for situations that are either implausible or irrelevant to an abuser's past or likely future circumstances. What is important is to recognise risky situations and behaviours for each individual, being clear how these relate to *his* past and possible future offending, with an understanding of how the situation or behaviour arose (whether through covert planning, misregulation, impulsivity, systematic planning or external circumstances). The abuser needs to identify the thoughts and feelings (positive, negative or ambivalent) associated with the situation or behaviour, and to develop strategies to cope with these thoughts and feelings without recourse to reoffending (e.g. through diversionary activity, self talk or specific avoidance behaviours). The abuser is again given homework to describe how the 'new me' will cope, and as before this is shared with the group, with more appropriate plans developed and tested in group discussion or through role play or sculpting.

Issues associated with urges and cravings are dealt with in the context of the problem of immediate gratification, presented to the group with a picture of a cartoon pig gorging itself on cake to reinforce the concept. The aim is to ensure that group members understand that it is not necessary to indulge a sexual urge, and that if it is not indulged it will dissipate like any other urge. In contrast, indulging an urge will make it stronger (like feeding the pig). The image of 'urge surfing' is also used to illustrate how, if one keeps in control at the crest of a wave, the wave will eventually subside, although it may be necessary to strain every sinew to retain control.

The short and long-term advantages of abusing and not abusing are entered on a decision matrix using stickers. Whilst there are inevitably more stickers identifying the advantages of not abusing than of abusing, the former tend to be long term and are often altruistic, whilst the latter are usually immediate and pleasurable. The task therefore is to help group members manage the immediate temptation with effective coping responses, rewarded by good feelings and the benefits of a positive abuse-free lifestyle. Strategies need to be individualised, and tend to involve an immediate reminder of the negative effects of 'giving in' (such as going to prison or causing harm to a victim), but it is also desirable for the abuser to plan a reward for success in abstaining. Where thoughts and feelings are very intrusive, group members may be referred to a forensic clinical psychologist for behavioural therapy, or to a psychiatrist for appropriate medication if necessary.

The final phase of the relapse prevention group is the presentation by each abuser of a 'New Life Plan'. This is a document developed in the Thames Valley Project sex abuser programme, and covers all aspects of an abuser's future life (Eldridge and Still 2001). Several sections of it are completed with workers outside of the group. This provides a positive conclusion to the group which reinforces the progress made within it.

OBJECTIVES

Below are suggested outcomes following intervention:

- the client will have acknowledged his potential to reoffend/reabuse
- the client will have articulated the need to sustain long-term efforts to avoid reoffending, i.e. beyond active treatment or intervention
- the client will have articulated an understanding of the possible routes or pathways to lapse and relapse
- the client will have articulated his pathway to lapse and relapse previously and likely pathways to lapse and relapse in the future
- for those clients who desire to avoid reoffending, they should be able to identify

  1. moods, sexual fantasies and thoughts which may trigger their desire to abuse others, including identification of events likely to prompt such moods, fantasies and thoughts

  2. situations or places to be avoided

  3. the characteristics of individuals who are most likely to be groomed and targeted for abuse, including here issues such as personality, age, physical appearance, demeanour and dress

- the client will have rehearsed strategies for dealing with moods, thoughts and fantasies which may increase his risk
- the client will have developed a lifestyle plan which assists in the avoidance of places, situations and people associated with increased risk
- the client will have rehearsed strategies for dealing with unexpected encounters with individuals associated with increased risk
- the client will have identified the actions he will take (the resources to be utilised) if he feels at significant risk of relapse
- the client will have rehearsed the actions to be taken, and particularly the cognitive strategies to be used if he has encountered a lapse situation/the potential abstinence violation effect
- the client will have rehearsed techniques for self monitoring of high risk situations
- the client will have rehearsed techniques for dealing with urges and cravings

- the client will have shared the detail of his relapse prevention plan and the actions inherent in the objectives above with his non-abusing partner/therapeutic chaperone.

INTERVENTIONS

There are several texts which give further and detailed guidance on techniques associated with the objectives above. We would refer the reader to the following: Eldridge (1998); Laws (1989); Laws, Hudson and Ward (2000); Morin and Levenson (2002); Steen (2001). For those clients whose desire to avoid reoffending is suspect (those who may follow what has been described as an approach pathway above), core work on motivation to change, on challenging attitudes supportive of abuse, on the management of abuse related sexual arousal and external surveillance and monitoring will be needed.

TIPS AND HINTS

Relapse prevention work should involve the client developing the skills of problem solving, self monitoring, impulse control and vigilance. Workers have to guard against prescription. In early stages of work with an abuser the worker may sometimes need to be quite directive. However, a different set of skills have to be emphasised in relapse prevention work. The worker has to be particularly encouraging of the client 'learning to learn', of the client being open to uncertainty, and of the client sometimes being ambivalent or anxious about independence and freedom from therapeutic oversight. Clearly the worker cannot be with the client '24/7' upon discharge from treatment or the completion of an order. Those clients who fare best are those who leave treatment with strategies in place to sustain focus on the need to maintain change, and with a flexible repertoire of skills to deal with both the expected and unexpected situations they may face in the future which might trigger risk.

The prevention of relapse will be assisted if there are those in the client's environment who can offer social support for change and the maintenance of relapse prevention plans. For that reason we would encourage the involvement of therapeutic chaperones/sponsors in relapse prevention work. This might be non-abusing partners (see Chapter 12) or others such as appropriately briefed and trained members of faith communities, other professionals or circles of support and accountability (see Chapter 2).

Those workers who have developed a credible and robust working relationship with the abuser might naturally be called upon by the client at times of perceived risk and need. Agencies might consider how best to promote the possibility of former clients being able to access help and guidance on a voluntary basis after the 'closure of the case' and termination of a licence. Not all abusers will access such a resource in our experience, though those who do so can often be helped before their problems escalate to lapse and relapse.

Even for those clients who desire to avoid reoffending, motivation to adhere to long-term vigilance and monitoring of high risk situations will fluctuate. It is useful if clients can be reminded of techniques for enhancing motivation to change (see Chapter 6), and for those offering guidance on relapse prevention to revisit evaluation of the client's motivation from time to time.

Relapse prevention is a skill and as such calls for the rehearsal and practice of techniques. 'Insight' alone is insufficient. Relapse prevention calls for active learning techniques such as role play with feedback. It lends itself to one-to-one work, with activity conducted on occasions away from the office/treatment room and in the client's 'natural environment'.

CHAPTER 12

Work with Non-abusing Partners

We are concerned in this chapter with the *context* of our work with the abuser and in particular the potential to influence outcomes through the inclusion of non-abusing partners in the therapeutic process.

The reality for many abusers is that if they are offered treatment this will be delivered away from their home, will entail their attendance at the office or group room of the treatment provider, and may only require attendance on a weekly or fortnightly basis. In our experience it is still only in a minority of cases that those who live with the abuser are drawn systematically into any therapeutic activity. In the case of those abusers who are in the community and who sustain their relationship with a partner, we believe that the involvement of the non-abusing partner in therapy has potential to optimise treatment effects, not least via the extension and consolidation of treatment gains. This chapter presents some preliminary thoughts as to how to work with non-abusing partners, drawing on the experience of the first author here in running groups for non-abusing partners and offenders, work co-facilitated over a 12-year period with fellow psychologist, Caroline Lovelock. We acknowledge also that more recently attention has been paid to the involvement of non-abusing partners via national initiatives, i.e. in that at least one of the accredited programmes sponsored by the English probation service, namely the Thames Valley Project, has prescribed work for this population.

In addition to this chapter and the work of the Thames Valley Project, we would encourage those who have an interest in this area to seek the texts by Levenson and Morin (2001a and b) and also Virginia Strand (2001).

TREATMENT RATIONALE

Some non-abusing partners choose to stay in relationships with abusers after the abuse has been disclosed. One purpose of work with them is to empower partners to make that decision on the basis of the fullest possible understanding of the abuser's behaviour and the consequences of their decision. If they do choose to maintain the relationship, their ability to protect their children must be maximised.

We believe that non-abusing partners have a unique perspective on the life of the abuser by virtue of their relationship history and (assumed) frequency of contact with the abuser. Whilst it is possible and on occasions likely that the abuser will be motivated to portray himself in a socially desirable light to the worker, we believe it is more difficult for the abuser to disguise issues such as mood, anxieties, aspects of lifestyle and his interpersonal functioning from his partner. (That is not to say, of course, that prior to disclosure of abuse the abuser did not groom the non-abusing partner and manipulate circumstances to disguise his intentions and behaviour.) The non-abusing partner can provide an additional source of information as to the abuser's functioning, validating or otherwise information the abuser has chosen to offer within therapy.

Many abusers we work with are keen to preserve their relationship. Often their denial of the extent of their past offending or minimisation of their responsibility for offending is driven by fear that were the non-abusing partner to learn the extent of their illegal sexual interests, the partner would leave them. In this context therefore we believe the non-abusing partner can play a role in motivating the abuser to address his abuse-related proclivities and to sustain efforts for therapeutic change.

Mann et al. (2002a), amongst others, have articulated so-called dynamic predictors of the risk of reconviction in sexual offenders. One example of these is the domain of social and emotional regulation. This includes issues such as intimacy and social skills. For those abusers within a relationship and suffering intimacy difficulties, the involvement of the non-abusing partner in relationship counselling and psycho-sexual therapy may be crucial. Hanson and Morton-Bourgon (2004) also emphasise ongoing relationship conflict as a potential dynamic risk factor.

Other risk predictors include the attitudes and beliefs the abuser has about his sexual abuse which may serve to promote offending, as well as any sex abuse-related sexual interests. Unsurprisingly, those who sustain generalised attitudes which support their offending are thought to be at increased risk of reabusing others. The circumstances of the abuser's life currently will be important in shaping his attitudes and beliefs. Again, we see an important role for the non-abusing partner, namely that of modelling appropriate and healthy attitudes towards children, women and issues of sexuality. The non-abusing partner may play a crucial role in challenging the abuser who sustains pro-abuse attitudes and may help support and promote positive attitude change.

In the domain of child protection, the non-abusing partner is often that individual in the family charged with the primary responsibility for oversight of children thought to be at risk, often being prescribed as the individual responsible for detecting any concerns a child might have and reporting any concerns about child protection matters to appropriate authorities. The involvement of the non-abusing partner in therapeutic work with the abuser should enrich that partner's knowledge of the abuser's offence history and modus operandi of offending. In turn, this should further advise their child protection strategies through a deeper understanding of the potential lapse and relapse patterns of their formerly abusive partner.

Given the above, therefore, there are several arguments as to why non-abusing partners might and indeed should be involved in supporting the management and treatment of the abuser. We are also concerned however to underline the issue of choice here and the proper support of the non-offending partner through any therapeutic process. We would not wish to see therapeutic work with the non-abusing partner lead to the victimisation or re-victimisation of that individual, or indeed any form of punishment of the non-abusing partner. Similarly, we would not wish work of this sort to imply inevitably any responsibility on the part of the non-abusing partner for the abuser's past actions, or indeed take away from the abuser his ultimate responsibility for his behaviour in the future. It is the abuser's responsibility to control his behaviour and live an offence-free life; if he fails to do so it will be his responsibility alone. However, the non-abusing partner may legitimately support and encourage his efforts towards behavioural control.

EXAMPLE OF AN INTERVENTION

The programme described in Figure 12.1 was developed for work with couples, in group.

Typically, these were couples in which the abuser was living outwith the home but in which both the abuser and partner wanted to achieve not only family resolution in the aftermath of the abuse but also family reunification. The non-abusing partner had expressed a commitment to child protection alongside their willingness to accept the abuser back into the home longer term. The abusers typically would have attended an abuser treatment group over two to three years prior to the couple's programme, that abuser treatment programme having been designed to address their offending behaviour and to promote a relapse prevention plan.

Four or five couples would form each programme, which was a closed group. The expectation of couples on joining was to work within the programme until all objectives were addressed. Typically, this meant that the work progressed over an 18-month minimum time period, often longer. Some couples would choose to repeat the programme, joining another cohort upon completion of their first programme. This would usually be at the request of the non-abusing partners who felt the work to be incomplete or who were not confident in their protective role. The abusers in this programme were all convicted offenders with histories of contact sexual offending against children. In some instances they sought to be reunited with families which included their victim, more usually they sought placement in families which did not include their victim. Sessions were held weekly, on average of two hours duration. The programme was coordinated by two clinical/forensic psychologists who also co-facilitated sessions alongside a third worker, either a probation officer or social worker. Figure 12.1 below describes the nine modules comprising the programme.

Module 1	The programme
	What is expected. The objectives. Introductions. Motivations for joining the programme. What will help, what will hinder? The distinct experiences of the abuser and the non-abusing partner.
Module 2	The research
	What is sexual abuse, who does it, what models help us understand abuse, who is at at risk, how long does the problem last, how do we try to protect children?
Module 3	The couple
	What does it mean to have a non-abusive relationship, what is healthy intimacy, how can we express and communicate emotional and physical needs, what is consent, what is responsibility?
Module 4	The offences
	Functional analysis of offending. 5 W-H of the index offence (who, what, where, when, why and how) and other known abusive acts.
Module 5	The effects
	Primary and secondary victims. Short and long-term effects. The context of the abuse. Other abusive behaviour.
Module 6	The underpinning problem
	Sexual arousal and fantasy, emotional congruence, intimacy skills and relationship deficits.
Module 7	The disinhibitors
	Excuse making, substance misuse, stress.
Module 8	The route to lapse and relapse
	Cycles and patterns of offending. Lapse and relapse models (to include high risk situations, seemingly irrelevant decisions, urge/cravings, abuse and non-abuse schemas, lifestyle changes).
Module 9	The future
	The family after reunification or separation. Boundary setting. The rights of the child. Support of the child. The child protection and criminal justice system. Maintenance of change. The non-abusing partner as leader of change. Practical resources to assist in change.

Figure 12.1: Overview of the couple's programme

The programme outlined above is based on the notion of the abuser and non-abusing partner working in collaboration with a co-working team, including male and female workers.

Our objectives for the non-abusing partners who attended the programme were:

1. that they would learn more of the behaviour of sexual abusers and their tactics for 'seducing' and molesting children

2. that they would learn the detail of their partner's sexually abusive behaviour and appreciate the implications of this for child protection

3. that they might realign their relationship with the abuser subsequent to the abuse so as to be empowered within the relationship and to attain non-abusive intimacy

4. that if they chose to remain in their relationship with the abuser that they understood the abuser's relapse prevention plan and could both monitor this and contribute to its nurturance, and

5. that if they chose to separate from their partner during the course of this programme they be assisted to do so from a position of dignity and strength and with due regard to the welfare of the child or children.

For the abusers our objectives reflected those above but with a particular anticipation that the programme would not only serve to extend and con-solidate the treatment gains made in the core programme, but would also enable the abuser to prioritise the needs of the children involved before their own. It was our expectation that by attending the couple's programme the abuser would learn in a very direct manner the importance of addressing the needs of others, most obviously the non-abusing partner, but also those others involved in the context of the offender's life.

The numbers who have attended the programme across the years were relatively small and we would hesitate to offer any quantitative evaluation of impact here. Questionnaire measures were administered to those who attended the programme at three stages: immediately prior to the programme start, at the nine-month stage, and upon completion of the programme. These measures were the Generalised Contentment Scale, the Index of Self Concept, the Index of Marital Satisfaction, and Index of Sexual Satisfaction (all referenced in Simmons 1986) and the Attitudes Towards Women Scale (Spence and Helmreich 1972).

Invariably, these questionnaire measures reflected change across time, the scores upon completion with few exceptions representing 'improve-ment' over the scores at the start of the programme. Intriguingly, at the nine-month stage scores would often suggest a worsening of the couple's situation. We suspect that when couples joined the programme they may have been motivated to under-represent difficulties. As they relaxed into the programme and began to trust the workers, we suspect they may have felt better able to disclose personal difficulties or deficits. The improved scores at the end of the programme on the psychometric measures reflect either general improvement across the programme or, alternatively, the client portraying themselves as improved so as to please the facilitators.

We note here that it is common practice to evaluate programmes via the use of psychometric tests, and in the absence of robust recidivism data to assume such psychometric measures are valid indices of change. We would recommend that psychometric measures are not used as the sole indices of change, given their transparency and susceptibility to socially desirable responses. We often bemoan that clients can learn to 'talk the talk' but not 'walk the walk'. Some clients 'talk the talk' in their answers to questionnaires.

THE THAMES VALLEY PROJECT PARTNER'S PROGRAMME

One of the treatment programmes accredited for sex offenders in England and Wales, the Thames Valley Project (Still *et al.* 2001), has recognised the need for intervention with the partners of offenders. 'Partner' here is a generic term, but essentially refers to women who may have children in their care who are potentially at risk. The women may include those who deny their partner did anything wrong and those who have little detailed knowledge of their partner's offending prior to attending.

The programme aims to help the partners make and maintain 'informed decisions about their relationship with the offender and their children's safety'. For the women who choose to remain with the abuser, the programme is designed to help them protect children from sexual abuse from whatever source and also assist in relapse prevention with the abuser. Each woman, regardless of whether they choose to stay in the relationship with the abuser, is offered help to understand and deal with the effects of their partner's abuse on the victim, family and themselves. If the woman chooses not to stay with the abuser, the programme aims to help that woman with child protection and protection of themselves.

The programme manual indicates that this is essentially a women only group based programme consisting of 18 sessions of two hours, run on a modular basis over 18 consecutive weeks at a set time. The authors specify a maximum of eight women per group. The work offered is based on the principle of gradual exposure, with general information offered about sexual abuse in the early stages, progressing to the specifics of their partner's behaviour and their situation. In outline the programme covers the following:

- an introduction to the programme, including ground rules and aims
- defining the problem to include a review of the impact of abuse and disclosure on the participants and their family life, to define what is meant by 'sexual abuse', and for participants to acknowledge and understand denial and its impact on others
- decision making and problem solving, including the participants identifying and prioritising decisions that need to be made in relation to themselves, the victim, their families and abuser
- general information about sex offenders (how sex offenders operate) and the application of theory here to their partner ('my partner's pattern of offending')
- victim awareness and communicating with children about sexual abuse
- the effects of abuse on family relationships, including handling the problem and opening up communication with the child
- the effects of the abuse on the non-offending partner, including impact on relationships with others, the empowerment of the non-abusing partner, dealing with other people's responses to the partner's offending and challenging the grooming behaviour of the abuser
- decision making: revisiting options and decisions made
- the drafting of a 'new family life plan', covering 'alert signs' to look out for in the offender, dealing with high risk situations, recognising signs of abuse in the child, strategies for child protection and responses to suspicions of abuse
- completion of evaluation materials (psychometrics).

The Partner's Programme here is set out in a detailed manual with the theoretical underpinnings outlined, alongside descriptions of each module and the support of materials necessary to progress the work. Readers are directed to the treatment manual for further information (Still, Faux and Wilson 2001).

BROADER THERAPEUTIC ISSUES WITH NON-ABUSING PARTNERS

Whilst the above represents attempts to engage non-abusing partners in work with abusers to promote child protection in those committed to family resolution, it is important to note the particular therapeutic needs of non-abusing partners. A landmark text by Virginia Strand (2002) is strongly recommended reading here. Strand focuses on interventions with non-offending mothers in incest families and argues that treatment with incest family members is often cost-effective when it is intensive and long term. Long term here is described as longer than six months. By 'intensive' she means that treatment is multi-modal, involving opportunities for individual, group, couple *and* family therapy. She describes six stages of work with mothers here, as follows.

1.   *Starting engagement and assessment:* includes an assessment of how traumatised the mother has been by her child's abuse. This builds on the traumagenic dynamics model put forward by Finkelhor and Browne (1985) by evaluating issues of 'betrayal', 'powerlessness', 'stigmatisation' and 'traumatic sexualisation'. Also assessed here, and from the 'strengths' perspective (Saleeby 1997), are issues of the woman's competencies in her roles as mother and wife. A sexual history is also taken.

2.   *Early intervention to address trauma effects*: addresses issues of powerlessness and betrayal in particular and the ambivalence mothers often feel in this situation as a result of the conflict between their allegiance to their partner and that to their children.

3.   *Strengthening coping strategies:* with a particular focus on helping the mother deal with anxiety, to ventilate feelings, to reduce faulty thinking about issues such as responsibility, guilt and the like, and to reduce depressive symptoms.

4.   *Surfacing traumatic effects of the incest behaviour:* the mothers are helped to explore the nature, duration and extent of the abuse and in so doing review core beliefs they may have had about themselves and thereby reassessing and re-evaluating their lives.

5.   *Identifying relationship consequences of the incest behaviour:* exploring the consequences of sexual abuse on women's roles as mothers and the consequences of the sexual abuse on a woman's role as a partner.

6.   *Working through a resolution:* including an emphasis on the mother committing to 'the process of establishing a closer and...more empathic relationship with her child'.

The reader is referred to Strand's text for further detail of both individual, group and family based therapeutic activities in incest cases.

FAMILY REUNIFICATION

The issue of when or whether an abuser should be rehabilitated to a family which includes children is a vexed one. There are those who believe (Elliott 2004) that the risk is too great under such circumstances and that the non-abusing partner should be encouraged to separate from the abuser, i.e. reunification should never occur. The current authors have encountered many treatment programmes which will not accommodate child abusers who live within families, in any circumstances. Passions often run high about these issues. It would seem that a starting point for any proposed rehabilitation of the abuser to the family must be an analysis of the particular family concerned, decision making being based on a case by case basis and with due respect for individual differences.

Levenson and Morin (2001b) have produced a useful 'safety checklist' to assist in the evaluation of abusers and non-offending parents. In the case of the non-abusing partner, they have articulated criteria for determining their capacity for reducing risk based on a competency framework, 'competency' here being described across various levels. At the lower levels, it is expected that the non-abusing partner will display knowledge and understanding of issues. At the higher levels, the non-abusing partner is expected to apply that knowledge and comprehension and solve problem situations as they arise.

The skills Levenson and Morin expect of the non-abusing partner are:

- acknowledgement of feelings
- acceptance of responsibility to manage risk factors in the home
- acknowledgement of the impact of child sexual abuse on children
- recognition of the indicators of child sexual abuse
- acknowledgement of own childhood sexual abuse
- understanding of the offender's patterns, chains, cycles and relapse prevention plan
- knowledge of how to protect children from sexual abuse
- implementation of family safety planning.

TIPS AND HINTS

In a chapter such as this we can only identify some of the key issues in work with non-abusing partners. We believe it is crucial that those who engage in this work should be well informed as to the impact of abuse on families, both the primary and secondary victims, but should also have an awareness of the broader context of the management of children with sexually abusive behaviour problems, not an uncommon sequelae of sexual abuse. We would recommend the text by Burton, Rassmussen and colleagues here, *Treating Children with Sexually Abusive Behaviour Problems* (Burton *et al.* 1998).

Our experience would suggest the importance of long-term follow-up in this area of work. Often couples work hard to achieve family reunification but can underestimate the difficulties of maintaining a relationship once therapeutic activity has ceased and surveillance by social work agencies has lessened. We advise that couples be provided with opportunities to call their therapists for support or 'booster' work as the need arises.

Where family reunification occurs it is important that issues beyond child protection be considered. It may be necessary to promote the general parenting skills of the abuser and non-abusing partner and referral for parenting skills training may be required. Similarly, in some cases it may be important to help the couple develop informal social support systems. In turn this may draw the couple into making decisions about who and what to tell of the abuser's history and circumstances. Again, the therapist may need to be available to counsel the couple here.

In working with couples and family reunification the worker needs to be informed of family traditions and structure. Lewis (2001) has commented on this issue and has suggested that mistakes can be made which may lead to the offender and family dropping out of therapy. He suggests that many African-American families for example maintain more role flexibility between spouses than do white families, and also that parenting by the oldest child may be more acceptable/expected in some families than others. He draws on the work of Minuchin (1974) and comments on how extended family structures may be vulnerable to boundary role and confusion. We would endorse Lewis' sentiments here and emphasise the importance of understanding the uniqueness of families and each family's culture when dealing with issues of family resolution and reunification.

Whether to work towards family reunification or not is an issue which generates professional anxiety and one which can lead to inter-professional hostility and suspicion. Reunification can only be promoted if based on a clear assessment of risk *and* a clear risk management strategy. Caution is expressed about the use of treatment providers in assessing risk, given the potential for their views to be skewed in the therapeutic relationship (see Chapter 3). Those who attempt to evaluate risk, including those who contribute to child protection conferences or indeed via the family courts, should seek detail from treatment providers as to objectives and methods used in work with the couple, the detail of how treatment integrity is maintained and how treatment is evaluated. They should seek information not only as to success but as to expectations not met and sessions which were non-productive. They should draw from the treatment provider information as to likely relapse issues. The therapist should be asked whether treatment was compromised in any way (e.g. by lack of resources or skills). The worker should be asked whether he or she formed any special allegiance with either partner and the reasons for this. Communication has to be a two-way process; the therapist must be prepared to have his or her work subject to detailed scrutiny, while the risk evaluator has an obligation and duty to ask challenging and probing questions.

CHAPTER 13

On-line Sexual Activity

It is evident from our consultancy practice nationwide that many staff face an increasing demand to manage those offenders whose behaviour has had a focus on on-line sexual activity, be that possessing illegal images, distributing offence-related pornography, or using electronic media to groom and entrap potential victims. In the companion text to this, little attention was paid to the evaluation of abusers in this domain. It is timely now to redress that balance and share our thoughts on the evaluation and management of those who use the Internet to sustain and promote their offence-related interests. We have a sense in drafting this chapter that work in this area is very much 'in progress'. There have been major contributions to the field from the COPINE project in Ireland (Quayle and Taylor 2003) and Elizabeth Griffin and David Delmonico (Delmonico, Griffin and Moriarity 2001) in the USA, who have developed and encouraged our professional endeavours in this area.

Notwithstanding the work of the projects referred to above, very fundamental questions have yet to be answered. For example, what should we make of a father convicted of possessing a collection of indecent images of children downloaded from the Internet and the likelihood of him molesting his own children, particularly in the absence of any other forensic history, including allegations of abuse? Should we treat all those who are convicted of possession of offence-related pornography as being likely to progress to 'hands on' abuse? If so, how do we determine the likely rate or timescale for escalation of abuse from possession to molestation? Similarly, what should be our strategy for working with offenders in this domain?

Our experience to date is that many of the men we have worked with who have offences related to the possession and distribution of pornography drawn from the Internet are often articulate, professional, assertive and well rehearsed in their arguments. They are often individuals whose response to attempts to counsel and guide them seems qualitatively different to that of many abusers we have worked with, particularly those abusers of a more passive nature. It has often seemed as if we are trying to manage the problem of recreational paedophilia in men whose fundamental value system believes in the legitimacy of using images of children for sexual pleasure.

We have other questions. In terms of our approaches to risk prediction, can we assume that the level of sophistication an abuser displays in the retrieval, storage and collection of images (including the level of sophistication of attempts to disguise or encrypt material) relates to risk? Similarly, can we assume that the diversity of images viewed in terms of gender and age of subject, the sexual acts portrayed and the like relates to risk? In this context do the same factors influence the risk of a repeat of the viewing of abusive images as the risk of committing contact offences?

Interesting ethical issues also arise. For example, given the extremely wide use of the Internet to access pornography, what percentage of workers have been or are regular users of Internet pornography and how does this impact on their approach to the management of those whose abuse stems from on-line sexual activity? It might be, for example, that the pornography using worker may be implicitly more tolerant of downloading offences than contact offences. Conversely, the worker may be more punitive in approach to downloading offences as if to distance the abuser's activity from their own. Clearly the opportunities for empirical research in these domains is vast and urgent.

ASSESSMENT

As with all abusers, it is important to conduct a proper assessment to guide management (including treatment) plans. To date the empirical basis for assessment is still developing. The work referred to so far makes some suggestions which have face validity but are not yet validated. Notably, we do not know how useful actuarial measures of static risk factors will prove to be with this population. (For a review of these instruments see Chapter 2 of this text or our companion text, Briggs et al. 1998.)

The actuarial tools in common usage were developed on samples of abusers who were convicted prior to the advent of the Internet. There have been no follow-up studies of sufficient length to guide us in their usage for this abuser population. We do not know if factors such as non-contact offences, stranger victim and male victim have the same aggravating effects as they have been shown to in relation to other abuse patterns (Hanson and Bussiere 1998; Thornton 2000). It may be wise therefore to avoid the application of actuarial instruments not standardised for the Internet abuser.

David Middleton (2003a) has reviewed evidence on the correlation between the use of child pornography and contact offending. Samples vary widely from a high of 40 per cent (actually based on abusers buying material by post, not Internet use and therefore not of direct relevance), downwards. We are not aware to date of any study which gives information about those factors which predict progression from viewing of images to contact offending.

We strongly advise that before any professional attempt to investigate an individual charged with offences involving on-line sexual activity is made that the assessor receive proper training in the infrastructure which may support this offending. In other words, workers should be familiar with the hardware and operating systems of computers, how sexually explicit images are retrieved, how contact can be established with those who share similar interests, the technology pertaining to the transmission of live sexual acts, the methodologies used to encrypt and disguise images, and how images are manipulated, can be categorised and stored. We are very aware that unless the worker has some degree of sophistication as to this technology that the abuser may mislead and misrepresent his actions, for example, suggesting that he inadvertently stumbled across sexually explicit images of children and the like.

Assessing the images

When attempting to evaluate the nature of the images used by the abuser we have found the following schema for classification drafted by the COPINE project to be useful (see Table 13.1) (Taylor *et al.* 2001).

Table 13.1 Classification of on-line images

Level	Category
1	Indicative
2	Nudist
3	Erotica
4	Posing
5	Erotic posing
6	Explicit erotic posing
7	Explicit sexual activity
8	Assault
9	Gross assault
10	Sadistic/bestiality

Level 1 images are described as those of children, clothed, but in which the way they are organised by the collector suggests 'inappropriateness'. Level 2 pictures ('nudist') are those of children who are naked or semi-naked, drawn from naturist settings. Level 3 images (erotica) may be of children in varying degrees of nakedness or in their underwear but with the pictures taken surreptitiously. Images at Level 4 are those of children deliberately posing (whether clothed or otherwise) but again with the context and organisation of the images giving rise to concern. 'Erotic posing' (Level 5) is used to describe those images of children in 'sexualised or provocative' poses, again regardless of the degree of clothing. Explicit erotic posing (Level 6) concerns a focus on the general area of the child. At Level 7 (explicit sexual activity) the images feature the child in sexual activity (e.g. masturbation and oral sex) but not including an adult. Level 8 images are of 'assault', i.e. the digital touching of the child by an adult. Gross assault images characterise Level 9, and are defined as 'grossly obscene pictures of sexual assault including penetration sex, masturbation or oral sex including an adult'. Finally, at Level 10, images are described as sadistic or bestial. These are pictures depicting an animal in some form of sexual contact with a child or the child appearing to be subject to pain, being held or bound.

This matter has also been considered by the Sentencing Advisory Panel (2003). Sentencers in England and Wales are recommended to consider both the nature of the indecent material and the offender's involvement with it in determining the seriousness of a particular offence. The Panel considered the COPINE classification and conflated some of the categories at the lower level. On this basis the courts, police and prosecuting authorities in England and Wales use the following classification:

- Level 1: Images depicting nudity or erotic posing with no sexual activity.
- Level 2: Sexual activity between children or solo masturbation by a child.
- Level 3: Non-penetrative sexual activity between adult(s) and child(ren).
- Level 4: Penetrative sexual activity between adult(s) and child(ren).
- Level 5: Sadism or bestiality.

ASSESSING THE ACTIVITY
It is important to begin to assess what is motivating the abuser's behaviour. As with all sexual abuse, motivating factors may be primarily sexual or be driven by a combination of other feelings and thoughts. Arousal and attitudes may be situational or generalised (see Chapter 2). Carnes, Delmonico and Griffin (2001) suggest four categories of 'cybersex user'. These are:

- 'recreational' users who have managed to remain oblivious of the social consequences of their behaviour
- 'discovery' users who may be driven by curiosity and excitement
- 'predisposed' users who may be feeding an interest which was controlled until there was easy access to stimuli, and
- 'lifelong compulsives' who may be sexually preoccupied and would also be likely to be acting out their urges in different ways.

They are mindful that distal events (such as an individual's early sexual experience) and proximal events (such as an existing sexual interest in children) in combination may form the 'setting' events which relate to both Internet use and the development of problematic cognitions. They make the point that engagement with the Internet is a dynamic process; some who misuse the Internet may *decrease* their level of engagement, some may increase their engagement. Where escalation occurs, processes such as the acquisition of computer skills and reinforcement by a community engaged in a similar behaviour may be relevant. Furthermore, escalation may be influenced by so-called 'cognitive-social factors', i.e. increased fantasy/sexual behaviour, reduced offline social contact, increased empowerment and control, and validation and normalisation. Internet use may escalate towards non-offending behaviour, e.g. involvement in other pornography or cybersex with adults. It may also escalate towards other offending behaviours such as downloading child pornography, the distribution and production of child pornography, engagement with Internet seduction of children, and contact offending.

We recommend when evaluating the abuser here that detailed questions are asked as to the nature and function of the on-line sexual behaviour. The framework below represents routine questions we would expect to be addressed in our evaluation of an abuser involved in inappropriate on-line sexual activity. This is developed from the work of Carnes, Delmonico and colleagues (Carnes, Delmonico and Griffin 2001; Delmonico, Griffin and Moriarity 2001).

SAMPLE TARGETS FOR INTERVENTION

History

1. When did the abuser first start their illegal on-line activity? How?
2. Have there been changes in frequency/usage/content/ involvement of others/change in their behaviour/change in

reported satisfaction or frustration levels/disruption in lifestyle/employment/risk taking on-line?

3. Have there been other life changes, e.g. relationship change, increase in use of alcohol/drugs or other disinhibitors?

4. What efforts has the abuser made in the past to stop?

5. What coping strategies does the abuser have in place to deal with issues such as stresses/mood/depression/anger?

6. Does the abuser have any preconvictions?

7. Have any fantasies been acted out with real adults or children (which may or may not be of an explicitly sexual nature)?

8. Have there been any attempts at contact in real life with people (adults/children) met on-line?

9. Have images been shared with others offline (work colleagues, children)?

10. Have images been exchanged with others? (How has this been done, what volume and what purpose did this serve?)

11. Have others been involved in creating or discussing images?

12. Status as a collector? Has the abuser provided missing bits of collections for others? Has the abuser distributed images to others?

13. Status as a teacher of others (wise ones)? Has the abuser recounted sexual experiences (adult/child) to others?

Action

1. What are the number of total hours that the abuser typically spends on-line in any one week?

2. What proportion of this time was spent in contact with others sexually interested in children or in downloading images?

3. How many times did the user switch on the computer for access to pornography? Briefest time......... Longest time.........?

4. What times of the day did the abuser access the Internet?

5. How many Internet media were accessed?

Newsgroups...
Internet relay chat...
Bulletin boards...
Email...
Video conferencing...
Other?...

6. How did the offender behave in respect of each? What level of pleasure was associated with these activities?

7. What nicknames did the abuser use (if any) and what did they mean to that person?

8. How was material from the Internet saved and organised (storage, labelling/filenames/encrypting)?

9. How much time did the abuser spend offline with collected material, editing, saving or as an aid to masturbation?

10. Have images been created through scanning from existing pictures or by digital camera (manipulating images or adding text)?

11. Did the abuser disrupt his employment in order to access pornography/equipment and/or potential victims?

Excitement/risk

1. Did the abuser take risks in terms of accessing the material (either because of others in the house or same room) or in storing it?

2. Have images been downloaded while others were in the room or in close proximity? If so, who, where, when?

3. Did the abuser experience a sense of excitement in anticipation of going on-line and/or a sense of frustration or irritation when blocked from doing so?

4. Did the abuser represent himself as other individuals (either same or other sex or age)?

5. What attempts did the abuser make to contact children through the Internet?

Reflection

1. What level of preoccupation did the abuser experience with regard to 'reliving' past experiences?

2. How much time did the abuser spend thinking about his latest Internet experience (chat or image) or planning the next?

3. Did the abuser keep details of other on-line people and reflect on these?

4. Did the abuser keep making promises to stop going on-line and then break them?

Arousal

1. What level of masturbation was associated with on-line activities?

2. Did masturbation take place on or offline?

3. What increase or change in sexual activities had occurred since accessing the Internet?

4. Did the individual engage in virtual sexual relationships with other (adults or children), e.g. through live chatrooms?

5. Had there been a change in the kinds of text or images accessed (age or other characteristics or the child, types of images and level of victimisation)?

6. Did arousal happen to other non-child images?

7. What types of images were viewed?
   - nudist
   - erotica
   - posing
   - erotic posing
   - explicit posing
   - explicit sex activity
   - assault
   - gross assault
   - sadistic/bestiality?

8. How diverse were the child images viewed?
   Age/sex/numbers/specific type etc.

Impact

1. What had been the level of general disruption to the abuser's life that being on-line had caused, particularly in relation to work or real-life social relationships?

2. Had there been a reduction in sexual interests with their partner (where relevant)?

3. Had there been emotional withdrawal from family members or friends?

4. Did the abuser experience a preoccupation with accessing the Internet such that there were ongoing difficulties in concentrating?

5. Did the abuser experience difficulties in concentrating on or keeping to offline commitments?

6. What are the abuser's existing social networks and levels of emotional support?

7. What level of social isolation is present?

Other sources of information

In addition to interviewing the abuser, it may be important also to interview those who have direct or indirect knowledge of the abuser's activities. The abuser's partner and in some cases his employer, for example, may help develop our understanding of the abuser's activity here, including the degree of secretiveness, 'obsessiveness' and costs involved in supporting the activity. Those who have gathered evidence and investigated the hardware and software of the abuser's personal computer may allow useful insights as to the level of sophistication of activity here, the extent of activity, and any pattern to on-line sexual activity, including frequency and duration of usage.

Self reporting of on-line sexual activity in response to questionnaires is a possibility and we are mindful of materials which are being developed for this purpose (O'Brien 2003).

ESCALATION

One area of particular concern to practitioners is that of whether on-line sexual activity will escalate into 'hands on' abuse. The following represents clinical signs to be considered in the evaluation of escalation. We believe we should treat the following behaviours with some concern:

- The abuser who takes more risks in indulging in on-line sexual activity, for example, the abuser who becomes less concerned if family members or work mates find him indulging in on-line sexual activity, the abuser who makes less effort to disguise or anonymise himself when indulging in chatroom activity and the like.

- Where the abuser makes deliberate effort to draw a child or vulnerable adult into the activity, for example, sitting a child on his knee whilst scanning the net for pornography.

- Where the offender makes effort to contact children via the Web and in the disguise of being another child or adolescent.

- Where the abuser seeks opportunity to observe on-line the molestation or seduction of children or the rape of vulnerable adults as it is actually occurring.

- Where there is progression in the intensity of images used, with collection moving from erotica through to imagery involving the penetrative abuse of others through to acts of sadism and bestiality.

- Where the offender's activity is reported by them to be no longer satisfying, particularly where the offender uses on-line sexual activity to facilitate masturbatory activity and where post-ejaculation feelings of psychological tension and craving still exist.

- Where the abuser makes connection with known sexual abusers who have actively molested children in the past.

- Where the on-line sexual activity co-exists alongside deterioration in the abuser's overall levels of self-regulation, for example, as typified by lapse into alcohol or substance misuse.

- Where images of a readily identifiable child are collected and where the location and whereabouts of that child are known to the abuser.

INTERVENTION
Objectives
These are suggested objectives following intervention:

- the abuser will have explored the pattern of his on-line sexual activity, will have determined those times at which he is most likely to engage in on-line sexual activity, any specific triggers to this, and strategies for managing such precursors or trigger events

- the abuser will have articulated why on-line activity should not be considered a 'victimless' crime

- the abuser will have been advised of the legal position regarding Internet offences, including sentencing guidelines and how offences are classified

- the abuser will have ensured that any personal computing equipment has been confiscated or destroyed or, where essential for work purposes, that appropriate physical or other safeguards have been drafted to curtail improper usage of the equipment

- the abuser will have explored the influence of Internet misuse on sexual fantasy, including offence related fantasies and will have developed strategies to deal with them

- the abuser will have learnt tactics to combat the sense of de-individuation and anonymity that may accompany problematic Internet usage

- the abuser will have detailed to his partner or therapeutic chaperone the nature and extent of his past on-line sexual activity and will have drafted an agreement with that partner or chaperone to ensure surveillance and monitoring of his future behaviour

- the abuser will have developed techniques to achieve a balanced lifestyle including healthy social outlets, and will have a repertoire of skills for the management of urges and cravings and generalised anxiety. For those clients who have used the Internet as a vehicle to avoid negative emotional states (e.g. boredom, anxiety), intervention should help the abuser understand how he uses the Internet to regulate and control his emotional state and to develop strategies for healthy emotional regulation.

Strategies for intervention

We have to determine how best to intervene with Internet offenders. It could be argued that existing group work programmes for sex offenders should be offered to Internet offenders, but with perhaps modification or additions made to address offence specific issues which relate to on-line offending. Alternatively, there is an argument that Internet offenders should be offered one-to-one work, rather than group work, as meeting with other offenders might feed that sense of being part of a larger group of like-minded individuals. (The risk here is that of the abusers' attitudes and beliefs about their Internet offending being consolidated by contact with others or of the abuser learning more sophisticated methods.) Further, some would argue that 'low risk' Internet offenders (notwithstanding the difficulties of identifying such a group on the basis of our limited research base to date) could be treated individually, high risk individuals should be treated in groups (see Middleton 2003a).

We do not know how best to address responsivity factors in the treatment of Internet offenders and we should be wary of premature confidence as to how best to intervene with them. That is not to say that we do not have useful pointers as to targets for intervention and tentative objectives for intervention have been suggested above. One of these relates to anonymity and de-individuation. Demetriou and Silke (2003) commented on the phenomenon of de-individuation. They describe this as a psychological state 'where inner restraints are lost when individuals are not seen or paid attention to as individuals'; such a state they suggest leads people to act aggressively and selfishly and less altruistically. They cite McKenna and Bargh (2000):

> Some of the outcomes of de-individuation include a weakened ability for an individual to regulate his or her behaviour, reduced ability to engage in

rational, long-term planning, and a tendency to react to immediate cues or based largely on his or her current emotional state. Furthermore, an individual will be less likely to care what others think of his or her behaviour and may even have a reduced awareness of what others have said or done. These effects can culminate in impulsive and disinhibited behaviour... (p.61)

Anonymity is said to be a key cause of de-individuation – we are more likely to misbehave if we believe our identity is unknown. The Internet offers an illusion of anonymity to the abuser. Techniques to combat the sense of anonymity include the abuser being instructed to imagine key individuals observing their on-line activity, individuals who would be disapproving of the activity. In imagination the abuser is asked to re-create the sequence of behaviour involved in Internet misuse but to imagine an observer or observers. The abuser may be encouraged to imagine the observers questioning him about his behaviour.

Concerning the objective of the abuser exploring the pattern to his Internet misuse, we refer back to Taylor and Quayle's (2003) model of potential problematic Internet use. In their pilot treatment manual (Version 3), Taylor and Quayle suggest that clients should apply the model and offer a written description of their offending, one which accords with that provided by police/forensic reports. They suggest that the client describes those factors that provided the context for their offending alongside the problematic self statements that facilitated the offending as well as writing the detail of the steps the abuser took in moving down the offence process. Whilst they encourage the client to outline any environmental facts that may have supported the offence behaviour, they also suggest the client describes what factors might have limited the offending behaviour.

Taylor and Quayle offer useful questions to be asked of the client and which may help the analysis above:

- Did the Internet change the way you were thinking and why?
- At any time did you feel what you were doing was a problem to you?
- What was the effect on the way you were feeling when you found child pornography?
- Have you at any time tried to stop using the Internet to access child pornography?
- Why do you think you were not successful?
- Does this affect the way you feel about your ability to control using it in the future?

Concerning the objective of the abuser articulating why on-line activity should not be considered as 'victimless' crime, first the client may be encouraged to articulate the child's experience. The client should explain the detail of one of the child sexual abuse images he has viewed (who was involved, what was depicted, where was the child). The abuser should then respond to questions such as:

- How old was the child when the image was taken (to include an estimate of the age of the child at youngest)?
- How would the child have been recruited?
- What was the child likely to have been thinking and feeling at the time?
- Would this be apparent from the way they looked?
- Why might the child have been unable to resist involvement?
- What long-term effects might the child experience, e.g. in their relationship with others, in their attitudes towards sex, in their well-being and adjustment, in their ability to disclose the abuse?

Similar questions can be asked about other children who have featured in on-line images.

One crucial aspect of empathy (see Chapter 9) is the excuses and distorted thinking the abuser may have used to accompany their Internet misuse. The abuser should be encouraged to list the beliefs he held as to why the offence was 'victimless'. Once these beliefs have been identified, the abuser should be assisted to generate counter arguments to the beliefs. The abuser may also consider the behaviour of the pornographer involved in obtaining and distributing the images. Questions such as 'how was the child directed when the images were taken?, 'how did the director ignore any resistance on the part of the child?, and 'what would the director have said to justify his/her behaviour?' might usefully be asked.

Other techniques for addressing empathy may be adapted from our treatment programmes for other sex offences, e.g. writing a victim apology letter and responding to questions asked by victims (e.g. why did you think it was acceptable to look at pictures of me and masturbate?), or sculpts or drawings depicting who might also be in the room with an abused child, e.g. to film or coerce them into posing for the image.

At the time of writing this text (autumn 2005), the National Probation Directorate is in the process of developing an accredited treatment programme for Internet sexual offenders (Hayes *et al.* 2005). It is offered as a group work or one-to-one programme and excludes high deviancy offenders who should be referred to longer mainstream accredited sex offender programmes (see Chapter 5).

The proposed dynamic risk factors to be targeted are drawn from the work of Thornton (1999), Middleton (2004), Middleton *et al.* (2005a, 2005b) and Quayle and Taylor (2002). These factors relate to motivation and readiness to change, intimacy, emotional loneliness, social skills and self-esteem associated with formation of insecure attachments, sexual preference for children, inability to deal with negative emotional affect and sexual preoccupation and lack of victim awareness and/or empathic response. Programme methods are similar in type to those used in the other accredited programmes (see Chapter 5) with content adapted to suit the particular nature of the offending and relevant dynamic risk factors.

TIPS AND HINTS

In the body of the text above suggestion has been made as to targets for the evaluation of on-line sexual activity and some of the methodologies which might be useful in this area. We would urge 'broad spectrum' thinking in the evaluation of those whose abuse relates to on-line sexual activity. In addition to evaluation of the nature and function of the on-line activity itself, we also suggest that the abuser's overall context be understood, i.e. that the offender's behaviour here is placed within the broader framework of his personal and sexual history. This should include other forensic history, current lifestyle and circumstances, and in particular ensure that evidence is gathered of other sex offence related sexual activities, of socio-affective functioning deficits, of problems in self-regulation or more pervasive attitudes that might support abuse.

It strikes us that this is an area which is fast developing. Each year our theorising and researching on this issue seems to expand. We strongly urge practitioners to keep abreast of this emerging field and to test continually the messages of this chapter. It may well be that much of what we have written here becomes outdated or overtaken by empirically guided strategies.

The phenomenology of on-line sexual activity often contains quite obsessive, if not compulsive, behavioural patterns. Indeed, those who indulge in such activity often comment on their sense of 'losing time' whilst indulging in their interests, but also of the psychological tension and anxiety they experience when they are frustrated in their attempts to indulge. Those who specialise in this area may find it useful to refresh their memory on the clinical literature concerning anxiety reduction, the management of obsessive/compulsive behaviours, as well as the more specific sex offender literature pertaining to urge and craving management, lifestyle change and the like.

In evaluating on-line sexual activity it may be useful to study the abuser's spending habits. Relapse may be associated, for example, with the purchase of new or more sophisticated equipment. Where the abuser is generally cooperative, he may be invited to share details of standing orders and the like which may give some indication as to spending patterns here.

We should note that, similar to our work with contact abusers, our experience is that it has proven invaluable to involve non-offending partners in the assessment and treatment of those Internet offenders who remain in an intimate relationship. In assessing the abuser we have often asked the partner to provide complementary information, e.g. her observations on the pattern of the abuser's Internet usage, how he has maintained privacy and secrecy for his illegal use, his mood, his engagement with the family, his comfort with and seeking of intimacy and his explanations/rationalisations for offending. We have invited non-offending partners to collaborate in treatment, for example, by inviting them to set ground rules for the offender's behaviour in the home. One partner determined that all magazine pornography and video-taped pornography that both she and her partner had enjoyed prior to discovering of his possession of Internet child pornography would be destroyed and no other such material would be brought into the home. Another partner of a man convicted of possession of child Internet pornography determined that whilst a laptop computer would remain in the home as it was necessary for her work, her partner would not be given permission to use the computer unless she was present in the room. Further, his use of the laptop would be confined to the family sitting room. We have encouraged the abuser and partner to develop or rekindle joint activities/hobbies that promote their social interaction with others as a couple and assist in addressing lifestyle imbalances. Where there have been issues of sexual dysfunction in the relationship we have made referral to appropriate sex therapists.

Finally, we should make comment on the use of child pornography images in treatment. The worker here must consider very carefully the appropriateness or otherwise of them viewing the images that have been involved in the client's offences. This is an ethical issue and there is a clear argument to be made that viewing such images constitutes a reabuse of the child. We do not think it is necessary or advisable for assessors or treatment providers to view the images in most cases. In our experience it is usually possible to get adequate description of the images to make clear what the abuser was seeing. Indeed, the names of websites being accessed give helpful clues. We believe that repeated exposure to such images has the potential to influence the psychological health and sexuality of those who view, unless very careful debriefing, counselling and support is offered on a regular basis to the worker concerned. Whilst on rare occasions it may prove useful to challenge the distorted perceptions of the abuser as to the age of the children involved, i.e. by confronting with a specimen image, this should be done as a last resort, we believe, and by selecting images ideally of children who are clothed or who fall at the lower level of the COPINE category.

We would hope that very clear guidelines and protocols will be in place determining which professionals should have access to images and under what circumstances.

CHAPTER 14

Resources

We conclude this text by highlighting resources we have found useful in supporting our work with sexual abusers. These are a range of organisations, texts and websites. The authors can be contacted via their email addresses and welcome feedback and comment on this text: DBriggsAsc@aol.com and roger5ken@aol.com

GOVERNMENTAL DEPARTMENTS

Department for Constitutional Affairs

www.dca.gov.uk

The website includes reference to the protocol for judicial case management in Public Law Children Act cases.

Home Office

www.homeoffice.gov.uk

The website includes sections on crime and policing, research and statistics, with useful links to information on current activity, e.g. the development of sexual assault referral centres (SARCs), action on drug assisted sexual assault, the rape action plan and issues in the disqualification of people working with children.

Sexual Crime Reduction Team

sexual.offences@homeoffice.gsi.gov.uk

The Scottish Executive

www.scotland.gov.uk

This website contains useful publications/research links.

ALSO

US Department of Health and Human Services

www.os.dhhs.gov

National Clearinghouse on Child Abuse and Neglect

http://nccanch.acf.hhs.gov

Office of Juvenile Justice and Delinquency Prevention

http://ojjdp.ncjrs.org

National Crime Victims Research and Treatment Centre

www.musc.edu/cvc/

This website is dedicated to victim treatment and research including victims of sexual crime.

Correctional Service Canada

www.csc-scc.gc.ca

This website includes extensive research reports.

ORGANISATIONS

National Organisation for the Treatment of Abusers

www.nota.co.uk

This organisation is committed to promoting effective sex offender management in the UK and Ireland.

The Association for the Treatment of Sexual Abusers

www.atsa.com

Based in North America, this international organisation focuses specifically on the prevention of sexual abuse through effective management of sex offenders.

Barnardo's

www.barnados.org.uk

This website contains useful resources, including links to 'research and publications' and 'internet safety'.

National Society for the Prevention of Cruelty to Children

www.nspcc.org.uk

This website contains links to 'Information and Resources' and to 'Publications/Research'.

British Association for the Study and Prevention of Child Abuse and Neglect

www.baspcan.org.uk

This charity aims to prevent physical, emotional and sexual abuse and neglect of children.

International Society for the Prevention of Child Abuse and Neglect

www.ispcan.org

Their mission is 'to support individuals and organisations working to protect children from abuse and neglect worldwide'.

American Professional Society on the Abuse of Children

www.apsac.org

The Family Violence and Sexual Assault Institute

www.fvsai.org

An international organisation providing information, networking, training, education and programme evaluation.

National Centre for Missing and Exploited Children

www.missingkids.com

Provides a range of services including a Cyber Helpline that the public may use to report child sexual exploitation as well as technical assistance to professionals involved in the prevention and investigation/prosecution of cases involving exploited children.

JOURNALS

Sexual Abuse: A Journal of Research and Treatment

Published by Plenum

Editor: Howard Barbaree

Visit: www.atsa.com and follow links.

Journal of Sexual Aggression

Published by NOTA and Taylor and Francis Journals

Editor: Simon Hackett

Visit www.nota.co.uk and follow links.

Child Abuse Review

Published by John Wiley and Sons Ltd

Editors: David Gough and Nicky Stanley

Journal of Interpersonal Violence

>   Published by Sage
>   Editor: Jon Conte

Child Abuse and Neglect: The International Journal

>   Published by Elsevier Ltd
>   Editor: John Leventhal

Child Maltreatment

>   (The Journal of the American Professional Society on the Abuse of Children)
>   Published by Sage
>   Editor: Steven Ondersma

Trauma Violence and Abuse: A Review Journal

>   Published by Sage
>   Editor: Jon Conte

Interpersonal Journal of Offender Therapy and Comparative Criminology

>   Published by Sage
>   Editor: George Palermo

INTERNET SAFETY

>   Thinkuknow.co.uk
>
>   A website for young people to help stay safe on-line, with on-line leaflet available also for parents and carers offering practical guidance.
>
>   Other sites useful in promoting internet safety include:
>
>   www.parentsonline.gov.uk
>   www.chatdanger.com
>   www.nch.org.uk and

Internet Watch Foundation

>   www.iwf.org.uk
>   A UK hotline for reporting illegal images.

ADDITIONAL RESOURCES

>   www.stopitnow.com
>
>   The website for Stop It Now!, a public education campaign to prevent child sexual abuse, that provides a helpline for those concerned.

References

Abel, G., Becker, J., Cunningham-Rathner, J., Rouleau, J., Kaplan, M. and Reich, J. (1984) *The Treatment of Child Molesters*. New York: SBC-TM.

Aberdeen City Council (1998) *Report on Investigation into Aberdeen City Council's Social Work Department's Handling of the Case of Mr Steven Leisk*. Aberdeen: Aberdeen City Council.

Ahmad, B. (1992) *Black Perspectives in Social Work*. Birmingham: Venture Press.

Alexander, M.A. (1999) 'Sex offender treatment probed anew.' *Sexual Abuse: A Journal of Research and Treatment 11*, 101–116.

Allam, J. (1998) *Community Based Treatment for Sex Offenders: An Evaluation*. Birmingham: West Midlands Probation Service and University of Birmingham.

All England Law Reports (1996) London: Butterworth.

Andrews, D.A. and Bonta, J. (1998) *The Psychology of Criminal Conduct (2nd edition)*. Cincinnati: Anderson.

Atkinson, R.L., Worsfold, H. and Fisher, P. (1998) 'Battle within borders.' In *Battle Without Borders* (conference abstracts). Beaverton: Association for the Treatment of Sexual Abuse.

ATSA (2004) *Public Health Approach To Sexual Abuse/Assault Fact Sheet*. Beaverton: Association for the Treatment of Sexual Abusers Public Policy Committee.

Baim, C., Brookes, S. and Mountford, A. (2002) *The Geese Theatre Handbook*. Winchester: Waterside.

Bakker, L., Hudson, S.M., Wales, D. and Riley, D. (1998) *An Evaluation of the Kia Marama Treatment Programme for Child Molesters*. Christchurch: New Zealand Department of Justice.

Barbaree, H.E., Peacock, E.J., Cortoni, F., Marshall, W.L. and Seto, M. (1998) 'Ontario penitentiaries program.' In W.L. Marshall, Y.M. Fernandez, S.M. Hudson, and T. Ward, *Sourcebook of Treatment Programs for Sexual Offenders*. New York: Plenum.

Barker, M. and Morgan, R. (1994) *Sex Offenders; A Framework for the Evaluation of Community Based Treatment*. London: Home Office.

Beckett, R.C. (1998) 'Community treatment in the United Kingdom.' In W.L. Marshall, Y.M. Fernandez, S.M. Hudson and T. Ward (eds) *Sourcebook of Treatment Programs for Sexual Offenders*. New York: Plenum.

Beckett, R.C., Beech, A., Fisher, D. and Fordham, A.S. (1994) *Community Based Treatment for Sex Offenders: An Evaluation of Seven Treatment Programmes*. London: Home Office.

Beech, A., Fisher, D. and Beckett, R.C. (1998) *Step 3: An Evaluation of the Prison Sex Offender Treatment Programme*. London: Home Office.

Beech, A. and Fordham, A.S. (1997) 'Therapeutic climate of sex offender programs.' *Sexual Abuse: A Journal of Research and Treatment 9*, 219–237.

Bickley, J. and Beech, A.E. (2002) 'An empirical investigation of the Ward and Hudson self-regulation model of the sexual offence process with child abusers.' *Journal of Interpersonal Violence 17*, 371–393.

Bickley, J. and Beech, A.R. (2003) 'Implications for treatment of sexual offenders of the Ward and Hudson Model of relapse.' *Sexual Abuse: A Journal of Research and Treatment 15*, 121–134.

Bickley, J., Fisher, D. and Beech, T. (2004) 'Identification and treatment implications of the Ward and Hudson pathways: a manualised approach.' Workshop presented to the Association for the Treatment of Sexual Abusers, Albuquerque, October 2004.

Blom-Cooper, L. (1987) *A Child in Mind.* London: Borough of Greenwich.

Bloom, M. (1996) *Primary Prevention Practices.* London: Sage.

Borduin, C.M., Henggeler, S.W., Blaske, D.M. and Stein, R.J. (1990) 'Multisystemic treatment of adolescent sexual offenders.' *International Journal of Offender Therapy and Comparative Criminology 34,* 105–114.

Bowden, K. (1994) '"No control of penis or brain?" Key questions in the assessment of sex offenders with a learning difficulty.' *Journal of Sexual Aggression 1,* 1.

Brandon, N. (1994) *The Six Pillars of Self Esteem.* New York: Bantam Books.

Briere, J., Berliner, L., Bulkley, J.A., Jenny, C. and Reid, T. (eds) (1996) *The APSAC Handbook of Child Maltreatment.* Thousand Oaks: Sage.

Briggs, D. (1994) 'The management of sex offenders in institutions.' In T. Morrison, M. Erooga and R. Beckett (eds) *Sexual Offending Against Children: Assessment and Treatment of Male Abusers.* London: Routledge.

Briggs, D., Doyle, P., Gooch, T. and Kennington, R. (1998) *Assessing Men Who Sexually Abuse. A Practice Guide.* London: Jessica Kingsley Publishers.

Budrionis, R. and Jongsma, A.E. (2003) *The Sexual Abuse Victim and Sexual Offender Treatment Planner.* New Jersey: Wiley.

Burton, J.E., Rasmussen, L.A., Bradshaw, J., Christopherson, B.J. and Huke, S.C. (1998) *Treating Children with Sexually Abusive Behaviour Problems.* New York: Haworth Maltreatment and Trauma Press.

Butler, C. and Hill, S. (2002) 'Partners for protection: an exploration of a developing initiative in working with children and families in danger.' Presentation at the annual conference of the National Organisation for the Treatment of Abusers. Lancaster.

Butler-Schloss, Rt. Hon. Lord Justice (1988) *Report of the Inquiry into Child Abuse in Cleveland, 1987.* London: HMSO.

Carnes, P., Delmonico, D.L. and Griffin, E. (2001) *In the Shadows of the Net: Breaking Free of Compulsive On-Line Sexual Behaviour.* Centre City: Hazelden.

Cautela, J.R. and Wisocki, P.A. (1971) 'Covert sensitization for the treatment of sexual deviations.' *The Psychological Record 21,* 37–48.

Clare, L., Scaife, J. and Buchan, L. (2002) 'Difference is in us, not just out there: diversity and clinical training.' *Clinical Psychology 11,* March 2002, 7–10.

Clarke, J. (2004) *The Psychosocial Impact on Facilitators of Working Therapeutically with Sex Offenders.* University of York: Unpublished PhD Thesis.

Coleman, E. and Haaven, J. (1998) 'Adult intellectually disabled sexual offenders: program considerations.' In W.L. Marshall, Y.M. Fernandez, S.M. Hudson and T. Ward (eds) *Sourcebook of Treatment Programs for Sexual Offenders.* New York: Plenum.

Cortoni, F. and Marshall, W.L. (1998) 'The relationship between attachment and coping in sex offenders.' Presentation at the Association for Treatment of Sexual Abusers 17th Conference, Vancouver.

Cortoni, F. and Marshall, W.L. (2001) 'Sex as a coping strategy and its relationship to juvenile sexual history and intimacy in sexual offenders.' *Sexual Abuse: A Journal of Research and Treatment 13,* 27–43.

Cowburn, M. (1996) 'The black male sex offender in prison, images and issues.' *The Journal of Sexual Aggression 2,* 2, 122–142.

Craissati, J. (1998) *Child Sexual Abusers. A Community Treatment Approach.* Hove: Taylor and Francis.

Cross, T.L., Bazron, B.J., Dennis, K.W. and Isaacs, M.R. (1989) *Towards a Culturally Competent System of Care.* Washington, DC: Child and Adolescent Service System Programme.

Cullen, M. and Freeman-Longo, R.E. (1995) *Men and Anger.* Brandon: Safer Society Press.

Daly, J.E., Power, T.G. and Goldolf, E.W. (2001) 'Predictors of batterer program attendance.' *Journal of Interpersonal Violence 16*, 10, October 2001, 971–991.

Davis, C.M., Yarber, W.L., Bauserman, R., Schreer, G. and Davis, S.L. (1998) (eds) *Handbook of Sexually Related Measures*. Thousand Oaks: Sage.

Davis, G., Hoyano, L., Keenan, C., Maitland, L. and Morgan, R. (1999) *The Admissibility and Sufficiency of Evidence in Child Abuse Prosecutions*. London: Home Office Research, Development and Statistics Directorate.

Delmonico, D.L., Griffin, E. and Moriarity, J. (2001) *Cybersex Unhooked: A Workbook for Breaking Free of Compulsive On-Line Sexual Behaviour*. Wickenburg: Gentle Path Press.

Demetriou, G. and Silke, A. (2003) 'A criminological internet sting.' *British Journal of Crimonology 43*, 213–222.

Department of Health (1989) *The Children Act*. London: Department of Health.

Department of Health (2000) *Care Standards Act 2000*. London: HMSO.

Department of Health, Department for Education and Employment, Home Office (2000) *Framework for the Assessment of Children in Need and their Families*. London: HMSO.

Derwent Initiative (2003) *Annual Report of the Derwent Initiative*. Newcastle: The Derwent Initiative.

Dodgson, P. (2003) 'Examination of attachment and interpersonal style of sexual offenders and the relevance of different treatment modalities.' ATSA 22nd Annual Research and Treatment Conference, St Louis, Missouri, 8–11 October.

Dominelli, L., Jeffers, L., Jones, G., Lisanda, S. and Williams, B. (1995) *Anti-racist Probation Practice*. Aldershot: Arena.

Doren, D.M. (2002) *Evaluating Sex Offenders*. Thousand Oaks, California: Sage.

Doyle, P. and Gooch, T. (1995) *The Mentally Handicapped as Offenders. Forensic Aspects of Mental Handicap*. Newcastle: Merit Publishers.

Doyle, P., Gooch, T., Harison, K., Ineson, L. and Kennington, R. (1998) *Sex Offender Programme Manual*. Newcastle: Northumbria Probation Service.

Eldridge, H. (1998) *Therapist Guide for Maintaining Change*. London: Sage.

Eldridge, H. and Saradjian, J. (2000) 'Replacing the function of abusive behaviours for the offender: remaking relapse prevention in working with women who sexually abuse children.' In D.R. Laws, S.M. Hudson and T. Ward (2000) *Remaking Relapse Prevention with Sex Offenders*. Thousand Oaks: Sage.

Eldridge, H. and Still, J. (2001) *Thames Valley Project Sex Offender Programme. Partner's Group Manual*. London: National Probation Directorate.

Elliott, M. (1993) *Female Sexual Abuse of Children: The Ultimate Taboo*. Harlow, Essex: Longman.

Elliott, M. (2004) Speaking on BBC *Woman's Hour*. 27 May 2004.

Ennis, L. and Horne, S. (2003) 'Predicting psychological distress in sex offender therapists.' *Sexual Abuse: A Journal of Research and Treatment 15*, 2, 149–158.

Erooga, M. (1994) 'Where the professional meets the personal.' In T. Morrison, M. Erooga and R.C. Beckett (eds) *Sexual Offending Against Children*. London: Routledge.

Erooga, M. and Masson, H. (eds) (1999) *Children and Young People who Sexually Abuse Others*. London: Routledge.

European Court of Human Rights (1996) Judgement in the case of Johansen v Norway. www.echr.coe.int

Farrenkopf, T. (1992) 'What happens to therapists who work with sex offenders?' *Journal of Offender Rehabilitation 18*, (3/4).

Fernandez, Y., Yates, P. and Mann, R. (2001) 'Process issues and content of an effective sexual offender treatment programme.' The Association for the Treatment of Sex Abusers 20th Annual Research and Treatment Conference. San Antonio, Texas: 7 November 2001.

Fernandez, Y.M., Marshall, W.L., Lightbody, S. and O'Sullivan, C. (1999) 'The child molester empathy measure: description and examination of its reliability and validity.' *Sexual Abuse: A Journal of Research and Treatment 11*, 1, 17–32.

Fernandez, Y.M. and Serran, G. (2002) 'Empathy training for therapists and clients.' In Y. Fernandez (ed) *In Their Shoes*. Oklahoma: Wood N. Barnes.

Findlater, D. and Hughes, T. (2004) 'Stop It Now! Making sex offending everybody's business.' Presentation at the annual conference of the National Organisation for the Treatment of Abusers, London.

Finkelhor, D. (1984) *Child Sexual Abuse: New Theory and Research*. New York: Free Press.

Finkelhor, D. and Associates (1986) *A Source Book on Child Sexual Abuse*. California: Sage.

Finkelhor, D. and Browne, A. (1985) 'The traumatic impact of child sexual abuse: a conceptualization.' *American Journal of Orthopsychiatry 55*, 4, 530–541.

Fisher, D. (2001) *Thames Valley Project: Victim Empathy Block Manual*. Oxford: Thames Valley Project.

Fisher, D. and Beech, T. (1998) 'Reconstituting families after sexual abuse: the offender's perspective.' *Child Abuse Review 7*, 1–15.

Fisher, D., Beech, T. and Browne, K. (1998) 'Locus of control and its relationship to treatment change and abuse history in child sexual abusers.' *Legal and Criminological Psychology 3*, 1–12.

Fisher, D. and Faux, M. (2001) *Thames Valley Sex Offender Groupwork Programme Foundation Block Manual*. London: National Probation Directorate.

Flaxington, F. and Procter, E. (1996) *Community Based Interventions Organised by the Probation Service*. London: Association of Chief Officers of Probation.

Frey, D. and Carlock, C.J. (1989) *Enhancing Self-Esteem*. Indiana: Accelerated Development Inc.

Furby, L., Weinott, M.R. and Blackshaw, L. (1989) 'Sex offender recidivism: a review.' *Psychological Bulletin 105*, 3–30.

Gahir, M. and Garrett, T. (1999) 'Issues in the treatment of Asian sex offenders.' *Journal of Sexual Aggression 4*, 2, 94–104.

Gallagher, C.A., Wilson, D.B., Hirschfield, P., Coggeshall, M.B. and Mackenzie, D.L. (1999) 'A quantitative review of the effects of sex offender treatment on sexual reoffending.' *Corrections Management Quarterly 3*, 19–29.

Geese Theatre Company (1994) Course materials presented to Northumbria Probation Service.

Gendreau, P., Little, T. and Goggin, C. (1996) 'A meta-analysis of the predictors of adult offender recidivism: What works?' *Criminology 34*, 575–607.

George, W.H. and Marlatt, G.A (1989) 'Introduction.' In D.R. Laws (ed) *Relapse Prevention with Sex Offenders*. New York: Guildford.

Goddard, C. and Carew, B. (1988) 'Protecting the child: hostages to fortune.' *Social Work Today 20*, 16.

Gordon, A. and Hover, G. (1998) 'The Twin Rivers Sex Offender Treatment Program.' In W.L. Marshall, Y.M. Fernandez, S.M. Hudson and T. Ward (eds) *Sourcebook of Treatment Programs for Sexual Offenders*. New York: Plenum.

Gothard, S., Ryan, B. and Heinrich, T. (2000) 'Treatment outcome for a maltreated population: benefits, procedural decisions and challenges.' *Child Abuse and Neglect 24*, 8, 1037–45.

Groth, A.N. and Birnbaum, H.J. (1979) *Men Who Rape*. New York: Plenum.

Grubin, D. (1996) 'Intervention and recidivism; some facts and some problems.' *Communiqué 4*, 1. Newcastle Upon Tyne: The Derwent Initiative.

Grubin, D. (1998) *Sex Offending Against Children: Understanding the Risk*. London: Home Office.

Grubin, D. (2000a) 'Complementing relapse prevention with medical intervention.' In R.D. Laws, S.M. Hudson and T. Ward *Remaking Relapse Prevention*. London: Sage.

Grubin, D. (2000b) 'SOTP Plus and the Sexual Behaviour Unit.' Newcastle: Unpublished Report to Mental Health Foundation.

Grubin, D., Madsen, L., Parsons, S., Sosnowski, D. and Warberg, B. (2004) 'A prospective longitudinal study of the impact of polygraphy on high-risk behaviours among adult sex offenders.' *Sexual Abuse; A Journal of Research Treatment and Therapy 16*, 3.

Grubin, D., McGregor, G. and Kennington, R. (2000) 'Rapists and child abusers, similarities and differences.' Presentation at National Organisation for the Treatment of Abusers Conference, November 2000.

Haaven, J., Little, R. and Petre-Miller, D. (1990) *Treating Intellectually Disabled Sexual Offenders.* Orwell: Safer-Society Press.

Hackett, S. (2000) 'Sexual aggression, diversity and the challenge of anti-oppressive practice.' *Journal of Sexual Aggression 5*, 1, 4–20.

Hall, G.C.N. (1995) 'Sexual offender recidivism revisited: a meta-analysis of recent treatment studies.' *Journal of Consulting and Clinical Psychology 63*, 5.

Hanna, F.J. (2002) *Therapy with Difficult Clients: Using the Precursors Model to Awaken Change.* Washington: American Psychological Association.

Hanson, R.K. (1997) *Rapid Risk Assessment of Sex Offender Recidivism.* Ottawa: Solicitor General of Canada.

Hanson, R.K. (2000) 'What is so special about relapse prevention?' In D.R. Laws, S.M. Hudson and T. Ward (eds) *Remaking Relapse Prevention with Sex Offenders: A Source Book.* London: Sage.

Hanson, R.K. (2003a) 'Assessing the recidivism risk of sexual offenders.' Paper presented at the Association for the Treatment of Sexual Abusers Conference, St Louis, October 2003.

Hanson, R.K. (2003b) 'Empathy deficits in sexual offenders: a conceptual model.' *Journal of Sexual Aggression 9*, 1.

Hanson, R.K. and Bussiere, M.T (1998) 'Predicting relapse: a meta-analysis of sexual offender recidivism studies.' *Journal of Consulting and Clinical Psychology 66*, 2, 348–362.

Hanson, R.K., Gordon, A., Harris, A.J.R., Marques, J.K., Murphy, W., Quinsey, V.L. and Seto, M.C. (2002) 'First report of the collaborative outcome data project on the effectiveness of psychological treatment for sex offenders.' *Sexual Abuse: A Journal of Research and Treatment,* 14–2, 169–194.

Hanson, R.K. and Harris, A. (1997) 'Dynamic risk factors project.' Presentation at the Association for the Treatment of Sexual Abusers Conference, Arlington.

Hanson, R.K. and Harris, A. (2000) *Sex Offender Needs Assessment Rating (SONAR).* Ottawa: Department of the Solicitor General of Canada.

Hanson, R.K. and Harris, A.J.R. (2002) 'Where should we intervene? Dynamic predictors of sex offence recidivism.' *Criminal Justice and Behaviour 27*, 6–35.

Hanson, R.K. and Morton-Bourgon, K. (2004) 'Predictors of sexual recidivism: an updated meta-analysis 2004–2.' Via Corrections Research, Public Safety and Emergency Preparedness, Canada.

Hanson, R.K., Steffy, R.A. and Gauthier, R. (1993) 'Long-term recidivism of child molesters.' *Journal of Consulting and Clinical Psychology 61*, 646–652.

Hare, R.D. (1994) *Without Conscience.* London: Warner.

Harris, G.T., Rice, M.E. and Quinsey, V.L. (1998) 'Appraisal and management of risk in sexual aggression: implications for criminal justice policy.' *Psychology, Public Policy and Law 4*, 1–2, 73–115.

Hart, S.D., Randall-Kropp, P., Laws, D.R., Klaver, J., Logan, C. and Watt, K. (2003) *The Risk for Sexual Violence Protocol (RSVP): Structuring Professional Guidelines for Assessing Risk of Sexual Violence.* British Columbia: Mental Health, Law and Policy Institute, Simon Fraser University.

Hay, J. (1992) *Transactional Analysis for Trainers.* Maidenhead: McGraw-Hill Education.

Hayes, E., Archer, D. and Middleton, D. (2005) *Internet Sexual Offending Treatment Programme.* London: National Probation Directorate.

Hebenton, W. and Thomas, T. (1997) *Keeping on Track? Observations on Sex Offender Registration in the US.* London: Home Office.

Hedderman, C. and Sugg, D. (1996) 'Does treating sex offenders reduce re-offending?' *Research Findings 45.* London: Home Office Research and Statistics Directorate.

Henry, F. (1999) 'Stop It Now! Campaign.' Presentation at joint National Organisation for Treatment of Abusers/Faithful Foundation Conference, London.

Heron, J. (1989) *The Facilitators Handbook.* London: Kogan Page.

HM Prison Service (2003) *Sex Offender Treatment Programme. Theory Manual.* London: HM Prison Service.

HM Prison Service Offending Behaviour Programmes Unit (2004) *SOTP 'Better Lives' Booster Programme.* London: HM Prison Service.

Hodge, J. (1985) *Planning for Co-leadership. A Practice Guide for Group Workers.* Newcastle: Groupvine.

Hogg, J. (2004) Personal communication.

Home Office (1991) *Criminal Justice Act.* London: HMSO.

Home Office (1997) Presentation at Northumbria Police Headquarters.

Home Office (1997a) *Crime (Sentences) Act.* London: HMSO.

Home Office (1997b) *Sex Offenders Act.* London: HMSO.

Home Office (1997c) *Home Office Circular 39/1977.* London: Home Office.

Home Office (1998) *Crime and Disorder Act 1998.* London: HMSO.

Home Office (1998a) *Human Rights Act.* London: Home Office.

Home Office (1998b) *Exercising Constant Vigilance: The Role of the Probation Service in Protecting the Public from Sex Offenders.* Report of a Thematic Inspection. London: Home Office.

Home Office (1999) *Prison Probation Review.* London: Home Office.

Home Office (2000) *The Criminal Justice and Court Services Act 2000.* London: Home Office.

Home Office (2001) *Criminal Justice and Police Act 2001.* London: HMSO.

Home Office (2003a) *Sexual Offences Act 2003.* London: Home Office.

Home Office (2003b) *Criminal Justice Act 2003.* London: Home Office.

Home Office and Department of Health (2004) *Dangerous People with Severe Personality Disorder Initiative.* www.dspd.gov.uk.

Home Office, Department of Health, Department of Education and Science, Welsh Office (1991) *Working Together.* London: HMSO.

Hopkinson, J. (1995) 'Some thoughts on working with sex offenders and racial difference.' *NOTA News 13.* Hull: National Organisation for Treatment of Abusers.

Hudson, S.M., Marshall, W.L., Wales, D., McDonald, E., Bakker, L. and MacLean, A. (1993) 'Emotional recognition in sex offenders.' *Annals of Sex Research 6,* 199–211.

Hudson, S.M. and Ward, T. (2000) 'Relapse prevention assessment and treatment implications.' In R.D. Laws, S.M. Hudson and T. Ward (eds) *Remaking Relapse Prevention with Sex Offenders.* London: Sage.

Hudson, S.M., Ward, T. and Laws, D.R. (2000) 'Whither relapse prevention?' In R.D. Laws, S.M. Hudson and T. Ward (eds) *Remaking Relapse Prevention with Sex Offenders.* London: Sage.

Hughes, J. (1998) 'Making inter-agency work work.' *NOTA News 28.* Hull: National Organisation for the Treatment of Abusers.

Jenkins, A. (1990a) *Invitations to Responsibility.* Adelaide: Dulwich Centre Publications.

Jenkins, A. (1990b) 'Invitations to responsibility: engaging adolescents and young men who have sexually abused.' In W.L. Marshall, Y.M. Fernandez, S.M. Hudson and T. Ward (eds) *Sourcebook of Treatment Programs for Sexual Offenders.* New York: Plenum.

Johnson, S. (2001) 'Changing the paradigm for young males.' Paper presented at the 2001 San Diego Conference on Child Maltreatment.

Joint Prison and Probation Accreditation Panel (2000) *Joint Prison and Probation Accreditation Criteria.* London: Home Office.

Jones, R.L., Loredo, C.M., Johnson, D.S. and McFarlane-Northern, G.H. (1999) 'A paradigm for culturally relevant sexual abuse treatment: an international perspective.' In A.D. Lewis *Cultural Diversity in Sexual Abuser Treatment.* Brandon: Safer Societies Press.

Jongsma, A.E. and Peterson, L.M. (1999) *The Complete Adult Psychotherapy Treatment Planner (2nd Edition).* New York: Wiley.

Kafka, M.P. (2002) 'The clinical importance of the thorough evaluation of axis I comorbid diagnoses in sex offenders.' *ATSA, Forum, Newsletter,* Fall 2002, 2–3.

Keenan, T. and Ward, T. (2003) 'Developmental antecedents of sexual offending.' In T. Ward, D.R. Laws and S.M. Hudson (eds) *Sexual Deviance: Issues and Controversies.* California: Sage.

Kennedy, H. and Grubin, D. (1992) '"Patterns of denial" in sexual offenders.' *Psychological Medicine* 22, 191–6.

Kennington, R. (2002) 'Accredited programmes for sex offenders in the community: some concerns and correspondence.' *NOTA News Issue 43,* September, 7. Hull: National Organisation for Treatment of Abusers.

Kennington, R., Dodds, M., McGregor, G. and Grubin, D. (2001) *Northumbria Sex Offender Programme Theory Manual.* London: National Probation Service.

Knight, R.A. and Prentky, R.A. (1990) 'Classifying sexual offenders: the development and corroboration of taxonomic models.' In W.L. Marshall, D.R. Laws and H. Barbaree *The Handbook of Sexual Assault.* New York: Plenum.

Knopp, F.H., Freeman-Longo, R.E. and Stevenson, W. (1992) *Nationwide Survey of Juvenile and Adult Sex-Offender Programs.* Orwell: Safer Societies Press.

Lane, S. (1997) 'The sexual abuse cycle.' In G. Ryan and S. Lane (eds) *Juvenile Sexual Offending: Causes, Consequences, and Correction.* San Fransisco: Jossey-Bass.

Langevin, R., Marentette, D. and Rosati, B. (1996) 'Why therapy fails with some sex offenders: Learning difficulties examined empirically.' In E. Coleman, S. Margretta, Dwyer and N. Pallone (eds) *Sex Offender Treatment.* London: The Harworth Press.

Langton, C.M. and Marshall, W.L. (2000) 'The role of cognitive distortions in relapse prevention programs.' In D.R. Laws, S.M. Hudson and T. Ward (eds) *Remaking Relapse Prevention with Sex Offenders. A Source Book.* London: Sage.

Laws, D.R. (ed) (1989) *Relapse Prevention with Sex Offenders.* New York: Guilford.

Laws, D.R. (1997) 'Harm reduction.' Paper presented to the conference of the Association for the Treatment of Sexual Abusers, Arlington.

Laws, D.R. (1998) 'Sexual abuse as a public health issue.' Presentation at National Organisation for Treatment of Abusers Conference, Glasgow.

Laws, D.R., Hudson, S.M. and Ward, T. (eds) (2000) *Remaking Relapse Prevention with Sex Offenders.* London: Sage.

Lees, S. (1989) 'Trial by rape.' *New Statesman.* 24 November 1989.

Letourneau, E.J. (2002) 'A comparison of objective measures of sexual arousal and interest: visual reaction time and penile plethysmography.' *Sexual Abuse: A Journal of Research and Treatment 14,* 3.

Levenson, J.S. and Macgowan, M.J. (2004) 'Engagement, denial and treatment progress among sex offenders in group therapy.' *Sexual Abuse: A Journal of Research and Treatment 16,* 1, January 2004, 49–63.

Levenson, J.S. and Morin, J.W. (2001a) *Connections Workbook.* London: Sage.

Levenson, J.S. and Morin, J.W. (2001b) 'Treating non-offending parents.' In *Child Sexual Abuse Cases: Connections for Family Safety.* London: Sage.

Lewis, A. (1999) *Cultural Diversity in Sexual Abuser Treatment: Issues and Approaches.* Brandon: Safer Societies Press.

Lewis, A.D. (2001) 'Working with culturally diverse populations.' In M.S. Carich and S.E. Mussack (eds) *Handbook for Sexual Abuser Assessment and Treatment.* Brandon. Safer Society Press.

Lillee and Reed v Newcastle City Council (2001) www.courtjudgements.gov.uk

Lord Chancellor's Department, Family Policy Division (2003) *Protocol for Judicial Case Management in Public Law Children Act Cases.* www.lcd.gov.uk

Lottes, I.L. (1998) 'Rape supportive attitude scales.' In C.M. Davis, W.L. Yarber, R. Bauserman, G. Schreer and S.L. Davis (eds) *Handbook of Sexuality Related Measures.* London: Sage.

Lund, C. (2000) 'Predictions of sexual recidivism. Did meta-analysis clarify the role and relevance of denial?' *Sexual Abuse: A Journal of Research and Treatment 12,* 4, 275–288.

Macgowan, M.J. (1997) 'A measure of engagement for social group work: the groupwork engagement measure.' *Journal of Social Service Research 23,* 2, 17–37.

Malamuth, N.M., Heavey, C.L. and Linz, D. (1993) 'Predicting men's anti-social behaviour against women: the interaction model of sexual aggression.' In G.C.N. Hall, R. Hirschman, J.R. Graham and M.S. Zaragoza (eds) *Sexual Aggression: Issues in Aetiology, Assessment and Treatment.* Washington, DC: Taylor and Francis.

Mann, R. (1998) 'Relapse prevention. Is that the bit where they told me all the things I couldn't do any more?' Presentation at Association for Treatment of Sexual Abusers conference, Vancouver.

Mann, R.E. (2000) 'Managing resistance and rebellion in relapse prevention intervention.' In D.R. Laws, S.M. Hudson and T. Ward (eds) *Remaking Relapse Prevention with Sex Offenders: A Sourcebook.* Thousand Oaks: Sage.

Mann, R.E. (2003) Personal communication, 10 April 2003.

Mann, R.E. and Beech, A.R. (2003) 'Cognitive distortions, schemas and implicit theories.' In T. Ward, D.R. Laws and S.M. Hudson (eds) *Sexual Deviance: Issues and Controversies.* London: Sage.

Mann, R.E., Daniels, M. and Marshall, W.L. (2002b) 'The use of role play in developing empathy.' In Y. Fernandez (ed) *In Their Shoes.* Oklahoma: Wood N. Barnes.

Mann, R. and Hollin, C. (2001) 'Schemas: a model for understanding cognition in sexual offending.' Paper presented at the 20th Annual Association for Treatment of Sexual Abusers research and treatment conference, San Antonio, Texas, November 2001.

Mann, R., O'Brien, M., Thornton, D., Rallings, M. and Webster, S. (2002a) *Structured Assessment of Risk and Need.* London: HM Prison Department.

Marlatt, G.A. and George, W.H. (1984) 'Relapse prevention: introduction and overview of the model.' *British Journal of Addiction 79,* 261–273.

Marquis, J. (1990) 'Orgasmic reconditioning: changing sexual object choice through controlling masturbation fantasies.' *Journal of Behaviour Therapy and Experimental Psychiatry 1,* 263–271.

Marques, J.K. (1999) 'How to answer the question "Does sex offender treatment work?"' *Journal of Interpersonal Violence 14,* 4, 437–451.

Marques, J.K., Nelson, C., Alarcon, J.M. and Day, D.M. (2000) 'Preventing relapse in sex offenders: what we learned from SOTEPs experimental treatment programme.' In D.R. Laws, S.M. Hudson and T. Ward (eds) *Remaking Relapse Prevention with Sex Offenders. A Source Book.* London: Sage.

Marshall, P. (1997) *The Prevalence of Conviction for Sexual Offending.* London: Home Office Research and Statistics Directorate.

Marshall, W.L. (1993) 'A revised approach to the treatment of men who sexually assault adult females.' In G.C.N. Hall, R. Hirschman, J.R. Graham and M.J. Zaragoza *Sexual Aggression: Issues in Aetiology, Assessment and Treatment.* Washington, DC: Taylor and Francis.

Marshall, W.L. (1999) 'What Works with Sex Offenders: An Overview of Research and Practice.' Address to National Organisation for Treatment of Abusers, conference, York.

Marshall, W.L. and Anderson, D. (2000) 'Do relapse prevention components enhance treatment effectiveness?' In R.D. Laws, S.M. Hudson and T. Ward (eds) *Remaking Relapse Prevention with Sex Offenders.* London: Sage.

Marshall, W.L., Anderson, D. and Fernandez, Y. (1999) *Cognitive Behavioural Treatment of Sexual Offenders.* Chichester: Wiley.

Marshall, W.L. and Barbaree, H.E. (1988) 'The long-term evaluation of a behavioural treatment program for child molesters.' *Behaviour Research and Therapy 26,* 499–511.

Marshall, W.L. and Bryce, P. (1996) 'The enhancement of intimacy and the reduction of loneliness among child molesters.' *Journal of Family Violence 11,* 3, 219–235.

Marshall, W. and Fernandez, Y.M. (2001) 'Empathy training.' In M.S. Carich and S.E. Mussack (eds) *Handbook for Sexual Abusers Assessment and Treatment.* Brandon: Safer Society Press.

Marshall, W.L., Fernandez, Y.M., Hudson, S.M. and Ward, T. (eds) (1998) *A Sourcebook of Treatment Programmes for Sexual Offenders.* New York: Plenum.

Marshall, W.L. and Marshall, L. (2000) 'Working with denial.' Presentation at Conference of the Association for the Treatment of Sexual Abuse, San Diego.

Marshall, W.L., Serran, G.A., Fernandez, Y.M., Mulloy, R., Mann, R.E. and Thornton, D. (2003) 'Therapist characteristics in the treatment of sex offenders: Tentative data on their relationship with indices of behaviour change.' *Journal of Sexual Aggression 9,* 1.

Matthews, J.K. (1998) 'An 11-year perspective of working with female sexual offenders.' In W.L. Marshall, Y.M. Fernandez, S.M. Hudson and T. Ward (eds) *Source Book of Treatment Programmes for Sexual Offenders.* New York: Plenum.

McGrath, R. (2001) 'Using behavioural techniques to control sexual arousal.' In M.S. Carich and S.E. Mussack (eds) *Handbook for Sexual Abuser Assessment and Treatment.* Brandon: Safer Society Press.

McGrath, R.J., Cumming, G. and Holt, J. (2002) 'Collaboration among sex offender treatment providers and probation and parole officers: the beliefs and behaviours of treatment providers.' *Sexual Abuse: A Journal of Research and Treatment 14,* 1, January, 49–66.

McGrath, R.J., Hoke, S.E. and Vojtisek, J.E. (1998) 'Cognitive and behavioural treatment of sex offenders.' *Criminal Justice and Behaviour 25,* 203–225.

McGregor, G., Kennington, R., Dodds, M. and Grubin, D. (2001) *Northumbria Sex Offender Programme. Core Programme Manual.* London: National Probation Directorate.

McKay, M. and Rogers, P. (2000) *The Anger Control Workbook.* Oakland: Newharbinger.

McKenna, K. and Bargh, J. (2000) 'Plan 9 from cyberspace: the implications of the internet for personality and social psychology.' *Personality and Social Psychology Review 4,* 57–75.

Menzies, I. (1970) 'A case study in the functioning of social systems as a defensive against anxiety.' *Social Relations 13,* 2.

Middleton, D. (2002) 'Accredited programmes for sex offenders in the community: an overview from the National Probation Service.' *NOTA News 43,* September 2002, 8–12.

Middleton, D. (2003a) *Assessment of Individuals Convicted of Child Pornography Offences.* Probation Circular 14/2003. London: National Probation Service for England and Wales.

Middleton, D. (2003b) Presentation at conference of the National Organisation for the Treatment of Abusers, Edinburgh.

Middleton, D. (2004) 'Current treatment approaches.' In M.C. Calder *Child Sexual Abuse and the Internet: Tackling the New Frontier.* Lyme Regis: Russell House Publishing.

Middleton, D., Beech, A.R. and Mandeville Norden, R. (2005b) *Analysis of National Psychometric Assessments of Internet Offenders*. London: National Probation Directorate (work in progress).

Middleton, D., Elliott, I.A., Mandeville-Norden, R. and Beech, A.R. (2005a) *An Investigation into the Applicability of the Ward and Seigert Pathways Model of Child Sexual Abuse with Internet Offenders*. In press.

Miller, P.A. and Eisenberg, N. (1988) 'The relationship of empathy to aggressive and externalising/antisocial behaviour.' *Psychology Bulletin 103*, 324–344.

Miller, W. and Rollnick, S. (1995) *Motivational Interviewing: Preparing People to Change Addictive Behaviour*. New York: Guilford Press.

Miller, W.R. and Rollnick, S. (1991) *Motivational Interviewing*. New York: Guilford.

Miller, W.R. and Rollnick, S. (2002) *Motivational Interviewing; Preparing People for Change*. 2nd Edition. New York: Guilford Press.

Minuchin, S. (1974) *Families and Family Therapy*. Cambridge, MA: Harvard University Press.

Mistry, T. and Brown, A. (1991) 'Black-White co-working in groups.' *Groupwork 4*, 2, 101–118.

Monk, D. (1999) 'The development of risk management panels on sex offenders and potentially dangerous offenders in London.' *VISTA 5*, 1.

Moos, R.H. (1986) *Group Environment Scale Manual*. Palo Alto, CA: Consulting Psychologists Press Ltd.

Morin, J.W. and Levenson, J.S. (2002) *The Road to Freedom*. Oklahoma: Wood 'N' Barnes.

Morrison, T. (1990) 'The emotional effects of child protection work on the worker.' *Practice 4*, 4.

Morrison, T. (1998) *Casework Consultation. A Practical Guide for Consultation*. London: Whiting and Birch and NOTA.

Morrison, T., Erooga, M. and Beckett, R. (eds) (1994) *Sexual Offending Against Children. Assessment and Treatment of Male Abusers*. London: Routledge.

Mothersole, G. (2000) 'Clinical supervision and forensic work.' *The Journal of Sexual Aggression 5*, 1, 45–58.

Murphy, W.D. (1990) 'Assessment and modification of cognitive distortions in sex offenders.' In W.L. Marshall, D.R. Laws and H.E. Barbaree *Handbook of Sexual Assault; Issues, Theories and Treatment of the Offender*. New York: Plenum.

Murphy, W.D. and Smith, T.A. (1996) 'Sex offenders against children: empirical and clinical issues.' In J. Briere, L. Berliner, J.A. Bulkley, C. Jenny and T. Reid *The APSAC Handbook on Child Maltreatment*. London: Sage.

Mussack, S.E. and Carick, M.S. (2001) 'Introduction.' In M.S. Carick and S.E. Mussack (eds) *Handbook for Sexual Abuser Assessment and Treatment*. Brandon: Safer Society Sex.

National Probation Directorate (2003) *Multi Agency Public Protection Arrangements. Guidelines for Practice*. London: Home Office.

National Probation Service (2000) *Thames Valley Sex Offender Groupwork Programme*. London: National Probation Service.

National Probation Service (2001) *Northumbria Sex Offender Groupwork Programme*. London: National Probation Service.

National Probation Service Northumbria (2003) *Multi Agency Public Protection Arrangements: Annual Report*. Newcastle: NPS Northumbria.

Nelson, C. and Jackson, P. (1989) 'High risk recognition: the cognitive behavioural chain.' In D.R Laws (ed) *Relapse Prevention With Sex Offenders*. New York: Guilford Press.

Nicholaichuk, T.P. (1996) 'Sex offender treatment priority: an illustration of the risk/need principle.' *Forum on Corrections Research 8*, 32.

Nicholaichuk, T., Gordon, A., Andre, G., Gu, D. and Wong, S. (1998) 'Outcome of the Clearwater Sex Offender Treatment Program: a matched comparison between treated and untreated offenders.' In press.

NOTA (1999) 'Dealing with diversity.' *NOTA News*. Hull: National Organisation for the Treatment of Abusers.

Nowicki, S. (1976) 'Adult Nowicki-Strickland Internal-External Locus of Control Scale.' Reproduced in A.C. Salter (1988) *Treating Child Sex Offenders and their Victims: A Practical Guide*. London: Sage.

O'Brien, M. (2003) *Internet Behaviours and Attitudes Questionnaire*. London: HM Prison Service, National Probation Directorate.

Parliament (2000) www.parliament.uk

Parton, N. (1986) 'The Beckford Report: a critical appraisal.' *British Journal of Social Work 16*, 5.

Patton, W. and Mannison, M. (1995) 'Sexuality attitudes: a review of the literature and refinement of a new measure.' *Journal of Sex Education and Theory 21*, 268–295.

Penzel, F. (2000) *Obsessive Compulsive Disorders*. Oxford: Oxford University Press.

Perry, D.A. (1998) *Effective Practice Initiative Pathfinder Project: Initial Assessment Checklist*. London: Her Majesty's Inspectorate of Probation.

Pithers, W.D. (1993) 'Treatment of rapists: reinterpretation of early outcome data and exploratory constructs to enhance therapeutic efficacy.' In G.C.N. Hall, R. Hirschman, J.R. Graham and M.S. Zaragoza (eds) *Sexual Aggression: Issues in Etiology Assessment and Treatment*. Washington, DC: Taylor and Francis.

Pithers, W., Kashima, K.M, Cumming G.F. and Beal, L.S. (1988) 'Relapse prevention; a method of enhancing maintenance of change in sex offenders.' In A.C. Salter *Treating Child Sex Offenders and Victims*. London: Sage.

Polaschek, D.L.L. (2003) 'Empathy and victim empathy.' In T. Ward, D.R. Laws and S.M. Hudson (eds) *Sexual Deviance: Issues and Controversies*. London: Sage.

Prentky, R.A. and Burgess, A.W. (1990) 'Rehabilitation of child molesters: a cost benefit analysis.' *American Journal of Orthopsychiatry 60*, 80–117.

Prochaska, J. and DiClemente, C. (1982) 'Transtheoretical therapy: towards a more integrative model of change.' *Psychotherapy. Theory Research and Practice 19*, 3.

Proeve, M.J. (2003) 'Responsivety factors in treatment.' In T. Ward, D.R. Laws and S.M. Hudson (eds) *Sexual Deviance: Issues and Controversies*. London: Sage.

Proulx, J., Ovimet, M., Pellerin, B., Paradis, Y., McKibben, A. and Aubut, J. (1998a) 'Post treatment recidivism in sexual aggressors.' Submitted for publication.

Proulx, J., Pellerin, B., McKibben, A., Aubut, J. and Ouimet, M. (1998b) 'Recidivism in sexual aggressors: static and dynamic predictors of recidivism in sexual aggressors.' In W.L. Marshall, D. Anderson and Y. Fernandez *Cognitive Behavioural Treatment of Sexual Offenders*. New York: Wiley.

Quayle, E. and Taylor, M. (2002) 'Child pornography and the Internet: perpetuating a cycle of abuse.' *Deviant Behaviour 23*, 4, 331–361.

Quayle, E. and Taylor, M. (2003) *Development of a Cognitive Behavioural Therapy (CBT) Module for People with a Sexual Interest in Children who Also Exhibit Problematic Internet Use*. University of Cork: COPINE Project.

Quinsey, V.L. and Earls, C.M. (1990) 'The modification of sexual preferences.' In W.L. Marshall, D.R. Laws and H.E. Barbaree (eds) *Handbook of Sexual Assault*. New York: Plenum.

Quinsey, V.L., Khanna, A. and Malcolm, P.B. (1998) 'A retrospective evaluation of the Regional Treatment Centre Sex Offender Treatment Program.' *Journal of Interpersonal Violence 13*, 621–644.

Quinsey, V., Rice, M.E. and Harris, G.T. (1995) 'Actuarial prediction of sexual recidivism.' *Journal of Interpersonal Violence 10*, 1, 85–105.

Rice, M.E., Harris, G.T. and Quinsey, V.L. (1993) 'Evaluating treatment programs for child molesters.' In J. Hudson and J. Roberts (eds) *Evaluating Justice: Canadian Policies and Programmes.* Toronto: Thompson.

Roberts, C. (1991) *What Works: Using Social Work Methods to Reduce Reoffending in Serious and Persistent Offenders.* Oxford: Applied Social Studies, University of Oxford.

Rogers, C. (1951) *Client Centred Therapy.* Boston, MA: Houghton-Mifflin.

Ryan, G. and Lane, S. (eds) (1987) *Juvenile Sex Offending – Causes, Consequences and Correction.* San Francisco: Jossey-Bass.

Ryan, G., Lane, S.R., Davis, J.M. and Isaac, C.B. (1987) 'Juvenile sex offenders: development and correction.' *Child Abuse and Neglect 2*, 385–95.

Saleeby, D. (1997) *The Strengths Perspective in Social Work Practice.* New York: Longman.

Salter, A.C. (1988) *Treating Child Sex Offenders and Victims.* California: Sage.

Salter, A.C. (1997) 'Special issues in risk assessment.' Address to the Annual Conference of the National Organisation for the Treatment of Abusers, Southampton.

Saradjian, J. (1996) *Women Who Sexually Abuse: From Research to Clinical Practice.* London: Wiley.

Schlank, A.M. and Shaw, T. (1997) 'Treating sexual offenders who deny – a review.' In B.K. Schwartz and H.R. Cellini (eds) *The Sex Offender: New Insights, Treatment Innovations and Legal Developments.* Kingston, NJ: Civil Research Institute.

Segal, Z.V. and Stermac, L.E. (1990) 'The role of cognition in sexual assault.' In W.L. Marshall, D.R. Laws and H.E. Barbaree (eds) *Handbook of Sexual Assault.* New York: Plenum Press.

Sentencing Advisory Panel (2003) *Annual Report of the Sentencing Advisory Panel, April 2002 – March 2003, Appendix D.* London: Home Office Communications Directorate.

Shapiro, L. (1993) *Building Blocks of Self Esteem.* King of Prussia, PA: Centre for Applied Psychology.

Sheath, M. (1990) 'Confrontative work with sex offenders: legitimised nonce-bashing.' *Probation Journal 37*, 4, 159–162.

Simmons, T. (1986) *Child Sexual Abuse: An Assessment Process.* NSPCC Occasional Papers. London: National Society for the Prevention of Cruelty to Children.

Social Work Services Inspectorate for Scotland (1997) *A Commitment to Protect: Supervising Sex Offenders: Proposals for More Effective Practice.* Edinburgh: Scottish Office.

Sonkin, D.J. and Durphy, M. (1997) *Learning to Live Without Violence. A Handbook for Men.* Volcano: Volcano Press Inc.

Smallbone, S.W. and Milne, L. (2000) 'Association between trait anger and aggression used in the commission of sexual offences.' *International Journal of Offender Therapy and Comparative Criminology 44*, 5.

Spence J.T. and Helmreich, R.L. (1972) 'The Attitudes Towards Women Scale.' *Psychological Documents 2*, 153.

Spencer, A. (2000) Personal Communication.

Steen, C. (2001) *The Adult Relaps Prevention Workbook.* Brandon, VT: Safer Society Press.

Steenman, H., Nelson, C. and Viesti, C. (1989) 'Developing coping strategies for high risk situations.' In R.D. Laws (ed) *Relapse Prevention with Sex Offenders.* New York: Guilford.

Stevenson, K., Davies, A. and Gunn, M. (2004) *Blackstone's Guide to the Sexual Offences Act 2003.* Oxford: Oxford University Press.

Still, J., Faux, M. and Wilson, C. (2001) *Thames Valley Project. The Partner's Programme.* London: National Probation Directorate.

Stoner, S.A. and George, W.H. (2000) 'Relapse prevention and harm reduction. Areas of overlap.' In D. Laws, S.M. Hudson and T. Ward (eds) *Remaking Relapse Prevention with Sex Offenders: A Source Book.* London: Sage.

Stop It Now! UK & Ireland (2005) *Annual Report April 2004 – March 2005*. Birmingham: The Lucy Faithfull Foundation.

Strand, V. (2002) *Treating Secondary Victims: Intervention with the Non-Offending Mother in the Incest Family*. Thousand Oaks: Sage.

Summit, R. (1983) 'The child sexual abuse accommodation syndrome.' *Child Abuse and Neglect 7*, 177–193.

Taylor, M., Holland, G. and Quayle, E. (2001) 'Typology of paedophilia picture collections.' *The Police Journal 74*, 2, 97–107.

Taylor, M. and Quayle, E. (2003) *Child Pornography: An Internet Crime*. Hove: Brunner-Routledge.

Taylor, R., Wasik, M. and Leng, R. (2004) *Blackstone's Guide to the Criminal Justice Act 2003*. Oxford: Oxford University Press.

Teerlink, R. (2000) 'Harley's Leadership U-turn.' *Harvard Business Review*, July–August 2000, 43–48.

Thornton, D. (1998) 'Structured anchored clinical judgement.' In D. Grubin *Sex Offending Against Children; Understanding the Risk*. London: Home Office.

Thornton, D. (1999) 'Structured risk assessment.' Presentation at National Organisation for Treatment of Abusers Conference, York.

Thornton, D. (2000) 'Risk Matrix 2000.' Presentation at Association for Treatment of Sexual Abusers Conference, San Antonio.

Thornton, D. (2002) 'Constructing and testing a framework for dynamic risk assessment.' *Sexual Abuse: A Journal of Research and Treatment 14*, 2, 139–154.

Underdown, A. (1998) *Strategies for Effective Offender Supervision*. London: Home Office.

Van den Broucke, S., Vandereycken, W. and Vertommen, H. (1995) 'Marital intimacy: conceptualisation and assessment.' *Clinical Psychology Review 15*, 3, 217–233.

Ward, T. (2002) 'Good lives and the rehabilitation of offenders: promises and problems.' *Aggression and Violent Behaviour 7*, 5, 513–528.

Ward, T. (in press) 'Toward a comprehensive theory of child sexual abuse: a theory knitting perspective.' *Psychology Crime and Law*.

Ward, T., Bickley, J., Webster, S.D., Fisher, D., Beech, A. and Eldridge, H. (2004) *The Self Regulation Model of the Offence and Relapse Process*. Victoria BC: Pacific Psychological Assessment Corporation.

Ward, T. and Hudson, S. (2000) 'A self regulation model of relapse prevention.' In D.R. Laws, S.M. Hudson and T. Ward (eds) *Remaking Relapse Prevention with Sex Offenders*. London: Sage.

Ward, T. and Mann, R. (2004) 'Good lives and the rehabilitation of offenders: a positive approach to sex offender treatment.' In A. Linley and S. Joseph *Positive Psychology in Practice*. Chichester: Wiley.

Webster, S.D. (2002) 'Assessing victim empathy in sexual offenders using the victim letter task.' *Sexual Abuse: A Journal of Research and Treatment 14*, 4, 281–300.

Webster, S.D. (2005) 'Pathways to sexual offence recidivism following treatment: an examination of the Ward and Hudson self-regulation model of relapse.' *Journal of Interpersonal Violence*. (Submitted for publication.)

Wilson, R.J., Picheca, J.E. and Serin, R.C. (2001) 'Circles of support and accountability: evaluating the efficacy of professionally supported volunteerism in the long term re-integration of high risk sexual offenders.' Paper presented at the 2001 Conference of the Association for the Treatment of Sexual Abusers, San Antonio, Texas.

Wolf, S. (1985) 'A multi factor model of deviant sexuality.' *Victimology: An International Journal 10*, 359–74.

Wolf, S. (1988) 'A model of sexual aggression/addiction.' *Journal of Social Work and Human Sexuality 7*, 1.

Yalom, I. (1975) *The Theory and Practice of Group Psychotherapy.* New York: Basic Books.

Yates, P.M., Kingston, D. and Hall, K. (2003) 'Pathways to sexual offending: validity of Ward and Hudson's (1998) self regulation model and relationship to static and dynamic risk among treated sexual offenders.' Paper presented to the Association for the Treatment of Sexual Abusers, St Louis, October 2003.

Yokley, J.M. (ed) (1990) *The Use of Victim Offender Communication in the Treatment of Sexual Abuse.* Orwell: Safer Society Press.

Subject Index

good lives theory 90
group cohesion 87, 94
Group Environment Scale 87
group work 19, 124

harm reduction approach 28
high risk offenders 34, 35–6
high risk situations 173, 176,
    182–3
HM Prison Service Sex
    Offender Treatment
    Programme (SOTP) 36–7,
    56, 87, 101, 165
Home Office Thematic
    Inspection 84
homophobia 68, 70
homosexual offenders 61, *64*
    68, 135
honesty 114
hope 99
hostels 38
House of Lords 41
Human Rights Act 1998 22,
    23
hyper caution 47

implicit theories 118, 119
impulsivity 70, 80, 81, 164–5
inadequacy 164, 165, 166, 175
incest 118, 143, 179, 193–4
incongruent behaviour 103,
    126
indecent exposure 135
indeterminate sentences of
    imprisonment for public
    protection 31
Index of Marital Satisfaction
    191
Index of Self Concept 191
Index of Sexual Satisfaction
    191
inhibitions, overcoming internal
    117, 118, 160
inter-agency working 28–9
interdependence 162
Internet *see* on-line sexual
    activity
interpreters 61–2, 68, 69
intimacy 89–90, 160–2, 163–5
    in childhood 160–1
    in relationships 161–2
intrusive thoughts 45–6, 47

job analysis 50

Kia Marama treatment
    programme 163
Kids and Sex Questionnaire
    125

lapses 173–4, 176, 182–3
leadership style 87
leading questions 22
learning difficulties, abusers
    with 11, 61, *64*, 68, 70,
    84
Learning from my Past
    questionnaire 105, *111*
Leisurewatch 25
letters, victim 152–3, 155, 209
lie detectors 43
life events
    destabilising 171–2, 175
    major 70–1
    and world views 119
lifestyles, abuse-free 12
Locus of Control questionnaire
    169
loneliness 166–7
loss 35
low risk offenders 79, 85

maltreatment, child 169–70
masturbation 135
masturbatory satiation
    technique 143
medical intervention, for
    deviant sexual interest
    144–5
mental distractors 141
meta-analysis 76, 77, 78, 96–7,
    147
meta-cognitive skills 177
minimisation 121, 122
misregulation 176, 177
mood, management 169
mood disorder 89
motivating statements 102
motivation
    to abuse 159–60
    staff 114
motivation to change 93–115
    action 93
    based on punishment 96
    and client histories 103
    conceptualisations of 95–9
    and denial 96–7
    evaluation 103–13, *106–13*

fluctuation across time
    95–6, 186
influences on 95
intervention examples
    100–13
intervention objectives
    99–100
low periods of 95–6, 186
maintenance 93
and motivational
    interviewing 100–1
and non-abusive partners
    188
precursors to change 98–9
reasons for change 102
and relapse 93, 98
and sanctions 115
and social factors 94–5
and social support 95,
    99–100, 103, *104*,
    109–10
and Socratic questioning
    101
stages of 93, 181
motivational interviewing
    100–1
Multi-Agency Public Protection
    Arrangements (MAPPA)
    22, 23, 32, 33–6
    framework 34
    and hostels 38
    levels of 35, 36
    risk assessment 34–6
Multi-Agency Public Protection
    Panel (MAPPP) 34, 35,
    53
multi-agency working 28–9

nave examiners 101
narcissism, of the therapist 82
National Assembly for Wales
    41
National Criminal Intelligence
    Service 28–9
National Probation Service
    Accredited Programmes
    56
necessity, sense of 98
needs of the abuser 18, 63
    see also anti-oppressive
    practice
networking, professional 59
New Family Life Plans 193
New Life Plans 183

Author Index